Ameri

Guide to Foreign Law Firms
Fifth Edition

Prepared with the cooperation of the
American Bar Association
Section of International Law

Edited by:
James R. Silkenat
Partner
Sullivan & Worcester LLP
New York, New York
and
William M. Hannay
Partner
Schiff Hardin LLP
Chicago, Illinois

Cover design by ABA Publishing

Page Layout by Quadrum Solutions (www.quadrumltd.com)

Printed in the United States of America.

14 13 12 11 10   5 4 3 2 1

Library of Congress Cataloging-in-Publication Data

Guide to foreign law firms / edited by James R. Silkenat and William M. Hannay; Section of International Law, American Bar Association. — 5th ed.

p. cm.

Includes bibliographical references and index.
ISBN-13: 978-1-61632-002-7 (alk. paper)
ISBN-10: 1-61632-002-8 (alk. paper)

1. Law firms—Directories. 2. Lawyers—Directories. I. Silkenat, James R. II. Hannay, William M., 1944- III. Silkenat, James R. Guide to foreign law firms. IV. American Bar Association. Section of International Law. V. Title: American Bar Association guide to foreign law firms. VI. Title: Guide to foreign law firms.

K68.G85 2010
340.06'01—dc22

2010026312

Introduction

When this series of volumes on "foreign law firms" began, more than 20 years ago, the number of law firms that engaged in cross border legal practice was much smaller than it is today. Global trade has skyrocketed, and with it the need for transnational legal counseling (and litigation help) has grown. The pace of change in law firm organization and structure, particularly among law firms that offer their services across national borders, has accelerated in the past few years in ways that, frankly, few of us could have predicted. Because of various law firm mergers, alliances, combinations and associations, it is no longer easy, in many cases, to identify a specific firm with the country of its origin. What does it mean to say that a particular law firm is "Brazilian," or "French" or even "American?" The answers are not as clear as they once were. The legal world is a much more complex realm these days, and it is becoming more so.

The First Edition of this *Guide* in 1988 filled a particular void in the area of reliable information on quality legal services in countries outside the United States. The political and economic world in which the First Edition was written (and the world of law firms that served it) has changed radically since that time and this Fifth Edition (as did the Second, Third and Fourth Editions in 1993, 1999 and 2004) reflects the revolution in legal practice that has accompanied it. This volume also reflects the overwhelmingly positive response to the first four Editions of the *Guide* and the felt need to continue the process.

As noted in the first four Editions of the *Guide*, the complexity and diversity of legal problems today frequently brings American lawyers and their clients into contact with the laws of foreign jurisdictions. In addition to American clients wanting to purchase from, invest in, or export to, other countries, there are numerous occasions during counseling and/or litigation when questions of foreign law arise. Because of the traditional American focus

1

on federal, state and local law in the United States, there is typically little familiarity in the U.S. either with the substantive content of foreign laws and regulations or with the identity and qualifications of foreign lawyers able to give advice on such laws and regulations.

This *Guide* is designed to assist both U.S. and non U.S. lawyers in identifying qualified legal counsel in the many foreign jurisdictions with which such lawyers are likely to come into contact, particularly those in countries emerging as significant factors in international commercial transactions.

This *Guide* has been prepared based on the recommendations and personal experiences of members of Section of International Law of the American Bar Association, as well as the knowledge, experience and viewpoint of the Editors. As the American Bar Association entity with the most detailed knowledge of foreign law issues, the Section of International Law has the broadest and most extensive contacts with a wide range of foreign lawyers. The authors being "of a certain age", have had the opportunity to work on projects involving lawyers in most of these jurisdictions over the years.

This *Guide* should not be viewed as an official recommendation by the ABA or the Section of International Law as to which legal counsel to use in a foreign jurisdiction. Nor should the failure of a firm to be listed in these pages be deemed any form of disapproval. Given the diversity of views within the ABA and the Section of International Law, that would be impractical, if not impossible. What the *Guide* does do is to list the foreign law firms most likely to be used or considered by the Editors and other contributing members of the Section when foreign law issues arise. This volume is intended to be a practical reference tool for lawyers, not an encyclopedic listing of all qualified lawyers in a particular foreign jurisdiction.

A number of difficult choices have had to be made in preparing this Fifth Edition of the *Guide*. Perhaps the most fundamental choice was what foreign countries to include. Essentially, the decision was to cover all of the major trading countries, plus other countries with which members of the Section have had a reasonable amount of experience. The country which posed the most serious questions for us in this regard was Canada. Canadian firms have made this situation even more complex by forming multi-tiered partnerships across Provincial boundaries in Canada and operating in some cases under a single firm name, although the original firms still exist. Almost any generalization we would make about law firms in Canada (other than their growth and their high level of expertise) would likely be in error in some material way. On balance, however, it was decided that listings for Canadian firms would be included in this Edition. Although the legal system in Canada is generally comprehensible to most American lawyers, we hope the *Guide* will be useful in identifying appropriate counsel in the respective Canadian Provinces.

Another difficult question was whether to list the overseas offices of North American and foreign firms in places other than their home country. Because most of these firms historically have had only a limited knowledge of local law (and, indeed, are prohibited in many cases from advising on local law questions), it was decided to omit such information from prior Editions of the *Guide* in the vast majority of cases. In this new Fifth Edition, however, we have included certain U.S.-based firms where (i) their foreign offices included a strong foreign law capacity from lawyers qualified in that particular jurisdiction and (ii) they were recommended on a reasonably consistent basis with regard to that non-U.S. jurisdiction. Since this is a new element in this Edition of the *Guide*, we have no doubt made mistakes, both of inclusion and exclusion. We hope to do better next time.

In prior Editions of the *Guide*, the general theory of the Editors has been to list only indigenous law firms for each foreign jurisdiction. With the advent of truly international law firms, however, and the changes that are taking place in the regulation of foreign lawyers, this is already in many ways an outmoded way of looking at the world. As noted at the outset, no longer is it possible to say with any degree of certainty whether a particular law firm is an American firm, a Swiss firm, a Swedish firm or a Japanese firm,

3

because the firm of the future (and, in many cases, the present) may have partners trained and located in each of those jurisdictions). While this revolution is only beginning to arrive with full force in some countries, we have decided to take the next step in this process (as hinted at in the Fourth Edition) and included some of the foreign offices of appropriate U.S. firms. We recognize the limitations and inconsistencies of our prior approach and are trying to find in this new Edition an acceptable alternative.

In reviewing this new Edition of the *Guide*, there are several caveats for the reader to keep in mind:

(i) For space reasons, firms have been listed only under what was deemed to be their "home" city. Although the other offices of firms were also listed, the addresses and other information typically only relate to the one city (even where some firms now maintain that they no longer have a headquarters city). Another limitation resulting from this approach is that the best law firm in a particular country may not be listed under the heading for that country, because the home office of that firm is based elsewhere. Indeed, in at least a few cases, the "best" law firm in a particular country may not even be allowed, officially, to practice local law because it is not allowed to employ locally qualified lawyers.

(ii) Various combinations of law firms in international "affiliations" or "associations" have been largely ignored for purposes of this volume. Such affiliations have taken many forms in recent years and are the subject, in some cases, of incomplete information. As a result, any attempt to recite or describe these relationships was doomed to failure. One would imagine that by the time the next Edition of the *Guide* is prepared, there will be greater stability in this area of legal practice and this will allow us to include more information about "affiliations" the next time around. Similar predictions were included in prior Editions of the *Guide*, but the situation has become even more complex since then.

(iii) The nature of what constitutes a law firm is also changing. Some of the largest "law firms" in some countries are now directly tied to (or grew out of) accounting firms. Similarly,

4

in the Netherlands, for example, tax had always been considered a discrete discipline. Now it has been merged, in most cases, into traditional law firm practice. The same is also true in certain other EU countries where prohibitions against multi-professional partnerships are being challenged.

(iv) In the few cases where there has been a truly cross-border merger of law firms, it has been decided that, if both of the prior firms are of sufficient strength, then the newly combined firm would be listed in this volume in both locations.

(v) Some countries, have been omitted either because they were too newly formed at the time of writing to have been included in our surveys or because they were in a state of disintegration or protracted warfare. In one or two instances, we simply could not identify a local counsel about whom we felt we had enough information to make a recommendation.

(vi) Finally, there are many things about foreign law firms and lawyers that the Editors still do not know, but would like to. Given the number of countries involved and the number of changes that have taken place (in the profession in general and in individual firms in particular), it would have been a unique achievement to get everything exactly right. We realize that we may have failed this test and hope that the errors that do exist in this volume do not cause great inconvenience. We have been shooting not only at a moving target, but at a target that occasionally shoots back (at least rhetorically).

It is our intention to update this *Guide* periodically to incorporate changes in addresses, qualifications and personnel in the firms listed and countries covered. Comments on the format or the listings contained herein from other lawyers, either from the United States or from abroad, would be both welcomed and appreciated by the Editors. We hope this effort is helpful to you.

James R. Silkenat
William M. Hannay
June 2010

The Editors

James R. Silkenat
Sullivan & Worcester LLP
(New York)

James R. Silkenat is a former Chairman of the 20,000 member American Bar Association Section of International Law and is a Partner in the New York office of Sullivan & Worcester LLP, where he helps coordinate the Firm's international practice. He specializes in the areas of international finance, banking, securities and corporate law. He is also a former Chairman of the ABA's Section Officers Conference, a member of the Executive Committee of the ABA's Board of Governors and Chairman of the ABA's Latin American Legal Initiatives Council.

From 1980 to 1986 Mr. Silkenat was Legal Counsel for the International Finance Corporation, the private sector-oriented affiliate of the World Bank in Washington, D.C., where he concentrated on privatization issues (including projects in Pakistan, Indonesia, Zimbabwe, China and other countries). He has also handled significant privatization efforts in Australia, Peru, South Africa and Turkey. He is the founder and a former Chairman of the American Bar Association's Committee on International Privatization.

Mr. Silkenat received his J.D. Degree from the University of Chicago Law School, where he was an Editor of the Law Review. He also received an LL.M. Degree in International Law from New York University School of Law.

Mr. Silkenat was formerly Chairman of the American Bar Association Committee on the People's Republic of China and was the founder of the *China Law Reporter*. He has led

Delegations to the Common Market and to Mexico for the American Bar Association and to China for the ABA, the Fellows of the American Bar Foundation and the Association of the Bar of the City of New York. He has also served as a Fellow of the National Endowment for the Humanities and as a Fellow in the U.S. State Department Scholar/Diplomat Program.

Mr. Silkenat is the Editor of: *The ABA Guide to International Business Negotiations (1st, 2nd and 3rd Editions)*; *The Moscow Conference on Law and Bilateral Economic Relations*; *The Law of International Insolvencies and Debt Restructurings*; *The Imperial Presidency and Consequences of 9/11*: *Lawyers React to the Global War On Terrorism*; *and the first four Editions of The ABA Guide to Foreign Law Firms*. He is also the author of more than 100 articles on international law, finance and public policy and has published articles in the *Harvard Law Review, Business Week Magazine, The New York Times* and *The Stanford Law Review,* among other publications. He also served as an Adjunct Professor of Law at Georgetown University Law Center from 1982 to 1986, where he taught a graduate seminar on international project financing. Mr. Silkenat also previously served as Chairman of both The Lawyers Committee for International Human Rights (now, Human Rights First) and The Council of New York Law Associates (now, The Lawyers Alliance for New York). He is a member of the ABA House of Delegates, a Life Fellow of the American Bar Foundation and a member of the Council on Foreign Relations. Mr. Silkenat is also a past Chairman of the International Human Rights Committee of the Association of the Bar of the City of New York and a former Chair of both the City Bar's Task Force on International Legal Services and its Council on International Affairs.

Mr. Silkenat is the recipient of the Lifetime Achievement Award from the American Bar Association Section of International Law and the Distinguished Alumni Award for Career Achievement from Drury University.

Currently, Mr. Silkenat serves as a Director of the World Justice Project and as a member of the ABA's Commission on Women in the Profession.

William M. Hannay

Schiff Hardin LLP
(Chicago)

William M. Hannay is a partner in the Chicago-based law firm of Schiff Hardin LLP and concentrates his practice in litigation and counseling with respect to competition and trade regulation law at home and abroad. He is the leader of the firm's Antitrust Practice Group.

Mr. Hannay chaired the American Bar Association's Section of the International Law and Practice in 1998-99 and later served as Chair of the ABA's Africa Law Initiative Council in 2000-02. In addition, Mr. Hannay is an Adjunct Professor at IIT/Chicago-Kent College of Law in Chicago, teaching courses in international business negotiations, antitrust law, unfair trade practices law, and international criminal law. He is a founding member of the Board of Governors of the African Law Institute and a member of the American Law Institute. He also co-chairs the ABA-NCCUSL International Joint Editorial Board.

He has written and lectured widely about antitrust and competition law, about how to avoid or resolve international disputes, and about the Foreign Corrupt Practices Act, including seminars or programs sponsored by the American Bar Association, the American Conference Institute, the Institute for International Research, the Practicing Law Institute, and the Southwestern Legal Foundation. He is the author of the newly-released *Designing an Effective FCPA and Anti-Bribery Compliance Program* (Thomson/West) and the author or co-author of *U.S. International Antitrust Enforcement* (Bureau of National Affairs), *Tying Arrangements: Practice Under Federal Antitrust, Patent and Banking Law* (Bureau of National Affairs), *Designing an Effective Antitrust Compliance Program* (Thomson/West) and *International Trade: Avoiding Criminal Risks* (Butterworth Legal Publishers), as well as a contributing author to *Antitrust*

Counseling and Litigation Techniques (Matthew Bender) and a co-author/editor of *A Lawyer's Guide to Doing Business in South Africa* (American Bar Association) and the Third and Fourth Editions of the *ABA Guide to Foreign Law Firms*.

Before joining Schiff Hardin in 1979, Mr. Hannay was an Assistant District Attorney under Robert Morgenthau in New York City and, prior to that, a law clerk to Justice Tom Clark of the U.S. Supreme Court. He served with commendation in Vietnam with the United States Army (1967-68). He received his B.A. from Yale University in 1966 and his J.D. from Georgetown University in 1973.

Acknowledgments

The Editors wish to acknowledge the contributions of the members of the Section of International Law of the American Bar Association, without whose assistance this *Guide* could not have been prepared. Particular credit should go to Marilyn J. Kamen, the Section's Publications Officer. The authors also wish to thank the current Chair of the Section, Glenn P. Hendrix, and Chair-Elect, Salli A. Swartz, for their assistance and support in this project.

The Section of International Law is currently composed of approximately 20,000 lawyers and foreign affiliate members. In responding to the interests of these members, the Section has formed more than 70 Committees and Task Forces to deal with specific substantive questions and geographic areas of practice related to foreign and international law. Typically, such Committees have between 30 and 400 members involved in their everyday activities (usually involving seminars, publications, draft legislation and speeches by governmental officials). The Committees within the Section which have a specific geographic focus or which have a particular business orientation were consulted extensively to develop the lists of foreign legal counsel that is included in this volume.

During the preparation of this volume, the Committees in the African/Eurasian Division of the Section (for which the Section's Divisional Chair, Edna Udobong, had responsibility) included: the Africa Committee (Gretchen Bellamy and Victor Mroczka, Co-Chairs); the Asia/Pacific Committee (Mohommad Syed and Albert Chang, Co-Chairs); the China Committee (Adam Bobrow and Elizabeth Cole, Co-Chairs); the Europe Committee (Violeta Balan and Malika Levarlet, Co-Chairs); the India Committee (Lalit Bhasin and Vandana Cyril Shroff, Co-Chairs); and the Russia/Eurasia Committee (Ekaterina Gill and Christopher Kelly, Co-Chairs).

In the Americas/Middle East Division (for which the Section's Divisional Chair, Robert Brodegaard, had responsibility), the following Committees of the Section were particularly helpful in providing information that was used in the preparation of this Edition of the *Guide*: the Canada Committee (John Boscariol and Marcela Stras, Co-Chairs); the Latin America and Caribbean Committee (Jean Paul Chabeneix and Marcos Rios, Co-Chairs); the Mexico Committee (Patrick Del Duca and Alejandro Suarez, Co-Chairs); the Middle East Committee (James Phipps and Katlyn Thomas, Co-Chairs); and the Islamic Finance Committee (Hdeel Abdelhady and Ali Ibrahim, Co-Chairs).

In Business Law Division I (for which Robert Brown, as Division Chair, had responsibility): the International M&A and Joint Venture Committee (Saul Feilbogen and Mark Greene, Co-Chairs); the International Commercial Transactions, Franchising and Distribution Committee (Alan Gutterman and Richard Kaye, Co-Chairs); the International Energy and Natural Resources Committee (Teresa Faria and Richard Silberstein, Co-Chairs); the International Transportation Committee (Mark Andrews and Catherine Pawluch, Co-Chairs); and the Cross-Border Real Estate Practice Committee (Duarte Athayde and Amy Sommers, Co-Chairs).

In Business Law Division II (for which Jason Matechak, as Division Chair, had responsibility): the Aerospace & Defense Industries Committee (William Black and Wendie Wigginton, Co-Chairs); the Information Services, Technology and Data Protection Committee (Mark Field and Jackie Klosek, Co-Chairs); the International Intellectual Property Rights Committee (Susan Brushaber and Jessica Darraby, Co-Chairs); and the International Procurement Committee (Paul Lalonde and Jeffrey Marburg-Goodman, Co-Chairs).

Also, in the Business Regulation Division (for which the Section's Divisional Chair, Matthew S. Dunne, had responsibility), the following Committees of the Section were quite helpful in providing information for this Edition of the *Guide*: the Customs Law Committee (Laura Fraedrich and Geoffrey M. Goodale, Co-Chairs); the Export Controls and Economic Sanctions Committee (Kay Georgi and Eric Hinton, Co-Chairs); the International Antitrust Law Committee

11

(Fiona Schaeffer and David A. Schwartz, Co-Chairs); and the International Trade Committee (Kristy Balsanek, Matthew R. Nicely and Amy Stanley, Co-Chairs).

In the Disputes Division (for which Louise Ellen Teitz, Division Chair, had responsibility): the International Arbitration Committee (Laurie Foster and Kevin O'Gorman, Co-Chairs); the International Courts Committee (Lee Caplan and Carl Nesser, Co-Chairs); the International Criminal Law Committee (Darryl Lew and Donald Shaver, Co-Chairs); the International Judicial Affairs Committee (Delissa Ridgeway, Chair); and the International Litigation Committee (Alex Blumrosen and Steven Richman, Co-Chairs).

In the Finance Division (for which Melida Hodgson, Division Chair, had responsibility): the International Mediation Committee (Duncan Cameron and Douglas McClaren, Co-Chairs); the International Financial Products and Services Committee (Lennaert Posch and Walter Stuber, Co-Chairs); the International Investment and Development Committee (Jean Paul Chabeneix and Daniel Moreno, Co-Chairs); the International Secured Transactions and Insolvency Committee (Robert Grossman, Chair); and the International Securities and Capital Markets Committee (Daniel Bushner and Adam Farlow, Co-Chairs).

In the Legal Practice Division (for which Christian Dilling Lundgren, Division Chair, had responsibility): the International Corporate Counsel Forum (Carole Basri and Richard Walsh, Co-Chairs); the Foreign Legal Consultant Committee (Albert Garrofe, Chair); the Transnational Legal Practice Committee (Wayne Carroll and Jennifer McCandless, Co-Chairs); and the U.S. Lawyers Practicing Abroad Committee (Linda Murnane and Laurence Wiener, Co-Chairs).

Finally, this *Guide* would not have been possible without the tremendous commitment of time and effort by Marisol Borja in assembling the information, typing it, preparing the volume for publication and overseeing the publication process.

J.R.S.
W.M.H.

Table of Contents

14

Albania

Kalo & Associates

Kavaja Avenue
G-Kam Business Center, 4th Floor
P.O. Box 235
Tirana
Albania

Telephone:	355-42 233 532
Fax:	355-42 224 727
E-Mail:	info@kalo-attorneys.com
Internet:	www.kalo-attorneys.com
Partners:	*Perparim Kalo*
	Alban Caushi
Number of Lawyers:	25
Other Offices:	Athens
	Belgrade
	Bucharest
	Istanbul
	Sofia
	Pristina
Areas of Practice:	Full Service

Albania *continued*

Boga & Associates

Green Park, Tower I
P.O. Box 8264
Tirana
Albania

Telephone:	355-42 251 050
Fax:	355-42 251 055
E-Mail:	boga@bogalaw.com
Internet:	www.bogalaw.com
Partners:	Genc Boga
	Vojo Malo
	Renata Leka
Number of Lawyers:	35
Other Office:	Pristina
Areas of Practice:	Full Service

Angola

Fatima Freitas Advogados

Edificio Monumental
Rua Major Kanhangulo, 290 - 1° dto.
C.P. 954, Luanda
Angola

Telephone:	244-222-372-030/57/92
Fax:	244-222-372-017
E-Mail:	Luanda@fatimafreitas.com
Internet:	www.fatimafreitas.com
Partner:	*Fatima Freitas*
Number of Lawyers:	22
Other Office:	Cabinda
Areas of Practice:	Labor
	Oil and Gass
	Real Estate

MG – Advogados

Rua Rainha Ginga, 80
Luanda
Angola

Telephone:	244-222-370019
Fax:	244-222-335497
E-Mail:	lawyers@mgadvogados.org
Partner:	*Manuel Goncalves*
Number of Lawyers:	13
Areas of Practice:	Full Service

Anguilla

Webster Dyrud Mitchell

Victoria House
P.O. Box 58
AI- 2640 The Valley
Anguilla, B.V.I.

Telephone:	264-461-2060
Fax:	264-461-3096
E-Mail:	trusts@websterdyrud.com
Internet:	www.websterdyrud.com
Partners:	*John Oliver Dyrud*
	Pamela J. Webster
Number of Lawyers:	8
Other Offices:	Nevis
	Miami
Areas of Practice:	Banking & Finance
	Litigation
	Corporate & Business
	Trusts

Keithley Lake & Associates

The Law Building
P.O. Box 14
The Valley
Anguilla, B.V.I.

Telephone:	264-497-2069
Fax:	264-497-3012
E-Mail:	lake@anguilla-attorney.com
Internet:	www.anguilla-attorney.com
Partners:	*Keithley F.T. Lake*
	Yvette Wallace
	Kenneth G. Porter

Number of Lawyers: 6
Areas of Practice: Banking & Finance
Corporate
Insurance
Litigation
Real Estate

J.A.G. Gumbs & Co.

P.O. Box 1398
The Valley
Anguilla

Telephone:	264-497-1212
Fax:	264-497-1214
E-Mail:	admin@jagcolaw.com
Internet:	www.jagcolaw.com
Partners:	*Toluloa Agbelus*
	Josephine A.G. Gumbs-Connor

Number of Lawyers: 3
Areas of Practice: Full Service

Antigua

Roberts & Co.
Roberts Building
60 Nevis Street
P.O. Box 1301
St. John's
Antigua

Telephone:	268-462-0076
Fax:	268-462-3077
E-Mail:	robertslaw@candw.ag
Internet:	www.lawyers.com/roberts&co
Partner:	*Clare K. Roberts*
Number of Lawyers:	3
Areas of Practice:	Full Service

Christian, Lovell, Walwyn & Co.
29 Redcliffe Street
P.O. Box 20
St. John's
Antigua

Telephone:	268-462-1136
Fax:	268-461-0767
E-Mail:	hlovell@candw.ag
Partner:	*Harold Lovell*
Areas of Practice:	Real Estate
	Litigation
	Business

Argentina

Marval, O'Farrell & Mairal

Av. Leandro N. C1001AAR
Alem 928 Buenos Aires
Argentina

Telephone:	54-11-4310-0100
Fax:	54-11-4300-0200
E-Mail:	marvel@marval.com.ar
Internet:	www.marval.com.ar
Partners:	*Alfredo M. O'Farrell*
	Hernan Slemenson
	Gabriel Gotlib
Number of Lawyers:	330
Other Offices:	Cordoba
	New York
Areas of Practice:	Full Service

Allende & Brea

Maipu 1300, 11th floor
C1006ACT Buenos Aires
Argentina

Telephone:	54-11-4318-9900
Fax:	54-11-4318-9999
E-Mail:	info@allendebrea.com.ar
Internet:	www.allendebrea.com
Partners:	*Pablo G. Louge*
	Diego Botana
	Osvaldo J. Marzorati

Number of Lawyers: 66
Areas of Practice: Full Service

M.&M. Bomchil

Suipacha 268, 12th Floor
C1008AAF Buenos Aires
Argentina

Telephone:	54-11-4321-7500
Fax:	54-11-4321-7555
E-Mail:	info@bomchil.com
Internet:	www.bomchil.com
Partners:	*Nestor Jose Belgrano*
	Marcelo Bombau

Number of Lawyers: 78
Areas of Practice: Full Service

Negri & Teijeiro Abogados

Av. Corrientes 316
Buenos Aires C1043AAQ
Argentina

Telephone:	54-11-5556-8000
Fax:	54-11-4328-5628
E-Mail:	Laurence_wiener@negri.com.ar
Internet:	www.negri.com.ar
Partners:	*Juan Javier Negri*
	Laurence Paul Wiener

Number of Lawyers: 37
Areas of Practice: Full Service

G. Breuer

25 de mayo 460
C1002ABJ Buenos Aires
Argentina

Telephone:	54-11-4313-8100
Fax:	54-11-4313-8180
E-Mail:	info@gbreuer.com.ar
Internet:	www.gbreuer.com.ar
Partners:	*Luis M. Casares*
	Diego M. Fissore

Number of Lawyers: 29
Areas of Practice: Full Service

Estudio Beccar Varela

Cerrito 740 Piso 16
C1010AAP Buenos Aires
Argentina

Telephone:	54-11-4379-6800
Fax:	54-11-4379-6860
E-Mail:	estudio@beccarv.com.ar
Internet:	www.beccarv.com.ar
Partners:	*Emilio Beccar Varela*
	Emilio Vogelius

Number of Lawyers: 103
Areas of Practice: Full Service

Alfaro Abogados

Av. del Libertador 498
C1001ABR Buenos Aires
Argentina

Telephone:	54-11-4393-3003
Fax:	54-11-4393-3001
E-Mail:	cealfaro@alfarolaw.com
Internet:	www.alfarolaw.com
Partners:	*Carlos Enrique Alfaro*
	Hernan Verly
	Martin Caselli
	Liliana Arauz
	Sebastian Carlos Rodrigo

Number of Lawyers: 35
Other Offices: New York
London
Madrid
Areas of Practice: Full Service

Perez Alati, Grondona, Benites, Arntsen & Martinez de Hoz (Jr.)

Suipacha 1111, 18th floor
C1008AAW Buenos Aires
Argentina

Telephone:	54-11-4114-3000
Fax:	54-11-4114-3001
E-Mail:	pagbam@pagbam.com.ar
Internet:	www.pagbam.com.ar
Partners:	*Jorge Luis Perez Alati*
	Alan Arntsen
	Betina Di Croce
Number of Lawyers:	114
Other Offices:	Mendoza
	New York
Areas of Practice:	Full Service

Sena & Berton Moreno

Rivadavia 611, 5th Floor
C1002AAE Buenos Aires
Argentina

Telephone:	54-11-4342-6809
Fax:	54-11-4331-7774
E-Mail:	law@sbm.com.ar
Internet:	www.sbm.com.ar
Partners:	*Enrique Gatti*
	Marcelo Saavedra
Number of Lawyers:	17
Areas of Practice:	Full Service

Brons & Salas

Maipu 1210, 5th Floor
C1006ACT Buenos Aires
Argentina

Telephone:	54-11-4891-2700
Fax:	54-11-4314-0399
E-Mail:	arovira@brons.com.ar
Internet:	www.brons.com.ar
Partners:	*Alfredo L. Rovira*
	Eduardo Represas
Number of Lawyers:	72
Other Offices:	Cordoba
	Rosario
	Montevideo
Areas of Practice:	Full Service

Vitale, Manoff & Feilbogen

Viamonte 1145
Buenos Aires C153ABW
Argentina

Telephone:	54-11-4371-6100
Fax:	54-11-4371-6365
E-Mail:	vmf@vmf.com.ar
Internet:	www.vmf.com.ar
Partner:	*Saul Ricardo Feilbogen*
Number of Lawyers:	66
Areas of Practice:	Full Service

Estudio Randle

Carlos Pellegrini 1135
Buenos Aires C1009ABW
Argentina

Telephone:	54-11-5252-0700
Fax:	54-11-5252-0706
E-Mail:	irandle@randlelegal.com
Internet:	www.randlelegal.com
Partner:	*Ignacio Randle*
Number of Lawyers:	9
Areas of Practice:	Full Service

Australia

Blake Dawson

Level 36
Grosvenor Place
225 George Street
Sydney, New South Wales 2000
Australia

Telephone:	61-2-9258-6000
Fax:	61-2-9258-6999
E-Mail:	legal.info@blakedawson.com
Internet:	www.blakedawson.com
Partners:	*John Field*
	David Williamson
	Adrian Morris
	Arthur Apos
Number of Lawyers:	750
Other Offices:	Melbourne
	Adelaide
	Singapore
	Canberra
	Perth
	Brisbane
	Shanghai
	Port Moresby
Areas of Practice:	Full Service

Corrs Chambers Westgarth

Governor Phillip Tower
1 Farrer Place
Sydney NSW 2000
Australia

Telephone:	61-2-9210-6500
Fax:	61-2-9210-6611
E-Mail:	john.denton@corrs.com.au
Internet:	www.corrs.com.au
Partners:	*John Denton*
	John Kelly
	Odette Gourley
Number of Lawyers:	295
Other Offices:	Perth
	Melbourne
	Brisbane
Areas of Practice:	Full Service

Allens Arthur Robinson

Level 27
530 Collins Street
Melbourne, Victoria 3000
Australia

Telephone:	61-3-9614-1011
Fax:	61-3-9614-4661
E-Mail:	contactus@aar.com.au
Internet:	www.aar.com.au
Partners:	*Tom Poulton*
	Zeke Solomon (Sydney)
	Michael Dowling
Number of Lawyers:	1240
Other Offices:	Bangkok
	Brisbane
	Hanoi
	Ho Chi Minh City
	Hong Kong
	Jakarta
	Perth
	Phnom Penh
	Port Moresby
	Shanghai
	Singapore
	Sydney
Areas of Practice:	Full Service

Freehills

MLC Centre
19 Martin Place
Sydney, New South Wales 2000

Telephone:	61-2-9225-5000
Fax:	61-2-9322-4000
E-Mail:	business.enquiries@freehills.com
Internet:	www.freehills.com.au
Partners:	*Gavin Ball*
	David Templeman
	Chris Robertson
Number of Lawyers:	850
Other Offices:	Melbourne
	Perth
	Brisbane
	Singapore
	Ho Chi Minh City
	Hanoi
	Jakarta
Areas of Practice:	Full Service

Minter Ellison

Aurora Place
88 Philip Street
Sydney, New South Wales 2000
Australia

Telephone:	61-2-9921-4941
Fax:	61-2-9921-4419
E-Mail:	mail@minterellison.com
Internet:	www.minterellison.com
Partners:	*Leigh Brown*
	Tom Read
	John Steven
	Bruce Cowley
Number of Lawyers:	1219
Other Offices:	Adelaide
	Brisbane
	Canberra
	Darwin
	Gold Coast
	Melbourne
	Perth
	Hong Kong
	Jakarta
	Shanghai
	Auckland
	Wellington
	London
Areas of Practice:	Full Service

Middletons

Level 25
Rialto South Tower
525 Collins Street
Melbourne, VIC 3000
Australia

Telephone:	61-3-9205-2132
E-Mail:	nick.nichola@middletons.com
Internet:	www.middletons.com
Partners:	*Nick Nichola*
	Debra Woodman
Number of Lawyers:	277
Other Offices:	Sydney
	Perth
Areas of Practice:	Full Service

Clayton Utz

Levels 19-35
No. 1 O'Connell Street
Sydney, New South Wales 2000
Australia

Telephone:	61-0-2-9353-4000
Fax:	61-0-2-8220-6700
E-Mail:	info@claytonutz.com
Internet:	www.claytonutz.com
Partners:	David Fagan
	Steve O'Reilly
	Michael Reade
	Joshua Fellenbaum
	Linda Evans
	Julie Levis
	Stuart Clark
Number of Lawyers:	1700
Other Offices:	Brisbane
	Canberra
	Darwin
	Melbourne
	Hobart
	Perth
Areas of Practice:	Full Service

Dobson Mitchell & Allport

59 Harrington Street
Hobart, Tasmania TAS 2612
Australia

Telephone:	61-36-222-1143
Fax:	61-36-223-6633
E-Mail:	tim.bugg@doma.com.au
Internet:	www.doma.com.au
Partner:	Timothy Bugg
Number of Lawyers:	23
Areas of Practice:	Full Service

Mallesons Stephen Jaques

Level 61
Governor Phillip Tower
1 Farrer Place
Sydney, New South Wales 2000
Australia

Telephone:	61-2-9296-2000
Fax:	61-2-9296-3999
E-Mail:	syd@mallesons.com
Internet:	www.mallesons.com
Partners:	*Robert Milliner*
	Stuart Fuller
	Tony O'Malley
	Nicola Wakefield Evans
	Tony Bancroft
	Larry Kwok
	John King
	Frank Zipfinger
Number of Lawyers:	1020
Other Offices:	Melbourne
	Perth
	Brisbane
	Canberra
	Hong Kong
	Beijing
	London
Areas of Practice:	Full Service

Jackson McDonald

140 St Georges Terrace
Perth, Western Australia
Australia

Telephone:	61-8-9426-6611
Fax :	61-8-9321-2002
E-Mail:	jacmac@jacmac.com.au
Internet:	www.jacmac.com.au
Partners:	*Gregory Boyle*
	Jeffrey Lin
	Peter Walton
Number of Lawyers:	164
Areas of Practice:	Full Service

Austria

Graf & Pitkowitz

Stadiongasse 2
A-1010 Vienna
Austria

Telephone:	43-1-401-170
Fax:	43-1-401-1740
E-Mail:	office@gpp.at
Internet:	www.gpp.at
Partners:	*Otto Waechter*
	Nikolaus Piktowitz
	Ferdinand Graf
Number of Lawyers:	17
Other Office:	Graz
Areas of Practice:	Full Service

Sehoenherr

Tuchlauben 17
A-1010 Vienna
Austria

Telephone:	43-1-534-370
Fax:	43-1-534-37-6100
E-Mail:	office@schoenherr.at
Internet:	www.schoenherr.eu
Partners:	*Christian Herbst*
	Christian Hauer
	Peter Madl
Number of Lawyers:	310
Other Offices:	Belgrade
	Brussels
	Bucharest
	Kiev
	Ljubljana
	Sofia
	Zagreb
	Bratislava
	Budapast
	Prague
Areas of Practice:	Full Service

Specht Rechtsanwalt GmbH

Teinfaltstrasse 8/5
A-1010 Vienna
Austria

Telephone:	43-1-219-6869
Fax:	43-1-219-6862-20
E-Mail:	vienna@specht-partner.com
Internet:	www.spechtpartner.com
Partners:	*Leopold Specht*
	Cweyda Akbal
Other Offices:	Moscow
	Belgrade
	Budapest
	Kiev
	Prague
	St. Petersburg
Areas of Practice:	Full Service

Binder Grosswang

Sterngasse 13
A-1010 Vienna
Austria

Telephone:	43-1-534-80
Fax:	43-1-534-808
E-Mail:	vienna@bindergroesswang.at
Internet:	www.bindergroesswang.at
Partners:	*Michael Binder*
	Michael Kutschera
Number of Lawyers:	41
Other Office:	Innsbruck
Areas of Practice:	Full Service

Masser & Partner Rechtsanwalte

Singerstrasse 27
A1010 Vienna
Austria

E-Mail:	rakanzlei@masser-partner.at
Internet:	www.masser-partner.at
Partners:	*Florian Masser*
	Robert Lirsch
Number of Lawyers:	8
Areas of Practice:	Full Service

Cerha Hempel Spiegelfeld Hlawati

Parkring 2
A-1010 Vienna
Austria

Telephone:	43-1-514-350
Fax:	43-1-514-3535
E-Mail:	office@chsh.at
Internet:	www.chsh.at
Partners:	*Benedikt Spiegelfeld*
	Peter Knobl
	Manfred Ton
Number of Lawyers:	92
Other Offices:	Bratislava
	Belgrade
	Brussels
	Budapest
	Bucharest
	Minsk
	Sofia
Areas of Practice:	Full Service

Dorda Brugger Jordis

Dr-Karl-Lueger-Ring 10
A-1010 Vienna
Austria

Telephone:	43-1-533-4795-0
Fax:	43-1-533-4797
E-Mail:	office@dbj.at
Internet:	www.dbj.at
Partners:	*Walter Brugger*
	Bernhard Reider

Number of Lawyers: 50
Areas of Practice: Full Service

Fellner Wratzfeld & Partner

Schottenring 12
1010 Vienna
Austria

Telephone:	43-1-537-700
Fax:	43-1-537-7070
E-Mail:	paul.luiki@fwp.at
Internet:	www.fwp.at
Partner:	*Paul Luiki*

Number of Lawyers: 43
Areas of Practice: Full Service

Wolf Theiss

Schubertring 6
A-1010 Vienna
Austria

Telephone:	43-1-515-10
Fax:	43-1-515-10-25
E-Mail:	wien@wolfftheiss.com
Internet:	www.wolftheiss.com
Partners:	*Andreas Theiss*
	Horst Eberhardt
Number of Lawyers:	166
Other Offices:	Belgrade
	Bratislava
	Bucharest
	Ljubljana
	Pragne
	Sarajevo
	Tirana
	Zagreb
Areas of Practice:	Full Service

DLA Piper Weiss-Tessbach

Schottenring 14
1010 Vienna
Austria

Telephone:	43-1-531-780
Fax:	43-1-533-5252
E-Mail:	Claudine.vartian@dlapiper.com
Internet:	www.dlapiper.com/austria1
Partner:	*Claudine Vartian*
Number of Lawyers:	70 in Austria
Other Offices:	Numerous
Areas of Practice:	Full Service

Bahamas

Graham, Thompson & Co.

Sasson House
Shirley St. and Victoria Avenue
P.O. Box N-272
Nassau, New Providence
Bahamas

Telephone:	242-322-4130
Fax:	242-328-1069
E-Mail:	info@gtclaw.com
Internet:	www.grahamthompson.com
Partners:	*Dana C. Wells*
	Pembroke H. Williams
	Tanya R. Hanna
Number of Lawyers:	16
Other Office:	Freeport
Areas of Practice:	Admiralty and Shipping
	Banking and Finance
	Corporate and Commercial
	Family Law
	Government Licenses and Approvals
	Immigration
	Litigation
	Personal Wealth Preservation
	and Planning
	Real Estate and Land Development

McKinney, Bancroft & Hughes

Mareva House
4 George Street
Nassau, New Providence
Bahamas

Telephone:	242-322-4195
Fax:	242-328-2520
E-Mail:	nassau@mckinney.com.bs
Internet:	www.mckinney.com.bs
Partners:	_Brian C. Moree_
	J. Oliver Liddell
Number of Lawyers:	28
Other Office:	Freeport
Areas of Practice:	Admiralty, Shipping and Aviation
	Commercial Property
	Family Law
	Litigation & Dispute Resolution
	Trusts and Estate Planning

Higgs & Johnson

Ocean Centre
Montagu Foreshore, East Bay Street,
P.O. Box N-3247, Nassau
Bahamas

Telephone:	242-502-5200
Fax:	242-502-5250
E-Mail:	nassaug@higgsiohnson.com
Internet:	www.higgsjohnson.com
Partners:	*Surinder Deal*
	Oscar N. Johnson, Jr.
	Sterling H. Caske
Number of Lawyers:	33
Other Offices:	Lyford Cay
	Freeport
	Abaco
	Grand Cayman
Areas of Practice:	Full Service

Bahrain

Haya Rashed Al Khalifa

First Floor
Bahrain Development Bank Building
P.O. Box 1188
Diplomatic Area, Manama
Bahrain

Telephone:	973-17-537771
Fax:	973-17-531117
E-Mail:	info@hraklf.com
Internet:	www.hraklf.com
Partners:	*Shaikha Haya Rashed Al Khalifa*
	Rashid Bo-Ghammar
Number of Lawyers:	14
Areas of Practice:	Banking and Finance
	Corporate and Commercial
	Litigation
	Bankruptcy

Bangladesh

Dr. Kamal Hossain & Associates

122-124 Motijheel Commercial Area
Chamber Building, 2nd Floor
Dhaka 1000
Bangladesh

Telephone:	8802-955-2946
Fax:	8802-955-2946
E-Mail:	khossain@citecho.net
Partners:	*Dr. Kamal Hossain*
	Sara Hossain
	Md. Abdul Wadud

Number of Lawyers: 21
Areas of Practice: Full Service

The Law Associates

203 Concord Tower, 2nd Floor
113 Kazi Nazrul Islam Avenue
Dhaka 1000
Bangladesh

Telephone:	880-2-933-0877
Fax:	880-2-933-7746
E-Mail:	amir@bdmail.net
Internet:	www.tlabd.org
Partners:	*M. Amir-Ul Islam*
	Tania Amir

Number of Lawyers: 11
Areas of Practice: Full Service

H&H Company

Shareef Mansion (Second Floor)
56/57 Motijheel Commercial Area
Dhaka
Bangladesh

Telephone:	880-2-955-0705
Fax:	880-2-955-2447
E-Mail:	hnh@bangla.net
Internet:	www.hnhcompany.com
Partners:	*Sayyid Shahid Hussain*
	Mollah M. Haque
	Rezwanul Haque
Number of Lawyers:	14
Other Offices:	Chiitangong
	Khulna
Areas of Practice:	International Financings
	Company Law
	Commercial Law
	Commercial Litigation

Barbados

George Walton Payne & Co.

Suite 205-207 Dowell House
Cr. Roebuck Street & Palmetto Sts.
Bridgetown
Barbados

Telephone:	246-426-0417
Fax:	246-228-5756
E-Mail:	gwp&co@caribsurf.com.
Internet:	www.gwpco.com.bb
Partners:	*George W. Payne*
	Dale D. Marshall
	Andrew V. Thornhill
	Tammy L. Bryan
	Diana R. Douglin

Number of Lawyers: 9
Areas of Practice: Full Service

Chancery Chambers

Chancery House
High Street
Bridgetown
Barbados

E-Mail:	chancery@chancerychambers.com
Internet:	www.chancerychambers.com
Partner:	*Trevor A. Carmichael*

Number of Lawyers: 8
Areas of Practice: Full Service

Belarus

Vlasova Mikhel & Partners

57-2 Parikovya Street
220114 Minsk
Belarus

Telephone:	375-17-211-8142
Fax:	375-17-211-8142
E-Mail:	info@vmp.by
Internet:	www.vmp.by
Partners:	*Liliya Vlasova*
	Konstantin Mikhel
	Tatiana Emilianova
	Ekaterina Zabello
Number of Lawyers:	14
Areas of Practice:	Full Service

Borovtsov & Salei

P.O. Box 86
Minsk 220029
Belarus

Telephone:	375-17-293-4418
Fax:	374-17-293-4422
E-Mail:	info@borovtsovsalei.com
Internet:	www.borovtsovsalei.com
Partner:	*Alexander Botian*
Number of Lawyers:	7
Areas of Practice:	Full Service

Belgium

Stibbe

Central Plaza
Loksumstraat 25 rue de Loxum
Rue Henri Wafelaertsstraat 47-51
BE-1000 Brussels
Belgium

Telephone:	32-2-533-5211
Fax:	32-2-533-5212
E-Mail:	info@stibbe.be
Internet:	www.stibbe.be
Partners:	*Vera von Hautte*
	Jan Peeters
Other Offices:	New York
	Amsterdam
	London
	Dubai
Number of Lawyers:	132 in Brussels
Areas of Practice:	Full Service

DLA Piper

106 Avenue Louise
B-1050 Brussels
Belgium

Telephone:	32-2-500-1500
Fax:	32-2-500-1600
E-Mail:	info@dlapiper.com
Internet:	www.dlapiper.com
Partners:	_Dirk Caesteker_
	Steven De Keyser
Number of Lawyers:	Over 3,200
Other Offices:	Numerous
Areas of Practice:	Full Service

Linklaters

Rue Brederode 13
1000 Brussels
Belgium

Telephone:	32-2-501-9411
Fax:	32-2-501-9494
E-Mail:	paul.vanhooghten@linklaters.com
Internet:	www.linklaters.com
Partners:	_Gerwin van Gerven_
	Paul van Hooghten
Number of Lawyers:	Numerous
Other Offices:	Numerous
Areas of Practice:	Full Service

Elegis, Huybrechts, Engels, Craen & Partners

Gateway House
Brussellstraat 59
2-2018 Antwerp
Belgium

Telephone:	32-3-244-1560
Fax:	32-3-238-4140
E-Mail:	hec@elegis.be
Internet:	www.elegis.be
Partners:	*Peter Engels*
	Edmond Brondel
	Marc Huybrechts
Number of Lawyers:	65
Other Offices:	Brussels
	Eupen
	Liege
	Namur
Areas of Practice:	Full Service

Cleary, Gottlieb, Steen & Hamilton

Rue de la Loi 57
1040 Brussels
Belgium

Telephone:	32-2-287-2000
Fax:	32-2-231-1661
E-Mail:	jmeyers@cgsh.com
Internet:	www.cgsh.com
Partners:	*Thomas Graf*
	Maurits Dolmans
	Jan Meyers
Number of Lawyers:	700
Other Offices:	Beijing
	Cologne
	Frankfurt
	Hong Kong
	London
	Milan
	Moscow
	New York
	Paris
	Rome
	Washington
Areas of Practice:	Full Service

LVP Law

6 Drêve des Renards/Vossendreef, b-1
1180 Brussels
Belgium

Telephone:	32-2-373-0910
Fax:	32-2-375-4525
E-Mail:	infobru@lvplaw.be
Internet:	www.lafili-law.be
Partners:	*Nicole Van Crombrugghe*
	Christine Sartini Vandenkerckhove
Number of Lawyers:	16
Other Offices:	Antwerp
	Kortrijk
Areas of Practice:	Full Service

Marx Van Ranst Vermeersch & Partners

Tervurenlaan 270
1150 Brussels
Begium

Telephone:	32-2-285-0100
Fax:	32-2-230-3339
E-Mail:	info@mvvp.be
Internet:	www.mvvp.be
Partner:	*Nicole Van Ranst*
Number of Lawyers:	26
Areas of Practice:	Full Service

Van Bael & Bellis

165 Avenue Louise
B-1050 Brussels

Telephone:	32-2-647-7350
Fax:	32-2-640-6499
E-Mail:	brussels@vanbaelbellis.com
Internet:	www.vanbaelbellis.com
Partners:	*Ivo Van Bael*
	Jean-Francois Bellis
Number of Lawyers:	61
Other Office:	Geneva
Areas of Practice:	Competition Law
	Trade & Customs Law
	Belgian Business Law
	EU Regulatory Law
	Regulated Industries

Loyens & Loeff

Woluwe Atrium
Neerveldstraat 101-103
B-1200 Brussels
Belgium

Telephone:	32-2-743-4343
Fax:	32-2-743-4310
Internet:	*www.loyens.com*
Partners:	*Peter Callens*
	Geert Bogaert
Number of Lawyers:	Numerous
Other Offices:	Numerous
Aeas of Practice:	Full Service

Nauta Dutilh

Chausee de La Hulpe 177
1170 Brussels
Belgium

Telephone:	32-2-566-8000
Fax:	32-2-566-8001
E-Mail:	info@nautadutilh.com
Internet:	www.nautadutilh.com
Partners:	*Didier de Vliegher*
	Derk van Gerven
Number of Lawyers:	72 in Brussels
Other Offices:	Amsterdam
	London
	Luxembourg
	New York
	Rotterdam
Areas of Practice:	Full Service

Freshfields Bruckhaus Deringer

Place du Champ de Mars 5
1050 Brussels
Belgium

Telephone:	32-2-504-7000
Fax:	32-2-504-7200
E-Mail:	info@freshfields.com
Internet:	www.freshfields.com
Partners:	*Onno Brouwner*
	John Davies
	Vincent Macq
	Geert Verhoeven
Number of Lawyers:	68 in Brussels
Other Offices:	Numerous
Areas of Practice:	Full Service

Simont Braun

Av. Louise 149
1050 Brussels
Belgium

Telephone:	32-2-543-7080
Fax:	32-2-543-7090
E-Mail:	info@simontbraun.eu
Internet:	www.simontbraun.be
Partners:	*Lucien Simont*
	Paul Alain Foriers
Number of Lawyers:	61
Areas of Practice:	Full Service

Liedekerke Wolters Waelbroeck Kirkpatrick

Boulevard de l'Empereur 3 Keizerslaan
B-1000 Brussels
Belgium

Telephone:	32-2-551-1515
Fax:	32-2-551-1414
E-Mail:	info@liedekerke.com
Internet:	www.liedekerke.com
Partners:	*Jacques Malherbe*
	Joe Sepulchre
	Yves Delacroix
Number of Lawyers:	79
Other Office:	London
Areas of Practice:	Full Service

Matray Matray & Hallet

7, Allee de Cloitre
B-1000 Brussels
Belgium

E-Mail: matray.hallet@matray.be
Internet: www.matray.be
Partner: *Francoise Vidts*
Number of Lawyers: 28
Areas of Practice: Full Service

VWEW Advocaten

Cluster Center
Leuvensesteenweg 369
B-1932 St. Stevens-Wolowe (Zaventem)
Belgium

Telephone: 32-2-725-6063
Fax: 32-2-725-7038
E-Mail: alain.vanderelst@vwew-law.be
Internet: www.vwew.be
Partners: *Alain Vanderelst*
Piet Everaert
Number of Lawyers: 16
Areas of Practice: Busienss Law
EU and Competition Law
Labor Law
Litigation

Belgium *continued*

Lorenz

Troonstraat 14-16
Brussels B 1000
Belgium

Telephone:	322-239-2000
Fax:	322-239-2002
E-Mail:	brussels@lorenz-law.com
Internet:	www.lorenz-law.com
Partner:	*Steven De Schrijver*
Number of Lawyers:	21
Other Offices:	Bishkek
	Geneva
Areas of Practice:	Full Service

Belize

Barrow & Williams

99 Albert Street
P.O. Box 617
Belize City
Belize

Telephone:	501-227-5280
Fax:	501-227-5278
E-Mail:	attorneys@barrowandwilliams.com
Internet:	www.barrowandwilliams.com
Partners:	*Dean O. Barrow*
	Rodwell Williams

Number of Lawyers: 4
Areas of Practice: Full Service

W.H. Courtenay & Co.

1876 Hutson Street
P.O. Box 160
Belize City
Belize

Telephone:	501-223-5701
Fax:	501-224-4248
E-Mail:	whc-co@hotmail.com
Internet:	www.courtenaylaw.com
Partners:	*Derek B. Courtenay*
	Shirley Rose Courtenay
	Jeremy D. Courtenay

Number of Lawyers: 5
Areas of Practice: Full Service

Bermuda

Appleby

Canon's Court
22 Victoria Street
P.O. Box HM 1179
Hamilton HM EX
Bermuda

Telephone:	441-295-2244
Fax:	441-292-8666
E-Mail:	info@applebyglobal.com
Internet:	www.applebyglobal.com
Partners:	*Cameron Adderley*
	Peter Bubenzer
	Judth Collis
	Shaun Morris
Number of Lawyers:	200 in Bermuda
Other Offices:	British Virgin Indies
	Cayman Islands
	Hong Kong
	Isle of Man
	Seychelles
	Jersey
	Zurich
	Bahrain
	London
	Mauritius
Areas of Practice:	Full Service

Conyers, Dill & Pearman

Clarendon House
2 Church Street
P.O. Box HM 666
Hamilton HM CX
Bermuda

Telephone:	441-295-1422
Fax:	441-292-4720
E-Mail:	bermuda@conyersdillandpearman.com
Internet:	www.cdp.bm
Partners:	*Graham Collis*
	Alec Anderson
	Peter Pearman
Number of Lawyers:	118
Other Offices:	Anguilla
	British Virgin Islands
	Cayman Islands
	Dubai
	Hong Kong
	London
	Sao Paolo
	Mauritius
	Moscow
	Singapore
Areas of Practice:	Full Service

Bolivia

C.R. & F. Rojas

Calle Federico Zuazo 1598
Edificio Park Inn, Piso 11
La Paz
Bolivia

Telephone:	591-2-211-3165
Fax:	591-2-237-6380
E-Mail:	Frojas@rojas-lawfirm.com
Internet:	www.rojas-lawfirm.com
Partners:	*Fernando Rojas*
	Carlos Ferreira
Number of Lawyers:	19
Other Office:	Santa Cruz
Areas of Practice:	Full Service

Guevara & Gutierrez

Calle 15 No. 7715
Esquina Calle Sanchez Bustamante
Torre Ketal, Piso 4 Oficina No. 2
La Paz
Bolivia

Telephone:	591-2-277-0808
Fax:	591-2-279-6462
E-Mail:	abogados@gg-lex.com
Partners:	*Ramiro Guevara*
	Primitivo Gutierrez
Number of Lawyers:	24
Other Office:	Santa Cruz
Areas of Practice:	Full Service

Bufete Aguirre Soc. Civ.

Arce No. 2071 ler Piso, Oficina 6
La Paz
Bolivia

Telephone:	591-2-244-0937
Fax:	591-2-244-0065
E-Mail:	abogados@bufeteaguirre-lawfirm.com
Internet:	www.bufeteaguirre-lawfirm.com
Partners:	*Ignacio Aguirre*
	Fernando Aguirre
	Perla Koziner
Areas of Practice:	General Commercial

Apt Law Firm

Capitan Ravelo 2328
P.O. Box 1261
La Paz
Bolivia

Telephone:	591-2-244-1809
Fax:	591-2-244-1088
E-Mail:	apt@legalapt.com
Internet:	www.legalapt.com
Partners:	*Wolfgang Apt*
	Miguel Apt
Number of Lawyers:	4
Areas of Practice:	Full Service

Botswana

Luke & Associates

Sable House
Plot 14416 Gabronne West Industrial Estates
Gaborone
Botswana

Telephone:	09-267-391-9345
Fax:	09-267-391-9345
E-Mail:	luke@info.bw
Internet:	www.attorneys.co.za/luke
Partner:	*Edward Fashole-Luke II*
Areas of Practice:	General Commercial Practice

Tengo Rubadiri Attorneys

Plot 7972, Letswai Rd BBS Mall
P/Bag BR 353
Gaborone
Botswana

Telephone:	267-391-1577
E-Mail:	rubadiri@global.bw
Partner:	*Tengo Rubadiri*

Rahim Khan & Company

Office #1, Plot 50362
Showgrounds Office Park
P.O. Box 1884
Gaborone
Botswana

E-Mail:	info@rahimkhan.co.bw
Partner:	*A.R. Khan*
Number of Lawyers:	3
Areas of Practice:	Full Service

Brazil

Demarest e Almeida

Av. Pedroso de Moraes, 1.201 Centro Cultural Ohtake
Sao Paulo, SP 05419-001
Brazil

Telephone:	55-11-2245-1800
Fax:	55-11-2245-1700
E-Mail:	da.sp@demarest.com.br
Internet:	www.demarest.com.br
Partners:	*Carolina Joop (New York)*
	Altamiro Boscoli
	Roberto Luiz Portella
Number of Lawyers:	320
Other Offices:	Campinas
	Fortaleza
	Porte Allegre
	Brasilia
	Rio De Janeiro
	Salvador
	Receife
	New York
Areas of Practice:	Full Service

Veriano E Advogados Associados

Ave. Presidente Wilson, 231
20030-021 Rio De Janeiro
Brazil

Telephone:	55-21-3824-4747
Fax:	55-21-2262-4247
E-Mail:	rh@veirano.com.br
Internet:	www.veirano.com.br
Partners:	*Ronaldo Veirano*
	Guido Vinci
Number of Lawyers:	218
Other Offices:	Sao Paulo
	Porto Allegre
	Brasilia
	Ribeirao Preto
Areas of Practice:	General Corporate
	Tax
	Banking
	Mergers and Acquisitions

Leite, Tosto e Barros

Doutor Renato Paes de Barros, 1.017
04530-001 Sao Paulo
Brazil

Telephone:	55-11-3847-3939
Fax:	55-11-3847-7446
E-Mail:	tostoadvsp@tostoadv.com
Partners:	*Ricardo Tosto de Oliveira Carvalho*
	Jorge Nemr
Number of Lawyers:	62
Other Offices:	Brasilia
	Rio de Janeiro
Areas of Practice:	Full Service

Noronha Advogados

Rua Alexandre Dumas, 1630
Sao Paulo
Brazil

Telephone:	55-11-5188-8090
Fax:	55-11-5184-0097
E-Mail:	noadsao@noranhaadvogados.com.br
Partners:	*D. de Noronha Goyos Jr.*
	Patricia Guidi
	Aarelio Gaazoni
Other Offices:	Rio de Janaeiro
	Brasilia
	Curitiba
	Porto Allegre
	Recife
	Belo Horizonte
	Buenos Aires
	Miami
	London
	Lisbon
	Shanghai
Areas of Practice:	Full Service

Lanna Peixoto Advogados

Rua Sergipe 925
Savassi, Belo Horizonte - MG
Brazil

Telephone:	55-31-3244-0076
Fax:	55-31-3244-0086
E-Mail:	bpeixoto@lpglobal.com.br
Internet:	www.lannapeixoto.com.br
Partner:	*Bruno Peixoto*
Number of Lawyers:	7
Other Offices:	Sao Paulo
	Brasilia
Areas of Practice:	Antitrust
	Regulated Industries
	International Trade
	Trademarks

Pinheiro Neto

Rua Hungaria, 1100
Sao Paulo 01455-000
Brazil

Telephone:	55-11-3247-8400
Fax:	55-11-3247-8600
E-Mail:	pna@pinheironeto.com.br
Internet:	www.pinheironeto.com.br
Partners:	*Antonio Mendes*
	Celso Cintro Mori
Number of Lawyers:	210
Other Offices:	Rio de Janeiro
	Brasilia
Areas of Practice:	Corporate Law
	Taxation
	Litigation

Wald & Associates

Av. Almiranta Barroso, 52
20031 000
Rio de Janeiro
Brazil

Telephone:	55-21-2272-9300
Fax:	55-21-2272-8789
E-Mail:	waldrj@wald.com.br
Internet:	www.wald.com.br
Partners:	*Antonio Tavares Paes*
	Alexandre Wald
Number of Lawyers:	72
Other Offices:	Sao Paulo
	Brasilia
Areas of Practice:	Full Service

Almeida Advogados

1461 Brigadeiro Farina Lima
01452-002 Sao Paulo/SP
Brazil

Telephone:	55-11-2714-6900
Fax:	55-11-2714-6901
E-Mail:	almedia@almeidalaw.com.br
Internet:	www.almeidaadvogados.com.br
Partner:	*Andre De Almeida*
Number of Lawyers:	33
Other Offices:	Rio de Janeiro
	Belo Horizonte
	Natal
Areas of Practice:	Full Service

Calvalho, Machado, Timm & Deffenti

Av. Carlos Gomes, 1340/602
90480-001 Puerto Alegre, RS
Brazil

Telephone:	55-51-3022-5550
Fax:	55-51-3022-6650
E-Mail:	carvalho@cmted.com.br
Internet:	www.cmted.com.br
Partners:	*Cristano Rosa de Carvalho*
	Fabiano Deffenti
Number of Lawyers:	9
Other Offices:	Sao Paulo
	Bento Goncalves
Areas of Practice:	Full Service

Tozzini Freire

Rua Borges Lago 1328
04038-904 Sao Paulo-SP
Brazil

Telephone:	55-11-5086-5000
Fax:	55-11-5086-5555
E-Mail:	mail@tozzini.com.br
Internet:	www.tozzinifreira.com.br
Partners:	*Claudia Muniz*
	Levasier Mahler
	Marcio Baptista
	Jose Luis de Salle Freire
	Jose Regazzini
Number of Lawyers:	326
Other Offices:	Rio de Janeiro
	Brasilia
	Porto Allegre
	Campinas
Areas of Practice:	Full Service

Suchodolski Advogados Associados

Rua Agusta 1819
Sao Paulo CAP 01413-000
Brazil

Telephone:	55-11-3372-1300
Fax:	55-11-3372-1301
Internet:	www.suchodolski.com.br
Partners:	*Beno Suchodolski*
	Maria Elvira Ramos
Number of Lawyers:	18
Areas of Practice:	International Transactions
	Mergers and Acquisitions
	Tax
	Corporate

Pinheiro, Mourao e Raso Advogados

SAUS Quadra 5
Conj. 302
Edificio OK Office Center
CEP 70.070-050
Brasilia
Brazil

E-Mail:	pmradv.com.br
Internet:	www.pmradv.com.br
Partners:	*Dafini de Araujo Peracio Manteiro*
	Adriana Mouralo Nogueira
Number of Lawyers:	18
Areas of Practice:	Full Service

Azevedo Sette Advogados

1ˢᵗ-Av. Das Nacoes Unidos
04578-908 Sao Paulo
Brazil

Telephone:	55-11-4083-7600
Fax:	55 11-4083-7601
E-Mail:	osette@azevedosette.com.br
Internet:	www.azevedosette.com.br
Partners:	*Fernando Azevedo Sette*
	Ordelio Azevedo Sette
Number of Lawyers:	160
Other Offices:	Belo Horizonte
	Goiania
	Vitoria
	Brasilia
	Rio de Janeiro
Areas of Practice:	Corporate Law
	Mergers and Acquisitions
	Project Finance
	General Practice

Mattos Filho, Veiga Filho, Marrey Jr. e Quiroga

Al. Joaquim Eugenio de Lima, 447
01403-001 Sao Paulo
Brazil

Telephone:	55-11-3147-7600
Fax:	55-11-3147-7770
E-Mail:	mattosfilho@mattosfilho.com.br
Partners:	*Otavio de Veiga Filho*
	Marcelo Mansour Haddad
	Jose Eduardo Carneiro Queiroz
Number of Lawers:	211
Other Offices:	Brasilia
	Rio de Janeiro
	New York
Areas of Practice:	Full Service

Trench, Rossi & Watanabe

Avenue Rio Branco, 1
20090-003 Rio de Janeiro
Brazil

Telephone:	55-21-2206-4960
Fax:	55-2206-4949
Internet:	trenchrossiewatanabe.com.br
Partners:	*Nazir Takieddine (Sao Paulo)*
	Fatima Carr (Sao Paulo)
	Ana Tavares de Mello
Other Offices:	Sao Paulo
	Brasilia
	Porto Allegre
Areas of Practice:	Full Service

Machado, Meyer, Sendacz e Opice

Av. Brigadeiro Faria Lima, 3.144
01451-000 Sao Paulo, S.P.
Brazil

Telephone:	55-113-150-700
Fax:	55-113-150-7071
E-Mail:	mmso@mmso.com.br
Internet:	www.mmso.com.br
Partners:	*Antonio Corred Meyer*
	Carlos Jose Rolim de Mello
	Jose Roberto Opice
Number of Lawyers:	380
Other Offices:	Brasilia
	Rio de Janeiro
	New York
	Belo Horizonte
	Salvador
	Porto Allegre
Areas of Practice:	Full Service

Felsberg & Associados

Avenida Paulista, 1294
Sao Paulo, SP
Brazil

Telephone:	55-11-31-41-3665
Fax:	55-11-31-41-9150
E-Mail:	neilmontgomery@felsberg.com.br
Internet:	www.felsberg.com.br
Partner:	*Neil Montgomery*
Number of Lawyers:	150
Other Offices:	Sao Paulo
	Rio de Janeiro
	Campinas
	Brasilia
	Shanghai
	Washington, D.C.
	New York
	Dusseldorf
Areas of Practice:	Full Service

Montaury Pimenta, Machado & Lioce

Av. Almirante Barroso, 139
20031-005 Rio de Janeiro
Brazil

Telephone:	55-21-2524-0510
Fax:	55-21-2240-1524
E-Mail:	mpml@montaury.com.br
Internet:	www.montaury.com.br
Partner:	*Luiz Montaury Pimenta*
Number of Lawyers:	72
Other Office:	Sao Paulo
Areas of Practice:	Intellectual Property
	Trademarks
	Patents

Oliveira Franco, Ribeiro, Kuster, Rosa Advogados Associados

Rua Visconde do Rio Branco, 237
Curitiba, PR 80410-000
Brazil

Telephone:	55-41-3028-8333
Fax:	55-41-3028-8300
E-Mail:	advocacia@oliveirafranco.com.br
Internet:	www.oliveirafranco.com.br
Partners:	*Christiano de Rocha Kuster Neto*
	Manoel Antonio de Oliveira Franco
	Alessandra Petry Ligocki
Number of Lawyers:	18
Areas of Practice:	Full Service

Brazil continued

Xavier, Bernardes, Braganca Sociedade de Advogados

Av. Rio Branco, 1-14
BR-20090-003
Rio de Janeiro-RJ
Brazil

Telephone:	55-21-2272-9200
Fax:	55-21-2283-0023
E-Mail:	xbblawriodejaneiro@xbb.com.br
Internet:	www.xbb.com.br
Partners:	*Roberto Liesegang*
	Horacio Bernades Neto
Number of Lawyers:	70
Other Offices:	Brasilia
	Sao Paulo
Areas of Practice:	Full Service

Duarte Garcia, Caselli Guimaraes e Terra Advogados

Rua Funchal, 129
045551-060
Sao Paolo, SP
Brazil

Telephone:	55-11-3841-7500
Fax:	55-11-3846-5028
E-Mail:	advogados@dgct.com.br
Internet:	www.dgcgt.com.br
Partners:	*Mario Sergio Duarte Garcia*
	Silvia Poggi de Carvalho
	Heloisa B. Nader D. CUnto
Number of Lawyers:	56
Other Offices:	Brasilia
	Beijing
Areas of Practice:	Full Service

Kourey Lopes Advogados

Av. Brigadeiro Faria Lima, 1355
Sao Paulo – SP 01452-919
Brazil

Telephone:	55-11-3799-8100
Fax:	55-11-3799-8200
E-Mail:	Kla@klalaw.com.br
Internet:	www.klalaw.com.br
Partners:	*Isabel Franco*
	Tiago Cortez
	Jorge Fernando Kourey Lopes

Number of Lawyers: 84
Areas of Practice: Full Service

British Virgin Islands

O'Neal Webster

Simmonds Building
30 Decastro Street
P.O. Box 961
Road Town, Tortola
British Virgin Islands

Telephone:	284-494-5808
Fax:	284-494-5811
E-Mail:	info@onealwebster.com
Internet:	www.onealwebster.com
Partners:	*Paul Dennis*
	Paul Webster
	Kerry Anderson
Number of Lawyers:	5
Areas of Practice:	Mutual Funds
	Banking & Finance
	Real Estate
	Shipping
	Litigation

Harney Westwood & Riegels

Craigmuir Chambers
P.O. Box 71
Road Town, Tortola
British Virgin Islands

Telephone:	284-494-2233
Fax:	284-494-3547
E-Mail:	bvi@harneys.com
Partners:	*Phillip Kite*
	Richard Peters
Number of Lawyers:	65
Other Offices:	Cayman Islands
	London
	Hong Kong
Areas of Practice:	Banking & Finance
	Investment Funds
	Tax

Appleby

Jayla Place
Wickhams Cay 1
P.O. Box 3190
Road Town, Tortola
British Virgin Islands

E-Mail:	info@applebyglobal.com
Internet:	www.applebyglobal.com
Partners:	*Valerie Georges-Thomas*
	Jeremy Leese
Number of Lawyers:	700
Areas of Practice:	Full Service

Brunei

Abrahams Damdson & Co.

Unit 1 and 2, Block B, Bangunan
Begawan Pehin Dato Haji Md. Yusof
Kampong Kiulap
Bandar Seri Begawan BE 1518
Brunei

Telephone:	673-224-2819
Fax:	673-224-2836
E-Mail:	adco@brunet.bn
Partner:	*James Chiew*
Areas of Practice:	Full Service

CCW Partnership

Units 9 and 10, 2nd Floor, Block C
Kianong Complex
Sultan Hassanal Bolkiah Highway
Bandar Seri Begawan BE1318
Brunei

Telephone:	673-245-1606
Fax:	673-245-1611
E-Mail:	ccw@pso.brunet.bn
Partner:	*Andrew Ong*
Areas of Practice:	Full Service

Bulgaria

Djingov, Gouginski, Kyutchukov & Velichkov

10 Tsar Osvoboditel Boulevard
Sofia 1000
Bulgaria

Telephone:	359-2-932-1100
Fax:	359-2-980-3586
E-Mail:	dgkv@dgkv.com
Internet:	www.dgkv.com
Partners:	*Assen A. Djingov*
	Zdrvaka Ugrinova
	Violette Kunze
	Georgi T. Gouginski
Number of Lawyers:	62
Other Office:	Frankfurt
Areas of Practice:	Full Service

Penkov, Markov & Partners

22-A Iztok Dstr.
1113 Sofia
Bulgaria

Telephone:	359-2-971-3935
Fax:	359-2-971-1191
E-Mail:	info@penkov-markov.eu
Partners:	*Vladimir Penkov*
	Dimitar Slavchev
Number of Lawyers:	22
Other Offices:	Bourgas
	Varna
	Lovech
	Pleveh
	Rousse
Areas of Practice:	Full Service

Boris Boyanov & Co.

82, Patriarch Evtimil Blvd.
Sofia, 1463
Bulgaria

Telephone:	359-2-8-055-055
Fax:	359-2-8-055-000
E-Mail:	mail@boyanov.com
Partners:	*Borislav Boyanov*
	Yordan Naydenov
	Alexander Chatalbashev
Number of Lawyers:	30
Areas of Practice:	Full Service

Cambodia

DFDL Mekong

45 Surgmarik Boulevard (P.O. Box 7)
Phnom Penh
Cambodia

Telephone:	855-2321-0400
Fax:	855-2342-8227
E-Mail:	info@dfdlmekong.com
Internet:	www.dfdlmekong.com
Partners:	*Alexander May*
	Martin DeSautels
Number of Lawyers:	78
Other Offices:	Bangkok
	Hanoi
	Ho Chi Minh City
	Phuket
	Vientiane
	Yangon
Areas of Practice:	Full Service

Cameroon

Ebong & Eben

Ruedes ecoles
Immeuble Supermont
P.O. Box 3540
Akwa-Douala
Cameroon

Telephone:	237-342-0796
Fax:	237-342-0796
E-Mail:	ebongebenlawfirm1@yahoo.fr
Internet:	www.ebongebenlawfirm.com
Partner:	*Emanuel Nzo Nguty Eben*
Number of Lawyers: 4	
Areas of Practice:	Full Service

Nico Halle And Co.

8, Avenue Douala Manga Bell
Immeuble Pharmacie Bell
Face SGBC Bali
Douala
Cameron

Telephone:	237-42-6479
Fax:	237-42-2634
E-Mail:	hallelaw@hallelaw.com
Partner:	*Nico Halle*
Number of Lawyers: 11	
Areas of Practice:	Full Service

The Abeng Law Firm

P.O. Box 4155
Duoala
Cameroon

Telephone:	237-3342-7320
Fax:	237-3343-7570
E-Mail:	roland@theabenglawfirm
Internet:	www.theabenglawfirm
Partner:	*Roland Abeng*
Number of Lawyers:	3
Areas of Practice:	Full Service

Canada

Alberta

Macleod Dixon

3700 Canterra Tower
400 Third Avenue S.W.
Calgary, Alberta T2P 4H2
Canada

Telephone:	403-267-8222
Fax:	403-264-5973
E-Mail:	info@macleoddix.com
Internet:	www.macleoddix.com
Partners:	*Joel Friley*
	Robert Malcolm
Number of Lawyers:	212
Other Offices:	Toronto
	Moscow
	Almaty
	Rio de Janeiro
	Caracas
Areas of Practice:	Full Service

Bennett Jones

4500 Bankers Hall East
855 2nd Street S.W.
Calgary, Alberta T2P 4K7
Canada

Telephone:	403-298-3100
Fax:	403-265-7219
E-Mail:	firmwatch@bennettjones.ca
Partners:	*William Osler*
	Milos Barutciski (Toronto)
	Jeff Kerbel (Toronto)
	Lenard Sali
Number of Lawyers:	236
Other Offices:	Edmonton
	Toronto
	Ottawa
Areas of Practice:	Full Service

British Columbia

Davis & Company

2800 Park Place
666 Burrand Street
Vancouver, British Columbia V6C 2Z7
Canada

Telephone:	604-687-9444
Fax:	604-687-1612
E-Mail:	webmaster@davis.com
Internet:	www.davis.ca
Partners:	*Dale Sanderson*
	Duncan Shaw
Number of Lawyers:	217
Other Offices:	Whitehorse
	Yellowknife
	Toronto
	Edmonton
	Tokyo
	Montreal
	Calgary
Areas of Practice:	Full Service

Richards Buell Sutton

700-401 West Georgia Street
Vancouver, British Columbia V6B 5A1
Canada

Telephone:	604-682-3664
Fax:	604-688-3830
Internet:	www.rbs.ca
Partners:	*Jeffrey J. Lowe*
	Jay Munsie

Number of Lawyers: 52
Areas of Practice: Full Service

Clark, Wilson

800-885 West Georgia Street
Vancouver, B.C. V6C 3H1
Canada

Telephone:	604-687-5700
Fax:	604-687-6314
E-Mail:	central@cwilson.com
Internet:	www.cwilson.com
Partners:	*Bill Holder*
	William Helgason
	Neil Melliship

Number of Lawyers: 88
Areas of Practice: General Practice
Corporate Law
Litigation
Intellectual Property
M&A

British Columbia

Lindsay Kennye

401 West Georgia Street
Vancouver, B.C. V6B 5A1
Canada

Telephone:	604-687-1323
Fax:	604-687-2347
E-Mail:	info@lklaw.ca
Internet:	www.lklaw.com
Partners:	*Richard Lindsay*
	Kelvin Stephens
Number of Lawyers:	72
Other Office:	Langley
Areas of Practice:	Full Service

Manitoba

Aikins, MacAulay & Thorvaldson

30th Floor, Commodity Exchange Tower
360 Main Street
Winnipeg, Manitoba R3C 4G1
Canada

Telephone:	204-957-0050
Fax:	204-957-0840
E-Mail:	amt@aikens.com
Internet:	www.aikens.com
Partners:	*Hugh Adams*
	Robert T. Gabor

Number of Lawyers: 87
Areas of Practice: Full Service

New Brunswick

Gilbert, McGloan, Gillis

22 King Street
P.O. Box 7174
Saint John, New Brunswick E2L 1G3
Canada

Telephone:	506-634-3600
Fax:	506-634-3612
E-Mail:	gmg@gmglaw.com
Internet:	www.gmglaw.com
Partners:	*Rodney Gillis*
	Warwick Gilbert

Number of Lawyers: 48
Areas of Practice: Full Service

Clark Drummie

40 Wellington Row
Saint John, New Brunswick E2L 4S3
Canada

Telephone:	506-633-3800
Fax:	506-633-3811
E-Mail:	cd@nbnet.nb.ca
Internet:	www.clarkdrummie.ca
Partners:	*Willard Jenkins*
	Norman Bosse

Number of Lawyers: 72
Other Office: St. Stephen
Areas of Practice: Full Service

Newfoundland

McInnes Cooper

10 Fort William Place
St. John's, New Foundland A1C 5X4
Canada

Telephone:	709-722-8735
Fax:	709-722-1763
E-Mail:	mesj@mcinnescooper.com
Internet:	www.mcinnescooper.com
Partners:	*Thomas Kendell*
	John Green
	Michael Crosbie
	Joe MacDonald
	Gavin Giles
Number of Lawyers:	714
Other Offices:	Charlottetown
	Fredericton
	Halifax
	Moncton
	Saint John
	Summerside
Areas of Practice:	Full Service

Nova Scotia

Stewart McKelvey Stirling Scales

Purdy's Wharf Tower One
1959 Upper Water Street
P.O. Box 997
Halifax, Nova Scotia B3J 2X2
Canada

Telephone:	902-420-3200
Fax:	902-420-1417
E-Mail:	halifax@smss.com
Internet:	www.smss.com
Partners:	*John D. Moore*
	Donald McDougall
Number of Lawyers:	186
Other Offices:	Fredricton
	Moncton
	Charlottetown
	Saint John
	St. John's
Areas of Practice:	Full Service

McInness Cooper

Purdy's Wharf Tower II
1300-1969 Upper Water Street
P.O. Box 730
Halifax, Nova Scotia B3J 2V1
Canada

Telephone:	902-425-6500
Fax:	902-425-6350
E-Mail:	mchfx@macinnescooper.com
Partners:	*Wyle Spicer*
	George Cooper
Number of Lawyers:	214
Other Offices:	Charlottetown
	Fredericton
	Moncton
	Saint John
	St. John's
	Summerside
Areas of Practice:	Full Service

Ontario

Stikeman Elliott

Suite 5300, Commerce Court West
199 Bay Street
Toronto, Ontario M5L 1B9
Canada

Telephone:	416-869-5500
Fax:	416-947-0866
E-Mail:	info@stikeman.com
Internet:	www.stikeman.com
Partners:	*Rod Barrett*
	Stuart Cobbett (Montreal)
	Edward Waitzer
	Philip J. Henderson
	Pierre Raymond
	Ross McDonald (Vancouver)
	Ken Ottenbreit (New York)
	Lou Cusano (Calgary)
	Stuart McCormack (Ottawa)
	W. Brian Rose
Number of Lawyers:	505
Other Offices:	Ottawa
	Montreal
	New York
	Calgary
	Vancouver
	London
	Sydney
Areas of Practice:	Full Service

Gowling Lafleur Henderson

1 First Canadian Place
100 King Street West
Suite 5800
Toronto, Ontario M5X 1G5
Canada

Telephone:	416-862-7525
Fax:	406-862-7661
Partners:	*Dean Saul (Ottawa)*
	Peter Lukasiewicz
	Catherine Pawluch
	Paul Blanchard (Ottawa)
Number of Lawyers:	720
Other Offices:	Ottawa
	Montreal
	Moscow
	Calgary
	London
	Vancouver
Areas of Practice:	Full Service

Blake, Cassels & Graydon

199 Bay Street, Suite 2800
Commerce Court West
Toronto, Ontario M5L 1A9
Canada

Telephone:	416-863-2400
Fax:	416-863-2653
E-Mail:	toronto@blakes.com
Internet:	www.blakes.com
Partners:	*Mark Adkins*
	Simon Finch
	Greg Karnargeliolis
	Dawn Jetten
Number of Lawyers:	541
Other Offices:	Ottawa
	Montreal
	New York
	Chicago
	Bahrain
	Shanghai
	Beijing
	Calgary
	Vancouver
	London
Areas of Practice:	Full Service

Borden Ladner Gervais

Scotia Plaza
40 King Street West
Toronto, Ontario M5H 3Y4
Canada

Telephone:	416-367-6000
Fax:	416-367-6749
E-Mail:	info@blgcanada.com
Internet:	www.blgcanada.com
Partners:	*Douglas Mitchell (Calgary)*
	Jeremy Farr (Ottawa)
	Ron Bozzer (Vancouver)
	Thomas Pepevnak (Calgary)
	Elinore Richardson
	Sean Weir
Number of Lawyers:	710
Other Offices:	Ottawa
	Vancouver
	Montreal
	Calgary
Areas of Practice:	Full Service

Davies Ward Phillips & Vineberg

1 First Canadian Place, Suite 4400
Toronto, Ontario M5X 1B1
Canada

Telephone:	416-863-0900
Fax:	416-863-0871
E-Mail:	info@dwpv.com
Partners:	_David Ward_
	Mark Katz
	Justin Vineberg (Montreal)
	Arthur Shiff
Number of Lawyers:	340
Other Offices:	Montreal
	New York
Areas of Practice:	Full Service

Fasken Martineau

66 Wellington Street West
Toronto Dominion Centre
Toronto Dominion Bank Tower
Toronto M5K 1N6
Canada

Telephone:	416-366-8381
Fax:	416-364-7813
E-Mail:	info@tor.fasken.com
Internet:	www.fasken.com
Partners:	*Alan Schwartz*
	Peggy McCallum
	David Doubilet
	Peter Kirby (Quebec)
	George C. Glover
	Walter Palmer
Number of Lawyers:	614
Other Offices:	Montreal
	London
	Vancouver
	Johannesburg
	Ottawa
	Paris
	Quebec City
	New York
Areas of Practice:	Full Service

Fraser Milner Casgrain

1 First Canadian Place
100 King Street West
Toronto, Ontario M5X 1B2
Canada

Telephone:	416-863-4511
Fax:	416-863-4592
E-Mail:	info@fmc-law.com
Internet:	www.fmc-law.com
Partners:	*John S. Elder*
	Michael Kaplan
	Dennis Wiebe
	Michel Brunet (Montreal)
	Richard A. Scott
Number of Lawyers:	551
Other Offices:	Montreal
	Ottawa
	Vancouver
	Calgary
	Edmonton
Areas of Practice:	Full Service

McCarthy Tetrault

66 Wellington Street West
Toronto Dominion Bank Tower
Suite 5300
Toronto, Ontario M5K 1E6
Canada

Telephone:	416-362-1812
Fax:	416-868-0673
E-Mail:	info@mccarthy.ca
Internet:	www.mccarthy.ca
Partners:	*Peter Beattie*
	Tom Bjarnason
	Niels Ortved
	John Boscariol
	Ian Scott (Montreal)
	Claude M. Jarry (Quebec City)
Number of Lawyers:	611
Other Offices:	London, Ontario
	Ottawa
	Quebec City
	Vancouver
	Calgary
	Montreal
	London, England
Areas of Practice:	Full Service

McMillan

Brookfield Place, Suite 4400
181 Bay Street
Toronto, Ontario M5J 2T3
Canada

Telephone:	416-865-7000
Fax:	416-865-7048
E-Mail:	info@mcmillan.ca
Internet:	www.mcmillan.ca
Partners:	_William Woloshyn_
	Graham Scott
	William Rowley
Number of Lawyers:	280
Other Offices:	Calgary
	Montreal
Areas of Practice:	Full Service

Shibley Righton

250 University Avenue
Suite 700
Toronto, Ontario M5H 3E5
Canada

Telephone:	416-214-5200
Fax:	416-214-5400
E-Mail:	admin@shibleyrighton.com
Internet:	www.shibleyrighton.com
Partners:	_Richard Shibley_
	William Northcote
Number of Lawyers:	35
Other Office:	Windsor
Areas of Practice:	Full Service

Osler, Hoskin & Harcourt

100 King Street West
One First Canadian Place
P.O. Box 50
Toronto, Ontario M5X 1B8
Canada

Telephone:	416-362-2111
Fax:	416-862-6666
Internet:	www.osler.com
Partners:	*J. Timothy Kennish*
	Brian M. Levitt
	Don Ross (New York)
	Christopher Portner
	Paul Cramton
	Dale Ponder
	Sahir Guindi (Montreal)
	Ronald C. Cheng (Ottawa)
Number of Lawyers:	497
Other Offices:	Ottawa
	Montreal
	Calgary
	New York
Areas of Practice:	Full Service

Fogler Rubinoff

99 Wellington Street West, #1200
Toronto, Ontario M5J 2Z9
Canada

Telephone:	416-864-9700
Fax:	416-941-8852
E-Mail:	thefirm@folgerrubinoff.com
Internet:	www.folgerrubinoff.com
Partners:	*Michael S. Slan*
	Michael Appleton
Number of Lawyers:	94
Other Office:	Ottawa
Areas of Practice:	Mergers and Acquisitions
	Real Estate
	Litigation
	Tax

Lang Michener

Brookfield Place
Suite 2500, 181 Bay Street
Toronto, Ontario M5J 2T7
Canada

Telephone:	416-360-8600
Fax:	416-365-1719
E-Mail:	info@langmichener.ca
Internet:	www.langmichener.ca
Partners:	*William J.V. Sheridan*
	Patrick J. Phelan
	Robert R. Cranston
	Cyndee Todgham-Cherniak
	Mark Richardson
	Manny Montenegrino
	Eugene Meehan
Number of Lawyers:	205
Other Offices:	Vancouver
	Hong Kong
	Ottawa
Areas of Practice:	Full Service

Goodmans

Bay Cidelarde Centre
333 Bay Street
Toronto, Ontario M5H 2S7
Canada

Telephone:	416-979-2211
Fax:	416-979-1234
E-Mail:	info@goodmans.com
Internet:	www.goodmans.com
Partners:	*Dale Lastman*
	Allan Leibel
Number of Lawyers:	368
Other Offices:	Vancouver
	Hong Kong
Areas of Practice:	Full Service

Torys

Suite 3000
79 Wellington Street West
Toronto, Ontario M5K 1N2
Canada

Telephone:	416-865-0040
Fax:	416-865-7380
Internet:	www.torys.com
Partners:	*James Baillie*
	Les Viner
Number of Lawyers:	246
Other Office:	New York
Areas of Practice:	Full Service

Aird & Berlis

Brookfield Place
181 Bay Street, Suite 1800
Toronto, Ontario M5J 2T9
Canada

Telephone:	416-863-1500
Fax:	416-863-1515
E-Mail:	jbernstein@airdberlis.com
Internet:	www.airdberlis.com
Partners:	*Jack Bernstein*
	Martin Kovnats
Number of Lawyers:	140
Areas of Practice:	Taxation
	Corporate Finance
	Real Estate
	Municipal and Administrative Law

Heenan Blaikie

200 Bay Street S Tower
Suite 2600
P.O. Box 185 Stn. Royal Bank
Toronto, Ontario M5J 2J4
Canada

Telephone:	416-3600-6336
Fax:	416-360-8425
E-Mail:	jbarnes@heenan.ca
Internet:	www.heenanblaikie.com
Partners:	*Jeffrey Barnes*
	Guy Tremblay (Montreal)
	Norman Bacal
	Paul Lalonde
Number of Lawyers:	514
Other Offices:	Montreal
	Vancouver
	Quebec City
	Calgary
	Victoria
	Paris
	Singapore
	Ottawa
Areas of Practice:	Full Service

Prince Edward Island

Campbell Lea

15 Queen Street
Charlottetown,
PEI CIA 7K7
Canada

Telephone:	902-566-3400
Fax:	902-566-9266
E-Mail:	office@campbelllea.com
Internet:	www.campbelllea.com
Partners:	*Paul Michael*
	Jane Ralling

Number of Lawyers: 9
Areas of Practice: Full Service

Quebec

Ogilvy Renault

Suite 2500
1 Place Ville Marie
Montreal, Quebec H3B 1R1
Canada

Telephone:	514-847-4747
Fax:	514-286-5474
E-Mail:	info@ogilvyrenault.com
Internet:	www.ogilvyrenault.com
Partners:	*Gerard Rochon*
	John Coleman
	William Hesler
Number of Lawyers:	372
Other Offices:	Ottawa
	Quebec City
	Toronto
	London
	Calgary
Areas of Practice:	Full Service

Desjardins Ducharme Stein Monast

600 de La Gauchetiere Street West, Suite 2400
Montreal, Quebec H3B 4L8
Canada

Telephone:	514-878-9411
Fax:	514-878-4800
E-Mail:	avocet@ddsm.ca
Internet:	www.desjardinsducharme.ca
Partner:	*Andre Vantour*
Number of Lawyers:	211
Other Office:	Quebec City
Areas of Practice:	Full Service

LaPointe Rosenstein

1250 René Levesque Boulevard West
Suite 1400
Montréal, Québec H3B 5E9
Canada

Telephone:	514-925-6300
Fax:	514-925-9001
E-Mail:	general@lapointerosenstern.com
Internet:	www.Lapointerosenstein.com
Partners:	*Howard W. Dermer*
	Brahm Gelfand
	Bruno Floriani
Number of Lawyers:	90
Other Office:	Longueuil
Areas of Practice:	Full Service

DeGrandepre Chait

1000, de la Gauchtetiere West
Montreal, Quebec H3B 4W5
Canada

Telephone:	514-878-4311
Fax:	514-878-4333
E-Mail:	info@degrandepre.com
Internet:	www.degrandepre.com

Partner: *Andre P. Asselin*
Number of Lawyers: 71
Areas of Practice: Full Service

Saskatchewan

MacPherson Leslie & Tyerman

1500 Hill Centre
1874 Scarth Street
Regina, Saskatchewan S4P 4E9
Canada

Telephone:	306-347-8000
Fax:	306-352-5250
Partners:	*Robert Pletch*
	Aaron Runge
	Don Wilson
Number of Lawyers:	114
Other Offices:	Saskatoon
	Calgary
	Edmonton
Areas of Practice:	Full Service

Cayman Islands

Walkers

Walker House
87 Mary Street
George Town, Grand Cayman
Cayman Islands

Telephone:	345-949-0100
Fax:	345-949-7886
E-Mail:	info@walkersglobal.com
Internet:	www.walkersglobal.com
Partners:	*Grant Stein*
	Mark Lewis
Number of Lawyers:	117
Other Offices:	British Virgin Islands
	London
	Dubai
	Jersey
	Hong Kong
	Singapore
Areas of Practice:	General Corporate
	Commercial Law
	Finance

Maples and Calder

Ugland House
P.O. Box 309
George Town, Grand Cayman
Cayman Islands

Telephone:	345-949-8066
Fax:	345-949-8080
E-Mail:	info@maplesandcalder.com
Internet:	www.maplesandcalder.com
Partners:	*Joanna Bodden*
	Grant Dixon
	Julian Reddyhough
	Charles Jennings
	Alasdair Robertson
Number of Lawyers:	180
Other Offices:	London
	Dublin
	British Virgin Islands
	Hong Kong
Areas of Practice:	Full Service

Cayman Islands *continued*

Higgs & Johnson

Anderson Square Building
Shedden Road
P.O. Box 866 GT
George Town
Grand Cayman
Cayman Islands

Telephone:	345-949-7555
Fax:	345-949-8492
E-Mail:	cayman@higgsjohnson.com
Internet:	www.higgsjohnson.com
Partners:	*Philip Boni*
	Gina Berry
Number of Lawyers:	9
Other Offices:	Nassau
	Lyford Cay
	Freeport
	Abaco
Areas of Practice:	Full Service

Appleby

Clifton house
75 Fort Street
Grand Cayman KY1-1104
Cayman Islands

Telephone:	345-949-4900
Fax:	345-949-4901
E-Mail:	sraftopoulos@applebyglobal.com
Internet:	www.applebyglobal.com
Partner:	*Simon Raftopoulos*
Areas of Practice:	Full Service

Channel Islands

Mourant de Feu & Jeune

22 Grenville Street
St. Helier, Jersey Je4 8PX
Channel Islands

Telephone:	44-1534-609-000
Fax:	44-1534-609-333
E-Mail:	enquiry@mourant.com
Internet:	www.mourant.com
Partner:	*Jonathan Rigby*
Number of Lawyers:	97
Other Offices:	Cayman Islands
	Dublin
	Guernsey
	Hong Kong
	London
	New York
	Luxembourg
	Singapore
Areas of Practice:	Full Service

Channel Islands *continued*

Carey Olsen

47 Esplanade
St. Heleier, Jersey JE1 OBD
Channel Islands

Telephone:	44-1534-88-8900
Fax:	44-1534-88-7744
Internet:	www.careyolsen.com
Partners:	*Tom Carey*
	Edward Quinn
Number of Lawyers:	66
Other Offices:	Guernsey
	London
Areas of Practice:	Full Service

Oglier & Le Masurier

Whitely Chambers, Don Street
St. Helier, Jersey JE4 9WG
Channel Islands

Telephone:	441-534-504000
Fax:	441-534-54444
E-Mail:	legal@ogier.com
Internet:	www.ogier.com
Partners:	*Peter Bertram*
	Richard Thomas
Number of Lawyers:	172
Other Offices:	Guernsey
	London
	Tokyo
	Bahrain
	British Virgin Islands
	Cayman Islands
	Dublin
	Hong Kong
Areas of Practice:	Full Service

Nigel Harris & Partners

Oak Walk
St. Peter Port, Jersey JE3 7EF
Channel Islands

Telephone:	44-1-534-495-555
Fax:	44-1-534-495-501
E-Mail:	nhp@nigelharris.com
Partner:	*Anita Lovell*

Number of Lawyers: 17
Areas of Practice: Full Service

Appleby

P.O. Box 207
13-14 Esplanade
St. Helier, Jersey JEI IBD
Channel Islands

Telephone:	44-1534-818025
E-Mail:	info@applebyglobal.com
Internet:	www.applebyglobal.com
Partners:	*Adrian O'Dell*
	Michael O'Connell

Number of Lawyers: 700
Areas of Practice: Full Service

Chile

Cariola Diez Perez-Cotapos y Cia

Av. Andres Bello 2711
Santiago
Chile

Telephone:	56-2-360-4000
Fax:	56-2-360-4030
E-Mail:	cariola@cariola.cl
Internet:	www.ingles.cariola.cl
Partner:	*Sebatian Obach*
Number of Lawyers:	84
Areas of Practice:	Full Service

Philippi, Yrarrazaval, Pulido y Brunner

Avenue El Golf 40
Las Condes, Santiago 7550107
Chile

Telephone:	56-2-364-7000
Fax:	56-2-364-3797
E-Mail:	philippi@philippi.cl
Internet:	www.philippines.cl
Partners:	*Juan Irarrazabal*
	Juan Francisco Gutierrez
Number of Lawyers:	48
Areas of Practice:	Foreign Investment Law
	Corporate Law
	General Practice

Carey y Cia

Miraflores 222
Santiago
Chile

Telephone:	56-2-365-7200
Fax:	56-2-633-1980
E-Mail:	carey@carey.cl
Internet:	www.carey.cl
Partners:	*Jorge Carey*
	Jaime Carey
	Marcos Rios
	Alfonso Silva
	Jaun Guillermo Levine
Number of Lawyers:	125
Areas of Practice:	Full Service

Claro y Cia

Apoquindo 3721
P.O. Box 1867
Santiago
Chile

Telephone:	56-2-367-3000
Fax:	56-2-367-3003
E-Mail:	claro@claro.cl
Internet:	www.claro.cl
Partners:	*Sebastian Eyzaguirre B.*
	Ricardo Claro V.
	Cristobal Eyzaguirre B.
Number of Lawyers:	68
Areas of Practice:	Full Service

Portaluppi, Guzman y Bezanilla

Av. El Golf 150
Las Condes, Santiago
Chile

Telephone:	56-2-461-7600
Fax:	56-2-362-0855
E-Mail:	pgb@pgb.cl
Internet:	www.pgb.cl
Partners:	*Jose Thomas Guzman*
	Juan Francisco Guzman
Number of Lawyers:	13
Areas of Practice:	Corporate Law
	Taxation
	Commercial and Civil Law
	Finance

Carey & Allende

Mira Flores 178
Santiago
Chile

Telephone:	56-2-485-2000
Fax:	56-2-633-4043
E-Mail:	careyallende@careyallende.com
Internet:	www.careyallende.cl
Partners:	*Guillermo Carey*
	Ramon Valdivieso
Number of Lawyers:	37
Areas of Practice:	Full Service

Alwin Abogados

Avda. Isidora Goyenechea, 3162
Las Condes, Santiago
Chile

Telephone:	56-2-245-6616
Fax:	56-2-245-6636
E-Mail:	aylwinabogados@alwinabogados.com.cl
Internet:	www.aylwinabogados@alwinabogados.com.cl

Partner: *Pedro Aylwin*
Number of Lawyers: 12
Areas of Practice: Corporate
Environmental
Energy
Taxation

China, People's Republic Of

King & Wood

40th Floor, Tower A,
Fortune Plaza
Zhonglu, Chaoyang
Beijing 100020
China

Telephone:	86-10-5878-5588
Fax:	86-10-5878-5599
E-Mail:	kingwoodbj@kingwood.com
Internet:	www.kingandwood.com
Partners:	*Wang Ling*
	James Jiang (New York)
	Susan Ning
	Jonathan Pan (New York)
	Su Zheng
Number of Lawyers:	784
Other Offices:	Chengdu
	Tokyo
	Guangzhou
	Xian
	Chongqing
	Hangzhou
	Tianjin
	New York
	Guangzhau
	Silicon Valley
	Shanghai
	Shenzen
Areas of Practice:	Full Service

Kang Da Law Firm

19 Jianguomenwei Avenue
Beijing 10004

Telephone:	86-10-8526-2828
Fax:	86-10-9526-2826
Internet:	www.kangda.com
Partner:	Fu Yang
Number of Lawyers:	207
Other Offices:	Shanghai
	Guangzhou
	Shenzhen
	Haikou
	Xian
	Taiyuan
	Hangzhou
	Nanjing
	Shenyang
Areas of Practice:	Commercial and Corporate Law
	Finance and Banking
	Litigation and Arbitration
	Foreign Investment

China, People's Republic Of

Jun He Law Office

China Resources Building
8 Jianguomenwei Avenue
Beijing 100005
China

Telephone:	86-10-8519-1300
Fax:	86-10-8519-1350
E-Mail:	junhebj@junhe.com
Internet:	www.junhe.com
Partners:	*Linfei Liu*
	Xiaolin Zhou (New York)
	Wei Xiao
	Adam Li (Shanghai)
	Chi Liu
	John Du (New York)
Number of Lawyers:	382
Other Offices:	Shanghai
	New York
	Haikou
	Shenzen
	Hong Kong
	Dalian
Areas of Practice:	Full Service

Allbright Law Offices

Citigroup Tower
14/F No. 33 Hua Yuan Shi Qiao Road
Pudong New Area 200120
Shanghai
China

Telephone:	86-21-61059000
Fax:	86-21-61059100
E-Mail:	huaqi@allbrightlaw.com
Internet:	www.allbrightlaw.com
Partners:	*Steve Zhu*
	Donna Li
Number of Lawyers:	200
Other Offices:	Beijing
	Hong kong
	Hagn shen
	Shen Zen
Areas of Practice:	Full Service

Grandall Legal Group

9/F, 6 Gongyan West Street
Jianguomenwei Avenue, Block E
Beijing100005
China

Telephone:	86-10-6517-1188
Fax:	86-10-6517-6800
Internet:	www.grandall-profile.com
Partners:	*Rubin Gerofsky Kaptzain (Shanghai)*
	Gregory Sy
Other Offices:	Shanghai
	Kumming
	Shenzen
	Guangzhou
	Hong Kong
Areas of Practice:	Full Service

China, People's Republic Of <small>continued</small>

Shepard Mullin Richter & Hampton LLP

41/F Raffles City Office Tower
268 Xizang Road Central, Huangpu
Shanghai 200001
China

Telephone:	86.21.2321.6000
Fax:	86.21.2321.6001
E-Mail:	tbissett@sheppardmullin.com
Internet:	www.sheppardmullin.com
Partner:	*Todd Bissett*
Number of Lawyers:	500 (11 in Shanghai)
Other Offices:	Numerous
Areas of Practice:	Full Service

Hylands Law Firm

5A1, Hanwei Plaza
No. 7, Guanghua Road
Chaoyang District
Beijing 100004
China

E-Mail:	hiwen@hylandslaw.com
Internet:	www.hylandslaw.com
Partners:	*Li Wen*
	Jiang Jiang
Number of Lawyers:	128
Areas of Practice:	Full Service

Jingtian & Gongcheng

34/F, Tower 3
China Control Place
77 JianGuo Road
Beijing 100025
China

Telephone:	86-10-5809-1000
Fax:	86-105809-1100
E-Mail:	job@jingtian.com
Internet:	www.jingtian.com
Partners:	*Zhang Hongjiu*
	Bai Fujun
Number of Lawyers:	122
Other Offices:	Shanghai
	Shenzen
Areas of Practice:	Full Service

East Associates

19th/F, Tower 2 "Landmark Towers"
8 North Dongsanhuan Road
Chaoyang District
Beijing 100004
China

Telephone:	86-10-6590-6639
Fax:	86-10-6590-6650
E-Mail:	office@ealawfirm.com
Internet:	www.ealawfirm.com
Partners:	*Dajin Li*
	Taili Wang
Number of Lawyers:	62
Other Offices:	Shanghai
	Tokyo
Areas of Practice:	Full Service

China, People's Republic Of

Liu, Shen & Associates

Hanhai Plaza
10 Caihefeng Road
Haidian District
Beijing 100080
China

E-Mail:	mail@liu-shen.com
Internet:	www.liu-shen.com
Partners:	*Jianyang Yu*
	Xiaonan Wu
Number of Lawyers:	40
Areas of Practice:	Intellectual Property
	Technology

Zhong Lun Law Firm

36-37/F, SK Tower
6A Jianguomenwei Avenue
Beijing 100022
China

Telephone:	86-10-5957-2288
Fax:	86-10-6568-1022
E-Mail:	wangxiaoying@zhonglun.com
Internet:	www.zhongonlun.com
Partner:	*Fei Wang*
Number of Lawyers:	511
Other Offices:	Shanghai
	Ghenzen
	Tokyo
	Wuhan
	Hong Kong
	Guangzhou
Areas of Practice:	Full Service

Global Law Office

15/F Tower 1
China Central Place
No. 81 Jianguo Road
Chaoyang District
Beijing
China

Telephone:	86-10-6584-6688
Fax:	86-10-6584-6666
E-Mail:	global@globallawoffice.com.cn
Internet:	www.globallawoffice.com.cn
Partner:	*Kevin H. Zeng*
Number of Lawyers:	114
Other Office:	Shanghai
Areas of Practice:	Full Service

Wang & Jing

14 F, South Tower
World Trade Center
No. 371-375 Huan Shi Dong Road
Guangzhou 510095
China

Telephone:	86-20-8760-0085
E-Mail:	wangjing@wjnco.com
Inernet:	www.wjnco.com
Partners:	*Jing Wang*
	Xiangman Shen
Number of Lawyers:	63
Other Office:	Shenzan
Areas of Practice:	Full Service

Colombia

Brigard & Urrutia

Calle 70 No. 4-41
Bogota
Colombia

Telephone:	571-744-2244
Fax:	571-310-0609
E-Mail:	currutia@bu.com.co
Internet:	www.bu.com.co
Partners:	*Carlos Urrutia*
	Carlos Umana
	Sergio Michelsen

Number of Lawyers: 64
Areas of Practice: Full Service

Lloreda Camacho & Co.

Calle 72 No. 5-83
Bogota
Colombia

Telephone:	571-326-4270
Fax:	571-326-4271
E-Mail:	jllcco@lloredacamacho.com
Internet:	www.lloredacamacho.com
Partners:	*Gustavo Tamayo*
	Enrique Alvarez

Number of Lawyers: 72
Areas of Practice: Full Service

Parra, Rodriguez & Cavelier

Carrera 9 No. 74-08, Suite 504
Edificio Profinanzas
Bogota
Colombia

Telephone:	571-376-4200
Fax:	571-376-1707
Internet:	www.rodriguezycavelier.com
Partner:	*Ernesto Cavelier*
Number of Lawyers:	34
Other Office:	Medellin
Areas of Practice:	Full Service

Prieto & Carrizosa

Carrera 9 No. 74-08 OF.305
Bogota
Colombia

Telephone:	571-326-8600
Fax:	571-326-8610
E-Mail:	info@prietocarrizosa.com.co
Internet:	www.prietocarrizosa.com
Partners:	*Juan Manuel Prieto*
	Martin Acero
Number of Lawyers:	88
Areas of Practice:	Full Service

Gomez-Pinzon Zuletta

Calle 67 No. 7-35
Of. 1204
Bogota
Colombia

Telephone:	571-319-2900
Fax:	571-321-0295
E-Mail:	gpa@gomezpinzon.com
Internet:	www.gpzlegal.com
Partner:	*Paula Samper-Salazar*
Number of Lawyers:	61
Other Office:	Medellin
Areas of Practice:	Full Service

Cardenas & Cardenas

Carrera 7 No. 71-52
Torre B, Piso 9
Santa Fe de Bogota, D.C.
Colombia

Telephone:	571-313-7800
Fax:	571-312-2410
E-Mail:	general@cardenasycardenas.com
Internet:	www.cardenas.com
Partners:	*Dario Cardenas*
	Bernardo Cardenas
	Eduardo Cardenas
Number of Lawyers:	28
Areas of Practice:	Full Service

Bernate & Gamboa

Carrera 7 # 26-20
Bogota
Colombia

Telephone:	571-210-6666
Fax:	571-210-7826
E-Mail:	post@bernateygamboa.com
Internet:	www.beranteygamboa.com
Partner:	*Rafael Hernando Gamboa*
Number of Lawyers:	14
Areas of Practice:	Full Service

Wiesner & Associates Ltda.

Carrera 9 No. 80-15
Santa Fe de Bogota, D.C.
Colombia

Telephone:	571-312-9541
Fax:	571-211-4919
E-Mail:	ewiesner@colomsat.net.co
Partner:	*Eduardo Wiesner*
Number of Lawyers:	12
Areas of Practice:	Full Service

Costa Rica

Gutierrez, Hernandez & Pauly

5.21, Ave. 6 & 8 No. 630
100 San Jose
Costa Rica

Telephone:	506-258-2270
Fax:	506-257-1623
E-Mail:	info@ghp.co.cr
Internet:	www.ghp.co.cr
Partner:	*Jose Manuel Gutierrez*
Number of Lawyers:	15
Areas of Practice:	Full Service

Lara, Lopez, Matamoros, Rodriguez & Tinoco

P.O. Box 4612-1000
San Jose
Costa Rica

Telephone:	506-2519-7500
Fax:	506-2519-7575
Internet:	www.lim.co.cr
Partners:	*Franklin Matamoros*
	Roberto Leon
Number of Lawyers:	22
Areas of Practice:	Full Service

Facio y Canas

Apartado 5173-1000
San Jose
Costa Rica

Telephone:	506-2256-5555
Fax:	506-2255-2510
E-Mail:	info@fayca.com
Internet:	www.fayca.com
Partners:	*Fernan Pacheco*
	Enrique Castillo
Number of Lawyers:	37
Areas of Practice:	Full Service

LEX Counsel

Escaza
Del costado sur Multiplaza 150
San Jose 1000
Costa Rica

Telephone:	506-201-0300
Fax:	506-201-0412
E-Mail:	info@lexcounsel.com
Internet:	www.lexcounsel.com
Partner:	*Alvaro Caraballo*
Number of Lawyers:	16
Areas of Practice:	Full Service

Soley, Saborio & Asociados

Oficentro Ejecutive La Sabana
San Jose
Costa Rica

Telephone:	506-2290-7200
Fax:	506-2290-7221
E-Mail:	sdeysoler@lawfirmcr.com
Internet:	www.lawfirmcr.com
Partner:	*Elias Soley*
Number of Lawyers:	18
Areas of Practice:	Full Service

Mora, Bolaños & Asociados

Apartado Postal 4309
1000 San Jose
Costa Rica

Telephone:	506-2222-8280
Fax:	506-2223-0190
E-Mail:	fermora@racsa.co.cr
Partners:	*Fernando Mora Rojas*
	Alfredo Bolaños Morales
Number of Lawyers:	4
Areas of Practice:	Full Service

Niehaus Abogados

P.O. Box 493-1000
San Jose
Costa Rica

Telephone:	506-2224-8282
Fax:	506-2225-0505
E-Mail:	info@ninclaw.com
Partners:	*Bernd Niehaus*
	Fernando Sdis
Number of Lawyers:	16
Areas of Practice:	Full Service

Cote d'Ivoire

N'Goan, Die-Kacou & Associes

World Trade Center
01 BP 3361
Abidjan
Cote d'Ivoire

Telephone: 225-214-424
Fax: 225-216-308
E-Mail: cabinetmas@aviso.cl
Partner: *Georges N'Goan*
Number of Lawyers: 8
Areas of Practice: Full Service

Bile-Aka, Brizoua-Bi & Associes

7, Boulevard Latrille
25 B.P. 945
Abidjan
Cote d'Ivoire

E-Mail: contact@bilebrizoua.net
Internet: www.bilebrizoua.ci
Partner: *Michael Brizoua-Bi*
Number of Lawyers: 8
Areas of Practice: Full Service

Croatia

Porobija & Porobija

Galleria Importanne
Iblerov trg 10/VII
1000 Zagreb
Croatia

Telephone:	385-1-4693-999
Fax:	385-1-4693-900
E-Mail:	porobija@porobija.hr
Internet:	www.probija.hr
Partner:	*Boris Porobija*
Areas of Practice:	Full Service

Vukic, Jelusic, Sulina, Stankovic, Jurcan & Jabuka

Nikole Tesle 9/V-VI
51 000 Rijeka
Croatia

Telephone:	051-211-600
Fax:	051-336-884
E-Mail:	info@vukic-lawfirm.hr
Internet:	www.vuckic-lawfirm.hr
Partner:	*Gordan Stankovic*
Number of Lawyers:	22
Areas of Practice:	Full Service

Cyprus

Dr. K. Chprysostomides & Co.

1 Lampousa Street
1095 Nicosia
Cyprus

Telephone:	357-22-777-000
Fax:	357-22-779-939
E-Mail:	kchprysos@logos.cy.net
Partner:	*Dr. Kyrpos Chprysostomides*
Number of Lawyers:	19
Areas of Practice:	Full Service

Andreas Neocleous & Co.

Neocleous House
195 Arch. Makarios III Avenue
3608 Limassol
Cyprus

Telephone:	357-25-110-000
Fax:	357-25-110-001
E-Mail:	info@neocleous.com
Internet:	www.neocleous.com
Partner:	*Andreas Neocleous*
Other Offices:	Moscow
	Budapest
	Kiev
	Prague
	Nicosia
	Paphos
	Sevastopol
	Brussels
Areas of Practice:	Full Service

Chrysses Demetriades & Co. LLC

Fortuna Court
284 Makarios III Avenue
3105 Limassol
Cyprus

Telephone:	357-25-800-000
Fax:	357-25-588-055
Internet:	www.demetriades.com
Partner:	*Christos Mavrellis*
Number of Lawyers:	47
Areas of Practice:	General Commercial Law
	Shipping
	Litigation

Tassos Papadopoulos & Associates

Chantecrair Building, 2nd Floor
2 Sofouli Street
1096 Nicosia
Cyprus

Telephone:	357-22-889-999
Fax:	357-22-889-988
Internet:	www.tplaw.com
Partners:	*Nicos Papaefstathipa*
	Alexia Kourtouri
Number of Lawyers:	16
Areas of Practice:	Full Service

Ioannides Demetriou LLC

2 Diagorou Street
ERA House
1097 Nicosia
Cyprus

Telephone:	357-220-22999
Fax:	357-220-22900
E-Mail:	info@idlaw.com.cy
Internet:	www.idlaw.com.cy
Partners:	*Pambos Ioannides*
	Andrew Demetriou
Number of Lawyers:	18
Other Offices:	Limassol
	Larnaca
Areas of Practice:	Full Service

Czech Republic

Cermak Horejs Matejka a spol.

Narodni 32
110 00 Prague 1
Czech Republic

Telephone:	420-296-167-111
Fax:	420-224-946-724
E-Mail:	info@apk.cz
Internet:	www.apk.cz
Partners:	*Karel Cermak*
	Karel Cermak, Jr.
	Jan Matejka
Number of Lawyers:	24
Areas of Practice:	Commercial Law
	Intellectual Property Law

Kocian Solc Balastik

Jungmannova 24
110 00 Prague
Czech Republic

Telephone:	420-224-103-316
Fax:	420-224-103-234
E-Mail:	ksbpraha@ksb.cz
Internet:	www.ksb.cz
Partners:	*Martin Solc*
	Jiri Balastik
Number of Lawyers:	54
Other Offices:	Karlovy Vary
	Ostrava
Areas of Practice:	Full Service

Peterka & Partners

Na Prikope 15
110 00 Prague 1
Czech Republic

Telephone:	420-246-085-300
Fax:	420-246-085-370
E-Mail:	office@peterkapartners.cz
Internet:	www.peterkapartners.com
Partner:	*Ondrej Peterka*
Number of Lawyers:	47
Other Offices:	Bratislava
	Kiev
	Sofia
	Moscow
Areas of Practice:	Full Service

Denmark

Philip & Partners

Vognmagergade 7
DK- 1120 Copenhagen
Denmark

Telephone:	45-33-13-11-12
Fax:	45-33-32-80-45
E-Mail:	lawoffice@philip.dk
Internet:	www.philip.dk
Partners:	*Mogens Yard*
	Henning Hansen

Number of Lawyers: 47
Areas of Practice: Full Service

Plesnar Svane Gronborg

Amerika Plads 37
2100 Copenhagen
Denmark

Telephone:	45-33-12-11-33
Fax:	45-33-12-00-14
E-Mail:	plesner@plesner.com
Internet:	www.plesner.com
Partners:	*Peter Fogh*
	Nicolai Orsted

Number of Lawyers: 201
Areas of Practice: Banking and Finance Law
Corporate Finance
Construction Law
Commercial Property
Corporate Law
EU and Competition Law

Stampe, Haume & Hasselriis

St. Kongensgade 42, 2
1022 Copenhagen
Denmark

Telephone:	33-15-15-32
Fax:	33-12-24-24
E-Mail:	tas@cphlaw.com
Internet:	www.cphlaw.com
Partner:	_Terry Selzer_
Number of Lawyers:	5
Areas of Practice:	Corporate
	Real Estate
	Litigation
	Insurance

Danders & More

Lautrupsgade 7
2100 Copenhagen
Denmark

Telephone:	45-33-12-95-12
Fax:	45-33-12-95-15
E-Mail:	anders.hansen@dandersmore.com
Internet:	www.dandersmore.com
Partner:	_Anders Hansen_
Number of Lawyers:	30
Areas of Practice:	Corporate and Financial Transactions
	Litigation

Kromann Reumert

Sunkrogsgade 5
DK-2100 Copenhagen
Denmark

Telephone:	45-70-12-12-11
Fax:	45-70-12-13-11
E-Mail:	cph@kromannreumert.com
Internet:	www.kromannreumert.com
Partners:	*Michael Budtz*
	Anders Lavesen
	Christian Lundgren
	Morten Kofmann
Number of Lawyers:	245
Other Offices:	London
	Aarhus
	Brussels
Areas of Practice:	Full Service

Bech-Bruun

Langelinie Alle 35
2100 Copenhagen
Denmark

Telephone:	45-72-27-00-00
Fax:	45-72-27-00-27
E-Mail:	info@bechbruun.com
Internet:	www.bechbruun.com
Partners:	*Per Hemmer*
	Randi Bach Poulsen
	Steen Halmind
Number of Lawyers:	230
Other Office:	Aarhus
Areas of Practice:	Full Service

Gorrissen Federspiel Kierkegaard

12 H.C. Andersen Boulevard
DK-1553 Copenhagen V
Denmark

Telephone:	45-33-41-41-41
Fax:	45-33-41-41-33
E-Mail:	gfk@gfklaw.dk
Internet:	www.gfklaw.dk
Partners:	*Henrik Lind*
	Niels Heering
Number of Lawyers:	145
Areas of Practice:	General Corporate
	Commercial Banking
	Banking and Finance

Lind Cadovius

Ostergade 38
DK-1019 Copenhagen K
Denmark

Telephone:	45-33-33-81-00
Fax:	45-33-17-81-01
E-Mail:	law.office@lindcad.dk
Internet:	www.lindcad.dk
Partner:	*Henrik Andresen*
Number of Lawyers:	46
Areas of Practice:	Full Service

Dania Law Firm

Bredgade 49
P.O. Box 9007
DK-1260 Copenhagen
Denmark

Telephone:	45-33-17-99-00
Fax:	45-33-17-99-01
E-Mail:	info@dania-law.dk
Internet:	www.dania-law.dk
Partner:	*Thomas Salicath*
Number of Lawyers:	39
Other Offices:	Svendborg
	Moscow
	Kiev
	Faroe Islands
	Greenland
Areas of Practice:	Full Service

Magnusson

Ny Kongensgade 10, 2
1472 Copenhagen
Denmark

Telephone:	45-82-51-51-00
Fax:	45-82-51-51-01
E-Mail:	copenhagen@magnusson.com
Internet:	www.magnusson.com
Partner:	*Anders Etgen Reitz*
Number of Lawyers:	114
Other Offices:	Gothenburg
	Minsk
	Moskow
	Stockholm
	Warsaw
	Wroclaw
Areas of Practice:	Full Service

Sirius Advokater

Holmens Kanal 7
1060 Copenhagen K
Denmark

Telephone:	45-88-88-85-85
Fax:	45-88-88-85-95
E-Mail:	pd@siriusadvokater.dk
Internet:	www.siriusadvokater.dk
Partners:	*Kristian Paaschburg*
	Peter Dyhr
	Rasmus Mehl
Number of Lawyers:	20
Areas of Practice:	Full Service

Dominican Republic

Troncoso y Caceres

Calle Socorro Sanchez 253, Apartado 1182
Santo Domingo
Domincan Republic

Telephone:	809-689-2158
Fax:	809-686-7212
E-Mail:	mail@troncoso-caceres.com
Internet:	www.troncoso-caceres.com
Partners:	*Manuel A. Troncoso*
	Marcos D. Troncoso
	Rafael Caceres
	Ana Isabel Caceres
Number of Lawyers:	18
Areas of Practice:	Full Service

Pellerano & Herrera

10 John F. Kennedy Avenue
Santo Domingo
Domincan Republic

Telephone:	809-541-5200
Fax:	809-567-0773
E-Mail:	ph@phlaw.com
Internet:	www.phlaw.com
Partner:	*Luis R. Pellerano*
Number of Lawyers:	34
Areas of Practice:	Full Service

Dhimes & Marra

Torre Elite
Ave 27 de Febrero No. 329
Santo Domingo
Domincan Republic

Telephone:	809-732-2035
Fax:	809-732-2062
E-Mail:	dhimesmarra@dhimesmarra-law.com
Internet:	www.dhimesmarra-law.com
Partners:	*Xavier Marra*
	Jacqueline Dhimes

Number of Lawyers: 10
Areas of Practice: Full Service

Ecuador

Bustamante & Bustamante

Avenues Patria & Amazonas
Cofiec Building
Quito
Ecuador

Telephone:	593-2-2562-680
Fax:	593-2-2564-628
E-Mail:	bustamanteybustmante@bustamante.com
Internet:	www.bustamante.com
Partner:	*Jose Rafael Bustamante*
Number of Lawyers:	35
Areas of Practice:	Full Service

Paz Horowitz Abogados

Whymper 1105 y Almagro
Edif. Tempo
P.O. Box 17-21-1533
Quito
Ecuador

Telephone:	593-2-222-057
Fax:	593-2-222-058
E-Mail:	info@pazhorowitz.com
Internet:	www.pazhorowitz.com
Partners:	*Bruce Horowitz*
	Jorge Paz
	Maria Edith Jativa
Number of Lawyers:	25
Areas of Practice:	Intellectual Property
	Mining and Natural Resources
	Banking
	Taxation
	Litigation

Romero Arteta Ponce

Av. 12 De Octubre N. 26-97
Quito
Ecuador

Telephone:	593-2-298-6666
Fax:	593-2-598-6664
E-Mail:	dromero@law.com.ec
Internet:	www.rap.com.ee
Partner:	*Gustavo Romero*
Number of Lawyers:	10
Areas of Practice:	Full Service

Perez, Bustamante y Ponce

Avenida Republica del Salvador 1082
Quito
Ecuador

Telephone:	593-2-2260-666
Fax:	593-2-2258-038
E-Mail:	pbp@pbblaw.com
Internet:	www.pbplaw.com
Partners:	*Jose Maria Perez-Areta*
	Jorge Cevallos

Number of Lawyers: 34
Areas of Practice: Full Service

Izurieta Mora Bowen

Estudio Juridico Av.
Amazonas 4000, Piso 5
P.O. Box 17-01-638
Quito
Ecuador

Telephone:	593-2-2263-500
Fax:	593-2-2462-562
E-Mail:	izurieta@izuri.etamorabown.com
Internet:	www.izurietamorabowen.com
Partner:	*Ricardo Izurieta Mora Bowen*

Number of Lawyers: 9
Areas of Practice: Full Service

Egypt

Kosheri, Rashed & Riad

16 Maamal El Sokkar Street
Garden City 11451
Cairo
Egypt

Telephone:	20-2-795-4795
Fax:	20-2-795-8521
E-Mail:	mailbox@krr-law.com
Internet:	www.krr-law.com
Partners:	*Hala Riad*

Number of Lawyers: 16
Areas of Practice: Full Service

Al Kamel Law Office

17 Nabil Al Wakad Street, Dokki
Giza
Egypt

Telephone:	20-2-3761-5271
Fax:	20-2-3761-5272
E-Mail:	kmlaw@kamelaw.com
Internet:	www.kamelaw.com
Partners:	*Dr. Mohammed Kamel*
	Rasheed Kamel

Number of Lawyers: 18
Other Office: Alexandria
Areas of Practice: Full Service

Shalakany Law Office

12, El Marashly Street, Zamalek
Cairo
Egypt

Telephone:	20-2-2728-8888
Fax:	20-2-2739-9399
E-Mail:	mail@shalakany.com
Internet:	www.shalakany.com
Partners:	*Khaled El-Shalakany*
	Sharif Shihata
Number of Lawyers:	45
Other Offices:	Alexandria
	Dubai
Areas of Practice:	Full Service

Zaki Hashem & Partners

23, Kasr El-Nil Street
Cairo
Egypt

Telephone:	20-2-393-3766
Fax:	20-2-393-3585
E-Mail:	law@hashemlaw.com
Internet:	www.hashemlaw.com
Partners:	*Tawfik Gamil Shehata*
	Zaki Hashem
Number of Lawyers:	47
Areas of Practice:	Full Service

Ibrachy & Dermarkar

16 Hussein Wassef Street
Messaha Square, Dokki
Giza
Egypt

Telephone:	202-3760-4592
Fax:	202-3760-4593
E-Mail:	inof@gibrachy-dermarkar.com
Internet:	www.ibrachy-dermarkar.com
Partners:	*Bahieldin Elibrachy*
	Menha A Samy
Areas of Practice:	Full Service

Denton Wilde Sapte

9 Shagaret El Dor Street
Zamatek
Cairo
Egypt

Telephone:	202-2735-0574
Fax:	202-2736-7717
E-Mail:	michael.lacey@dentonwildesapte.com
Internet:	www.dentonwildesapte.com
Partner:	*Michael Lacey*
Number of Lawyers:	23 in Egypt
Areas of Practice:	Full Service

El Salvador

Romero Pineda & Asociados

World Trade Center 1, Suite 305, Col. Escalon
San Salvador
El Salvador

Telephone:	503-2505-5555
Fax:	503-2505-5500
E-Mail:	info@romeropineda.com
Internet:	www.romeropineda.com
Partners:	*Jose Roberto Romero*
	Roberto Romero Pineda

Number of Lawyers: 25
Areas of Practice: Full Service

Espino Nieto & Asociados

83 Avenida Norte No. 138 Col. Escalon,
P.O. Box 2224
San Salvador
EL Salvador

Telephone:	503-2263-7522
Fax:	503-2264-3198
E-Mail:	info@espinolaw.com
Internet:	www.espinolaw.com
Partners:	*Luis Miguel Espino*
	Rafael Mendoza

Number of Lawyers: 10
Areas of Practice: Full Service

Delgado & Cevallos

67 Avenida Sur
San Salvador
El Salvador

Telephone:	503-298-3900
Fax:	503-298-3939
E-Mail:	info@delgadocevallos.com
Internet:	www.delgadocevallos.com
Partners:	*Ricardo Cevallos*
	Aquiles A. Delgado
Number of Lawyers:	11
Areas of Practice:	Full Service

Arias & Munoz

Calle La Mascota 533
San Benito
El Salvador

Telephone:	503-2257-0900
Fax:	503-2257-0901
E-Mail:	elsalvador@ariaslaw.com
Internet:	www.ariaslaw.com
Partner:	*F. Armando Arias*
Number of Lawyers:	130
Other Offices:	Guatamala City
	San Pedro Sula
	Tegucigalpa
	Managua
	San Jose
Areas of Practice:	Full Service

Estonia

Lepik & Luhaaar

Niguliste Street 4
Tallinn 10130
Estonia

Telephone:	372-630-6460
Fax:	372-630-6463
E-Mail:	Tallinn@lawin.ee
Internet:	www.lawin.ee
Partners:	*Peeter Lepik*
	Liina Linsi
Number of Lawyers:	27
Areas of Practice:	Full Service

Tark & Co.

2 Roosikrantsi Street
Tallinn 10119
Estonia

Telephone:	372-6-110-900
Fax:	372-6-110-911
E-Mail:	tarkco@tarkco.ee
Internet:	www.tarkco.com
Partner:	*Aare Tark*
Number of Lawyers:	40
Areas of Practice:	Full Service

Raidla Lejins & Norcous

2 Roosikrantsi Street
Tallinn 10119
Estonia

Telephone:	372-6-407-170
Fax:	372-6-407-171
E-Mail:	rln@rln.ee
Internet:	www.raidla.ee
Partner:	*Juri Raidla*
Number of Lawyers:	23
Areas of Practice:	Full Service

Glimstedt Straus & Partners

Ravala pst 5
Tallinn 10143
Estonia

E-Mail:	ilmar.straus@glimstedt.ee
Internet:	www.glimstedt.ee
Partner:	*Ilmar Straus*
Number of Lawyers:	15
Areas of Practice:	Full Service

Ethiopia

Teshome Gabre-Mariam Bokan

P.O. Box 101485
Addis Ababa
Ethiopia

Telephone:	251-1-551-8484
Fax:	251-11-551-3500
E-Mail:	tgmb@telcom.net.et
Partner:	*Teshome Gabre-Mariam Bokan*
Areas of Practice:	Corporate
	Intellectual Property
	Natural Resources

Fiji

Howards Lawyers

Level 7, FNPF Place
Victoria Parade
GPO Box 13687
Suva
Fiji

E-Mail: wclarke@howardslaw.com.fj
Internet: www.howardslaw.com.fi
Partner: *Wylie Clarke*
Number of Lawyers: 7
Areas of Practice: Full Service

Finland

Roschier

Keskuskatu 7 A
00100 Helsinki
Finland

Telephone:	358-20-506-6000
Fax:	358-20-560-6100
Internet:	www.roschier.com
Partners:	*Christian Wik*
	Jon Unnerus
Number of Lawyers:	160
Other Offices:	Stockholm
	Vaasa
Areas of Practice:	Full Service

Castren & Snellman

Erottajankatu 5 A
00130 Helsinki
Finland

Telephone:	38 20 7765 765
Fax:	358 20 7765 001
E-Mail:	info@castren.fi
Internet:	www.castren.fi
Partners:	*Pekka Jaatinen*
	Jan Orndahl
Number of Lawyers:	100
Other Offices:	St. Petersburg
	Moscow
Areas of Practice:	M&A
	Banking
	Insolvency
	Intellectual Property
	Dispute Resolution

Fondia Ltd.

Lonnrotinkatu 5
FI-00120 Helsinki
Finland

Telephone:	358-20-7205-400
Fax:	358-20-7205-499
E-Mail:	fondia@fondia.fi
Internet:	www.fondia.fi
Partners:	*Arto Lindfors*
	Janne Haapakeri (Tampere)
	Ville Heikkinen (Oulu)
Number of Lawyers:	50
Other Offices:	Turku
	Tampere
	Oulu
	Jyvaskyla
	Vaasa
Areas of Practice:	Full Service

Hannes Snellman

Etelaranta 8
FIN 00130 Helsinki
Finland

Telephone:	358-9-228-841
Fax:	358-9-177-393
E-Mail:	hannes.snellman@hannassnellman.fi
Internet:	www.hannessnellman.fi
Partner:	*Johan Aalto*
Number of Lawyers:	175
Other Offices:	Moscow
	St. Petersburg
	Stockholm
Areas of Practice:	Full Service

HH Partners, Ltd.

Mannerheimintie 14A
00100 Helsinki
Finland

Telephone:	358-9-177-613
Fax:	358-9-653-873
E-Mail:	hhpartners@hhpartners.fi
Internet:	www.hhpartners.fi
Partner:	*Arto Kukkonen*
Number of Lawyers:	12
Areas of Practice:	Full Service

Waselius & Wist

Etelaesplanadi 24A
00130 Helsinki
Finland

Telephone:	358-9-668-9520
Fax:	358-9-668-9522
E-Mail:	jan.waselius@ww.fi
Internet:	www.ww.fi
Partners:	*Jan Waselius*
	Tarja Wist
Number of Lawyers:	23
Areas of Practice:	General Corporate
	Business Law
	Capital Markets
	Tax

LMR

Mannerheimintie 14A
00100 Helsinki
Finland

Telephone:	358-9-5860-100
Fax:	358-9-5860-1060
E-Mail:	mail@lmr.fi
Internet:	www.lmr.fi
Partners:	*Jukka Luostarinen*
	Kimmo Mettala
Number of Lawyers:	22
Areas of Practice:	Full Service

Procope & Hornborg

Keskaustatu 8
00101 Helsinki
Finland

Telephone:	358-10-3090-300
Fax:	358-10-3090-333
E-Mail:	lawfirm@procope.fi
Internet:	www.procope.fi
Partners:	*Kalevi Tervanen*
	Kari Helio
	Ismo Hentula
Other Offices:	Tampere
	Jyvaskyla
Number of Lawyers:	32
Areas of Practice:	Full Serivce

Veikko Paolotie & Co.

Aleksanterinkatu 44
FIN –101 Helsinki
Finland

Telephone:	358-9-2288-3100
Fax:	358-9-2288-3300
Internet:	www.veikkopalotie.fi
Partners:	*Ossi Sokka*
	Mika Pakorinen
Number of Lawyers:	20
Areas of Practice:	Insolvency
	M&A
	Corporate Law

France

Jeantet Associes

87 Avenue Kleber
75784 Paris
France

Telephone:	33-1-45-05-80-08
Fax:	33-1-47-04-20-41
E-Mail:	info@jeantet.fr
Internet:	www.jeantet.fr
Partners:	*Thierry Brun*
	Yvon Dreano
Number of Lawyers:	82
Other Office:	New York
Areas of Practice:	Full Service

Thieffry & Associes

29, rue de Lisbonne
75008 Paris
France

Telephone:	33-1-45-62-45-54
Fax:	33-1-42-25-80-07
E-Mail:	thieffry-paris@thieffrey.com
Internet:	www.thieffry.com
Partners:	*Patrick Thieffry*
	Jean Thieffry
Number of Lawyers:	11
Areas of Practice:	Full Service

France _{continued}

Bredin Prat

130 Rue du Faubourg St.-Honore
75008 Paris
France

Telephone:	33-1-44-353-535
Fax:	33-1-44-891-073
E-Mail:	info@bredinprat.com
Internet:	www.bredinprat.fr
Partners:	*Jean-Francois Prat*
	Pascal Lagesse
Other Office:	Brussels
Areas of Practice:	Full Service

Vatier & Associes

12 rue D Astorg
Paris 75008
France

Telephone:	33-1-5343-1555
Fax:	33-1-5343-1578
E-Mail:	contact@vatier-associes.com
Partner:	*Bernard Vatier*
Number of Lawyers:	15
Areas of Practice:	Full Service

Delsol & Associes

38, rue Saint Ferdinand
75017 Paris
France

Telephone:	33-1-53-70-69-69
Fax:	33-1-53-70-69-60
E-Mail:	fbuffaud@delsoladvocats.com
Internet:	www.delsoladvocats.com
Partner:	*Frank Buffaud*
Number of Lawyers:	52
Other Offices:	Lyon
	Marseille
Areas of Practice:	Full Service

Freshfields Bruckhaus Deringer

2 rue Paul Cezanne
75008 Paris
France

Telephone:	33-1-44-56-44-56
Fax:	33-1-44-56-44-00
Internet:	www.freshfields.com
Partners:	*Jean-Luc Michaud*
	Elie Kleiman
Number of Lawyers:	182 in Paris
Other Offices:	Numerous
Areas of Practice:	Full Service

Jobard Chemla & Associes

50, Boulevard de Courcelles
75017 Paris
France

Telephone:	33-1-42-67-11-70
Fax:	33-1-42-67-11-83
E-Mail:	pe@jbard-chemla.com
Internet:	www.jbard-chemla.com
Partner:	*Pierre-Emmanuel Jobard*

Number of Lawyers: 11
Areas of Practice: Full Service

Cabinet van Hagen

6, Avenue George V
75008 Paris
France

Telephone:	33-1-4720-0064
Fax:	33-1-4720-2509
E-Mail:	van.hagen@wanadoo.fr
Partner:	*Anthony van Hagen*

Number of Lawyers: 9
Areas of Practice: Full Service

Bernard Hertz Bejot

8 rue Murillo
75008 Paris
France

Telephone:	33-1-43-18-80-80
Fax:	33-1-43-18-80-90
E-Mail:	ablumrosen@bhbfrance.com
Internet:	www.bhbfrance.com
Partner:	*Alex Blumrosen*

Number of Lawyers: 15
Areas of Practice: Full Service

Phillips Giraud Naud & Swartz

49 Boulevard de Courcelles
Paris 75008
France

Telephone:	33-14-429-2323
Fax:	33-14-227-9085
E-Mail:	sswartz.pgparis.com
Internet:	www.pgparis.com
Partner:	*Salli Swartz*

Number of Lawyers: 7
Areas of Practice: Full Service

France *continued*

Vogel & Vogel

30 Avenue d' Iena
75016 Paris
France

Telephone:	33-1-53-67-76-20
Fax:	33-1-53-67-76-25
E-Mail:	info@vogel-vogel.com
Internet:	www.vogel-vogel.com
Partners:	*Louis Vogel*
	Joseph Vogel
Number of Lawyers:	33
Other Offices:	Brussels
	Frankfurt
Areas of Practice:	Full Service

Gide Loyrette Nouel

26, Cours Albert ler
75008 Paris
France

Telephone:	33-1-40-75-60-00
Fax:	33-1-43-59-37-79
E-Mail:	info@gide.com
Internet:	www.gide.com
Partners:	*Jean-Marie Burgaburu*
	Frederic Nouel
	Philippe Despres
	Robert MacDonald (New York)
	Pierre Raoul-Duval
	Philippe Xavier-Bender
Number of Lawyers:	589
Other Offices:	Numerous
Areas of Practice:	Full Service

KGA Avocats

44, Avenue des Champs Elysees
75008 Paris
France

Telephone:	33-1-44-95-20-00
Fax:	33-1-49-50-03-97
E-Mail:	thklein@kga.fr
Partner:	*Theodore Klein*
Number of Lawyers:	37
Other Offices:	Lyon
	Marseille
	Brussels
Areas of Practice:	Full Service

Fromont Briens & Associes

5, rue Boudreau
F-75009 Paris
France

Telephone:	33-1-44-51-63-80
Fax:	33-1-44-51-63-89
E-Mail:	info@fromont-briens.com
Internet:	www.fromont-briens.com
Partners:	*Mikael Pelan*
	Cedric Guillon
	Guillaume Desmoulin
Number of Lawyers:	104
Areas of Practice:	Labor and Employment Law

Lamy & Associes

6, Square de l'Opera
Louis-Jouvet
F-75009 Paris
France

E-Mail:	info@lamy-associes.com
Internet:	www.lamy-associes.com
Partners:	_Christoph-Martin Radtke_
	Nathalie Biltz
Number of Lawyers:	45
Other Office:	Lyon
Areas of Practice:	Full Service

Nixon Peabody LLP

32, rue de Monceau
75008 Paris
France

Telephone:	33 1 70 72 36 00
Fax:	33 1 70 72 36 01
E-Mail:	adesenilhes@nixonpeabody.com
Internet:	www.nixonpeabody.com
Partner:	_Arnaud de Senilhes_
Number of Lawyers:	800 (29 in Paris)
Other Offices:	Numerous
Areas of Practice:	Full Service

PDGB Avocats

174, Avenue Victor Hugo
75116 Paris
France

Telephone:	33-1-44-05-21-21
E-Mail:	roy.arakelian@pdgb.com
Internet:	www.pdgb.com
Partners:	*Roy Arakelian*
	Christian Roth
	Alexandre de Gouyon Matignon

Number of Lawyers: 47
Areas of Practice: Full Service

Germany

Heuking Kuhn Lue Wojtek

Georg-Glock-Strasse 4
D-40474 Dusseldorf
Germany

Telephone:	49-211-600-5500
Fax:	49-211-600-5505
E-Mail:	dusseldorf@heuking.de
Internet:	www.heuking.de
Partners:	*Wolfgang Kuhn*
	Ulrich Wittkop (Hamburg)
	Ralf Wojtek (Hamburg)
Number of Lawyers:	204
Other Offices:	Frankfurt
	Paris
	Berlin
	Chemnitz
	Brussels
	Zurich
	Hamburg
	Munich
	Cologne
Areas of Practice:	Full Service

Salger Rechtasanwalte

Darmstadter Landstrasse 125
60598 Frankfurt-Sachsenhausen
Germany

Telephone:	49-69-66-40-88-0
Fax:	49-69-66-40-88-10
E-Mail:	info@salge.com
Internet:	www.salger.com
Partners:	*Hanns-Christian Salger*
	Thomas Foersterling

Number of Lawyers: 7
Areas of Practice: Full Service

Noerr LLP

Brienner Str. 38
80333 Munich
Germany

Telephone:	49-89-286280
Fax:	49-89-280110
E-Mail:	info@.noerr.com
Internet:	www.noerr.com
Partners:	_Thomas Schultz_
	Ronald Frohne (New York)
	Dirk Lentfer (Berlin)
	Georg Jahn
Number of Lawyers:	450
Other Offices:	Frankfurt
	New York
	Berlin
	Dresden
	Prague
	Budapest
	Warsaw
	Moscow
	Bucharest
	Dusseldorf
	Budapest
	Prague
	Bratislava
	Kiev
Areas of Practice:	Full Service

Thuemmel Schuetze & Partner

Urbanstrasse 7
D-10783 Stuttgart
Germany

Telephone:	49-711-16-67-156
E-Mail:	roderich.thuemmel@tsp-law.com
Internet:	www.tsp-law.com
Partner:	*Roderich C. Thuemmel*
Other Offices:	Berlin
	Dresden
Number of Lawyers:	50
Areas of Practice:	Full Service

Hengeler Mueller

Benrather Strasse 18-20
D-40213 Dusseldorf
Germany

Telephone:	49-211-8304-0
Fax:	49-211-8304-170
E-Mail:	info@hengeler.com
Internet:	www.hengeler.com
Partners:	*Klaus Bohlhoff*
	Joachim Rosengarten
	Gerd Krieger
	Matthias Braun
Number of Lawyers:	262
Other Offices:	Frankfurt
	London
	Berlin
	Brussels
	Budapest
	Prague
Areas of Practice:	Full Service

Freshfields Bruckhaus Deringer

Bockenheimer Anloge 44
60329 Frankfurt
Germany

Telephone:	49-69-273-080
Fax:	49-69-232-664
Internet:	www.freshfields.com
Partners:	*Peter Chrocziel (Munich)*
	Burkhard Bastuck (Cologne)
	Helmut Begmann (Berlin)
Other Offices:	Numerous
Number of Lawyers:	2,776
Areas of Practice:	Full Service

Loschelder Rechtsanwaelte

Konrad-Adenauer Ufer 11
D-50668 Cologne
Germany

Telephone:	49-221-650-65-220
Fax:	49-221-650-65-225
Partners:	*Henning Wahlers*
	Thilo Klingbeil
	Frank Heerstrassen
Number of Lawyers:	32
Areas of Practice:	Full Service

Gleiss Lutz

Maybachstrasse 6
Germany
D-70469 Stuttgart

Telephone:	49-711-8997-0
Fax:	49-711-855-096
E-Mail:	info@gleisslutz.com
Internet:	www.gleisslutz.com
Partner:	*Gerhard Wegen*
Other Offices:	Frankfurt
	Berlin
	Brussels
	Dusseldorf
	Munich
Number of Lawyers:	312
Areas of Practice:	Full Service

Taylor Wessing

Hanseatic Trade Center
Am Sandtorkai 41
D-20457 Hamburg
Germany

Telephone:	49-40-36-80-30
Fax:	49-40-36-32-80
E-Mail:	hamburg@taylorwessing.com
Internet:	www.taylorwessing.com
Partners:	*Jorg Wimmers*
	Andreas Meissner
Number of Lawyers:	618
Other Offices:	Numerous
Areas of Practice:	Full Service

SKW Schwarz

Wittlelsbacherplatz 1
D-80333 Munich 2
Germany

Telephone:	49-89-28-64-00
Fax:	49-89-280-94-32
E-Mail:	muenchen@skwschwarz.de
Internet:	www.skwlschwarz.de
Partners:	*Sebastian von Wallwitz*
	Mathias Schwarz
Number of Lawyers:	152
Other Office:	Frankfurt
Areas of Practice:	Full Service

GORG

Klingelhoferstrasse, 5
10785 Berlin
Germany

Telephone:	49-30-884503-149
Fax:	49-30-884503-174
E-Mail:	hmgiessen@george.de
Internet:	www.georg.de
Partner:	*Hans-Michael Giessen*
Number of Lawyers:	150
Other Offices:	Essen
	Frankfurt
	Cologne
	Munich
Areas of Practice:	Full Service

Clifford Chance

Mainzer Landstrasse 46
60325 Frankfurt am Main
Germany

Telephone:	49-69-7199-01
Fax:	49-69-7199-4000
E-Mail:	kersten.schenck@cliffordchance.com
Internet:	www.cliffordchance.com
Partners:	*Kersten Von Schenck*
	Thomas Gasteyer
Number of Lawyers:	420 in Germany
Other Offices:	Numerous
Areas of Practice:	Full Service

SIBETH Partnerschaft

Ander Hauptwache 7
Frankfurt 60313
Germany

Telephone:	49-69-71-58-99-6-0
Fax:	49-69-71-58-99-6-99
E-Mail:	frankfurt@sibeth.com
Internet:	www.sibeth.com
Partner:	*Susanna Fuchsbrunner*
Number of Lawyers:	53
Other Offices:	Berlin
	Munich
Areas of Practice:	Full Service

Oppenhoff & Partner

Borsenplatz 1
50667 Cologne
Germany

Telephone:	49-221-2091-100
Fax:	49-221-2091-333
E-Mail:	klaus.guenther.oppenhoff.eu
Internet:	www.oppenhoff.eu
Partners:	*Ronald Meissner*
	Klaus Guenther

Number of Lawyers: 81
Areas of Practice: Full Service

Ghana

Bruce-Lyle, Bannerman & Thompson

87 Liberty Avenue
Accra
Ghana

Telephone:	233-21-221-491
Fax:	233-21-773-738
E-Mail:	BLBandT@ghana.com
Partner:	*Reginald E. Bannerman*
Areas of Practice:	Full Service

Bentsi-Enchill, Letsa & Ankomah

Teachers Hall Annex
4 Barnes Close
Accra
Ghana

Telephone:	233-21-221-171
Fax:	233-21-226-129
E-Mail:	belm@africaonline.com.gh
Partner:	*Kojo Bentsi-Enchill*
Number of Lawyers:	13
Areas of Practice:	Full Service

Sam Okudzeto & Associates

Total House, 3rd Floor
P.O. Box 5520
Accra - North
Ghana

Telephone:	233-21-666-377
Fax:	233-21-666-545
E-Mail:	okudzeto@ghana.com
Partners:	*Sam Okudzeto*
	Nene Amegatcher

Number of Lawyers: 8
Areas of Practice: Commercial Law
Minerals and Mining
Corporate Law

Saah & Company

Chadwick House
8 Birim Street
Asylum Down
Accra
Ghana

Telephone:	233-21-232-008
Fax:	233-21-230-084
E-Mail:	jsaah@saahpartners.com
Internet:	www.saahpartners.com
Partner:	*Jacob Saah*

Number of Lawyers: 3
Area of Practice: Full Service

Laryea, Laryea & Company, P.C.

No. 5 Mankralo Close
East Cantonments
Accra
Ghana

Telephone:	233-21-775282
Fax:	233-21-755690
E-Mail:	laryea@africaonline.com.gh
Partner:	*Kenneth D. Laryea*
Number of Lawyers:	7
Areas of Practice:	Full Service

Gibraltar

Hassans

57/63 Line Wall Road
Gibraltar

Telephone: 350-200-79000
Fax: 350-200-71966
E-Mail: info@hassans.gi
Internet: www.hassans.gi
Partners: *James Levy*
Tony Provasoli
Michael Castiel
Javier Chincotta
Number of Lawyers: 79
Areas of Practice: Full Service

Triay & Triay

28 Irish Town
Gibraltar

Telephone: 350-200-72020
Fax: 350-200-72270
E-Mail: triay@triay.com
Internet: www.triay.com
Partner: *Raymond Triay*
Number of Lawyers: 24
Areas of Practice: Full Service

Greece

Zepos & Yannopoulos

75, Katehaki & Kifissias Avenue
Athens 115 25
Greece

Telephone:	30-210-69-70-000
Fax:	30-210-69-94-640
E-Mail:	info@zeya.com
Internet:	www.zeya.com
Partners:	*Constantine Yannopoules*
	Dimitros Zepos

Number of Lawyers: 46
Areas of Practice: Full Service

Massouridis-Stavropoulos & Associates

39, Panepistimiou Street
10564 Athens
Greece

Telephone:	30-210-322-2409
Fax:	30-210-322-0902
E-Mail:	mass@otenet.gr
Partner:	*Anthony Massouridis*

Number of Lawyers: 8
Areas of Practice: Full Service

KGDI

28, Dimitriou Soutson St.
Athens
Greece

Telephone:	30-210-817-1500
Fax:	30-210-685-6657
Internet:	www.kgdi.gr
Partner:	_Panou Nikas_
Number of Lawyers:	67
Other Offices:	Thessaloniki
	Piraeus
Areas of Practice:	Full Service

Bahas, Gramatidis & Parnters

26 Filellinon Street
10558 Athens
Greece

Telephone:	30-210-331-8170
Fax:	30-210-331-8171
E-Mail:	law-firm@bahagram.com
Internet:	www.bahagram.com
Partner:	_Nassos Felonis_
Number of Lawyers:	28
Areas of Practice:	Commercial Law
	Corporate and Business Law
	Litigation

Elias Paraskevas Attorneys

7 Asklepiou Street
Athens 10679
Greece

Telephone:	30-210-361-0333
Fax:	30-210-364-5329
E-Mail:	paraskeu@hol.gr
Partner:	*Eirrini Charisiadou*
Number of Lawyers:	26
Areas of Practice:	Full Service

IKRP

25 Boukourestiou St.
Athens 10671
Greece

Telephone:	30-210-36-16-816
Fax:	30-210-36-15-425
E-Mail:	athens@rokas.com
Internet:	www.rokas.com
Partners:	*Ioannis K. Rokas*
	Alkistis Christofilou
Number of Lawyers:	31
Other Offices:	Numerous
Areas of Practice:	Full Service

M. & P. Bernitsas

5 Lykavittou Street
Athens 10672
Greece

Telephone:	30-210-36-15-395
Fax:	30-210-36-40-805
E-Mail:	bernitas@bernitaslawoffices.gr
Internet:	www.bemitsaslawoffices.gr
Partners:	*Panayotis Bernitsas*
	Nikos Papachristopoulos

Number of Lawyers: 34
Areas of Practice: Full Service

Panagopoulos, Vainanidis, Schina, Economou

32 Acadimias Street
106-72 Athens
Greece

Telephone:	30-210-36-43-846
Fax:	30-219-36-04-611
E-Mail:	pvse-law@otenet.gr
Internet:	www.pyse-law.gr
Partners:	*Aida Economou*
	Costas Vainanidis

Number of Lawyers: 14
Areas of Practice: Full Service

Grenada

Wilkinson, Wilkinson & Wilkinson

Lucas Street
St. George's
Grenada

Telephone:	473-440-3578
Fax:	473-440-4172
E-Mail:	wilkinson@spiceisle.com
Partners:	*Ernest Wilkinson*
	Magaret Wilkinson
Areas of Practice:	Full Service

Guam

Blair Sterling Johnson Martinez & Leon Guerro

1008 DNA Building
238 Archibishop F.C. Flores Street
Hagatana 96910-5205
Guam

Telephone:	671-477-7587
Fax:	671-472-4290
Partner:	*Richard Johnson*
Number of Lawyers:	9
Areas of Practice:	Full Service

Teker Torres & Teker

Suite 2-A
130 Aspinall Avenue
Hagatana 96910
Guam

Telephone:	671-477-9891
Fax:	671-472-2601
E-Mail:	tekerciville@guamattorneys.com
Partner:	*Phillip Torres*
Number of Lawyers:	16
Areas of Practice:	Full Service

Guatemala

Mayora & Mayora

Edificio Plaza Centrica
01010 Guatemala City
Guatemala

Telephone:	502-222-368-68
Fax:	502-236-625-40
E-Mail:	mayora&mayora@gua.gbm.net
Internet:	www.mayora-mayora.com
Partner:	*Eduardo Mayora Dawe*
Number of Lawyers:	16
Areas of Practice:	Full Service

Bonilla, Montano, Toriello & Barrios

Avenida Reforma 15-54, Zona 9 01009
Guatemala City
Guatamala

Telephone:	502-2334-0704
Fax:	502-2334-2361
E-Mail:	info@bonilla.com.gt
Internet:	www.bonilla.com.gt
Partners:	*Jorge Rolando Barrios*
	Saul Guillermo Bonilla
Number of Lawyers:	12
Areas of Practice:	Full Service

Rodriguez, Archila, Castellanos, Solares & Aguilar

Diagonal 6, 10-01 Zona 10
Centro Gerencial Las Margaritas
Torre II, Oficina 1101
01010 Guatemala City
Guatemala

Telephone:	502-2339-3139
Fax:	502-2324-3939
Internet:	www.racsa.com.gt
Partner:	*Alfredo Rodriquez Mahuad*
Number of Lawyers:	20
Areas of Practice:	Full Service

Carrillo & Asociados

Diagonal 6, Zona 10
Guatemala City 01010
Guatemala

Telephone:	502-2421-5700
Fax:	502-2421-5724
E-Mail:	info@carillolaw.com
Internet:	www.carillolaw.com
Partner:	*Alfonso Carillo M*
Number of Lawyers:	26
Areas of Practice:	Full Service

Guyana

Luckhoo & Luckhoo

Whitehall
1 Croal Street
Georgetown
Guyana

Telephone:	592-225-9232
Fax:	592-225-6301
Partner:	*Edward A. Luckhoo*
Areas of Practice:	Full Service

Haiti

Cabinet Sales

62, Rue Geffard
Petion-ville
Haiti

Telephone:	502-2510-3991
Fax:	502-2256-5107
E-Mail:	info@cabinetsales.com
Partner:	*Jean-Frederic Sales*
Number of Lawyers:	14

Cabinet de Me Louis Gary Lissade

8, Rue Louissant Bourdon
Port-au-Prince
Haiti

Telephone:	509-2245-4980
Fax:	509-2245-9958
E-Mail:	glissade@haitionline.com
Partner:	*Louis Gary Lissade*
Areas of Practice:	Full Service

Honduras

Gutierrez Falla & Associados

Avenida La Paz 2702
Tegucigalpa
Honduras

Telephone:	504-238-2455
Fax:	504-238-6109
E-Mail:	info@gutierrezfalla.com
Partner:	*Mauricio Villena Bermudez*
Number of Lawyers:	6
Areas of Practice:	Full Service

Bufete Ortez Colindres y Asociados

Edificio El Centro
Tegucigapa
Honduras

Telephone:	504-375-687
Fax:	504-372-572
E-Mail:	eortezc@multivisionhn.net
Partner:	*Enrique Ortez Colindres*
Areas of Practice:	Full Service

J.R. Paz y Asociados

Col. Palmira, Ave. Republica de Argentina
Tegucigalpa
Honduras

Telephone:	504-239-1300
Fax:	504-235-5868
E-Mail:	legibus@lexhon.hn
Internet:	www.lexhon.hn
Partner:	*Jose R. Paz*
Number of Lawyers:	20
Other Office:	San Pedro Sula
Areas of Practice:	Full Service

Lopez Rodezno & Asociados

Edificio Palmira 5 Piso
Ave. Republica de Chile No. 1701
Tegucigala
Honduras

Telephone:	504-232-8114
Fax:	504-232-4116
E-Mail:	lr@lopezrodezno.com
Internet:	www.lopezrodezno.com
Partner:	*Rene Lopez Rodezno*
Areas of Practice:	Full Service

Hong Kong

Deacons

Alexandra House
18 Chater Road, Central
Hong Kong

Telephone:	852-2-825-9211
Fax:	852-2-810-0431
E-Mail:	hongkong@deacons.com
Internet:	www.deaconslaw.com.hk
Partners:	*James Bertram*
	Keith Cole
	David Lyons (Brisbane)
	Charmaine Koo
Number of Lawyers:	92
Other Offices:	Kuala Lumpur
	Beijing
	Shanghai
	Guangzhou
	Taipei
	Bangkok
Areas of Practice:	Full Service

Mayer Brown JSM

Prince's Building
10 Chater Road, Central
Hong Kong

Telephone:	852-2-843-2211
Fax:	852-2-845-9121
E-Mail:	info@mayerbrownjsm.com
Internet:	www.mayerbrownjsm.com
Partners:	*David Ellis*
	Irene Lau
	Alastair MacAulay
Number of Lawyers:	230
Areas of Practice:	Full Service

Wilkinson & Grist

Prince's Building, 6th Floor,
Chater Road, Central
Hong Kong

Telephone:	852-2-524-6011
Fax:	852-2-527-9041
E-Mail:	partners@wilgrist.com
Internet:	www.wilgrist.com
Partners:	*Michael Chan*
	Catherine Chong
Number of Lawyers:	68
Other Office:	Beijing
Areas of Practice:	Full Service

Siao Wen & Leung

Wing On Central Building
26 Des Voeux Road, Central
Hong Kong

Telephone:	852-2103-9888
Fax:	852-2525-4630
Partner:	*Kenneth Siao*

Number of Lawyers: 36
Areas of Practice: Full Service

Sit, Fung, Kwong & Sham

Gloucester Towa, The Landmark
11 Pedder Street, Central
Hong Kong

Telephone:	852-2522-8101
Fax:	852-2845-9292
E-Mail:	webmaster@sfks.com.hk
Internet:	www.sfks.com.hk
Partner:	*C.K. Kwong*

Number of Lawyers: 31
Areas of Practice: Full Service

Boughton Petersen Yang Anderson

409 Jardine House
1 Conaught Place, Central
Hong Kong

Telephone:	852-2298-7618
E-Mail:	klee@bpya.com.hk
Internet:	www.bpya.com.hk
Partners:	*Kevin Lee*
	Victor Yang

Number of Lawyers: 18
Areas of Practice: Full Service

Hungary

Danubia

16 Bajcsy-Zsilinszky
Budapest H-1051
Hungary

Telephone:	36-1-411-8800
Fax:	36-1-266-5770
E-Mail:	central@danubia.com
Internet:	www.danubia.hu
Partner:	*Michael Lantos*
Number of Lawyers:	54
Areas of Practice:	Intellectual Property

Nagy & Trocsanyi

Ugocsa Utca 4/B
H-1126 Budapest
Hungary

Telephone:	36-1-487-8700
Fax:	36-1-478-8701
Internet:	www.nt.hu
Partners:	*Peter P. Nagy*
	Tibor Bogdan
Number of Lawyers:	26
Other Office:	New York
Areas of Practice:	Full Service

Szecskay Law Firm

Kossuth Square 16-17
H-1055 Budapest
Hungary

Telephone:	36-1-472-3000
Fax:	36-1-472-3001
E-Mail:	info@szecskay.com
Internet:	www.szecskay.hu
Partner:	*Andras Szecskay*

Number of Lawyers: 28
Areas of Practice: Full Service

Gardos, Furedi, Mosonyi, Tomori

Vaci Utca 81
Vaci Utca Center
1056 Budapest
Hungary

Telephone:	36-1-235-7560
Fax:	36-1-327-7561
E-Mail:	postmaster@gfmt.hu
Internet:	www.gfmt.hu
Partner:	*Katalin Furedi*

Number of Lawyers: 16
Areas of Practice: Full Service

Bogsch & Partners

Kiralyhago ter 8-9
H-1126 Budapest
Hungary

Telephone:	36-1-318-1945
Fax:	36-1-318-7828
E-Mail:	central@bogsch-partners.hu
Internet:	www.bogsch-partners.hu
Partner:	*Tamas Godolle*
Number of Lawyers:	14
Areas of Practice:	Corporate Law
	Mergers & Acquisitions
	Intellectual Property
	EU Law
	Real Estate

Burai-Kovaes & Partners

Andrassy ut 100
Budapest H-1062
Hungary

Telephone:	36-1-354-4300
Fax:	36-1-354-4399
E-Mail:	office@burai-kovacs.hu
Internet:	www.burai-kovacs.hu
Partner:	*Dezso Perlaki*
Number of Lawyers:	14
Areas of Pratice:	Full Service

Iceland

Logos Legal Servcies

Efstaleiti 5
103 Reykjavik
Iceland

Telephone:	354-1-540-0300
Fax:	354-1-540-0301
E-Mail:	logos@logos.is
Internet:	www.logos.is
Partners:	*Arni Vilhjalmsson*
	Einar Axelsson
	Gunnar Sturluson
Other Offices:	London
	Frederiksberg
Areas of Practice:	Full Service

Pacta Law Office

Laugavegi 99
Reykjavik
Iceland

Telephone:	354-440-7900
Fax:	354-440-7901
E-Mail:	pall@pacta.is
Internet:	www.pacta.is
Partner:	*Pall Arnor Palsson*
Number of Lawyers:	20
Other Offices:	Akureyri
	Egilsstadir
	Isafjordur
Areas of Practice:	Full Service

India

Amarchand & Mangaldas & Suresh A. Shroff & Co.
Peninsula Chambers, Peninsula Corporate Park,
Marg, Lower Parel
Mumbai 400 013
India

Telephone:	91-22-566-04455
Fax:	91-22-566-28466
E-Mail:	Cyril.shroff@amerchand.com
Internet:	www.amarchand.com
Partners:	*Shardul Shroff*
	Cyril Shroff
Other Offices:	New Delhi
	Bangalore
	Hyderabad
	Kolkata
Number of Lawyers:	475
Areas of Practice:	Full Service

Rajinder Narain & Co.

Shiram House
14F Connaught Place
New Delhi 110 001
India

Telephone:	91-11-2331-3251
Fax:	91-11-2335-3164
E-Mail:	rnc@vsnl.net
Internet:	www.rajindernarainco.com
Partner:	*Ravinder Nath*
Number of Lawyers:	25
Areas of Practice:	Full Service

Priti Suri & Associates

E-601 Guari Sadan
S. Hailey Road
New Delhi 110001
India

Telephone:	91-11-4350-0500
Fax:	91-11-4350-0502
E-Mail:	psuri@psalegal.com
Internet:	www.psalegal.com
Partner:	*Priti Suri*
Number of Lawyers:	11
Areas of Practice:	Full Service

Juris Chamber

E-55, L.G.F. Panchsheel Park
New Delhi
India

Telephone:	91-98-1109-8069
Fax:	91-11-4101-2330
E-Mail:	info@jurischamber.com
Internet:	www.jurischamber.com
Partner:	*Ajay Verma*
Areas of Practice:	Full Service

Majmudar & Co.

96, Free Press House
Free Press Journal Road
Nariman Point
Mumbai 400 021
India

Telephone:	91-22-6630-7272
Fax:	91-22-6630-7252
E-Mail:	mailbox@majmudarindia.com
Internet:	www.majmudarindia.com
Partner:	*Akil Hirani*
Number of Lawyers:	32
Other Office:	Bangalore
Areas of Practice:	Full Service

Singhania & Partners

B-92, 9th Floor, Himalaya House 23
Kasturba Gandhi Marg
New Delhi, 110 001
India

Telephone:	91-120-463-1000
Fax:	91-120-463-1001
E-Mail:	info@singhania.in
Internet:	www.singhania.net
Partners:	*Ravi Singhania*
	J.K. Gupta
	Sameer Rastogi
Number of Lawyers:	67
Other Offices:	Bangalore
	Hyderabad
	Mumbai
Areas of Practice:	Full Service

Lawquest

522, Maker Chambers V
211 Nariman Point
Mumbai 400 021
India

Telephone:	91-22-6615-6555
Fax:	91-22-2287-2080
E-Mail:	poorvi@lawquestinternatinoal.com
Internet:	www.lawquestinternational.com
Partner:	*Poorvi Chothani*
Areas of Practice:	Full Service

225

Kochhar & Co.

S-454, Greater Kailash II
New Delhi 110048
India

Telephone:	91-11-2921-5477
Fax:	91-11-2921-9656
E-Mail:	delhi@kochhar.com
Internet:	www.kochhar.com
Partners:	*Rohit Kochhar*
	Dhruv Wahi
Number of Lawyers:	77
Other Offices:	Bangalore
	Hyderabad
	Gurgaon
	Singapore
	Atlanta
	Tokyo
	Chennai
	Mumbai
Areas of Practice:	Full Service

Fox Mandal Little

Central Bank Building
MG Road
Mumbai 400 023
India

Telephone:	91-22-2265-2739
Fax:	91-22-2265-9918
E-Mail:	Mumbai@foxmandallittle.com
Internet:	www.foxmandallittle.com
Partners:	*Dara Mehta*
	Zubin Morris
Number of Lawyers:	88
Other Offices:	Hyderabad
	London
	Dhaka
	Bangalore
	Chennai
	New Delhi
	Kolkota
Areas of Practice:	Full Service

Mulla & Mulla & Craigie Blunt & Caroe

Mulla House
51 Mahatma Gandhi Road Fort
Mumbai 400 001
India

Telephone:	91-22-2204-4960
Fax:	91-22-2204-0246
E-Mail:	info@mullaandmulla.com
Internet:	www.mullaandmulla.com
Partners:	*E.A.K. Faizullabhoy*
	Shardul Thacker
	Yazdi Dandiwala
	E.B. Desai
Number of Lawyers:	140
Other Offices:	Bangalore
	New Delhi
Areas of Practice:	Full Service

Malvi Ranchoddas

Yusuf Building, 3rd Floor
Mahatma Gandhi Road
Mumbai 400 001
India

Telephone:	91-22-6633-1801
Fax:	91-22-6633-1802
E-Mail:	malvirco@vsnl.com
Partner:	*Prakash Mehta*
Number of Lawers:	14
Areas of Practice:	Full Service

J. Sagar Associates

84-E, Lane C-6
Sainik Farms
New Delhi – 110 062
India

Telephone:	91-11-4311-0600
Fax:	91-11-4311-0617
E-Mail:	sajai@jsalaw.com
Internet:	www.jsalaw.com
Partner:	*Sajai Singh*
Number of Lawyers:	157
Other Offices:	Gurgaon
	Hyderabad
	Bangalore
	Mumbai
Areas of Practice:	Full Service

AZB Partners

Express Towers
Nariman Point
Mumbai 400021
India

Telephone:	91-22-6639-6880
Fax:	91-22-6639-68888
E-Mail:	Mumbai@azbpartners.com
Internet:	www.azbpartners.com
Partner:	*Zia Mody*
Number of Lawyers:	222
Other Offices:	New Delhi
	Bangalore
Areas of Practice:	Full Service

Bhasin & Co.

10 Hailey Road
New Delhi 110001
India

Telephone:	91-123-322-2601
Fax:	91-123-329-273
E-Mail:	lbhasin@gmail.com
Partner:	*Lalit Bhasin*
Other Office:	Mumbai
Areas of Practice:	Full Service

Indonesia

Ali Budiardjo, Nugroho, Reksodiputro

Graha Niaga, 24th Floor
Jalan Jenderal Sudirman Kav. 58
Jakarta 12190
Indonesia

Telephone:	62-21-250-5125
Fax:	62-21-250-5001
E-Mail:	info@abnrlaw.com
Internet:	www.abnrlaw.com
Partner:	*Mardjono Reksodiputro*
Number of Lawyers:	45
Other Office:	Singapore
Areas of Practice:	Full Service

Wiriadinata & Saleh

Graha Niaga, 26th Floor
Jalan Jenderal Sudirman Kav. 58
Jakarta 12190
Indonesia

Telephone:	62-21-250-5175
Fax:	62-21-250-5185
Internet:	www.wands-law.com
Partners:	*Hoesein Wiriadinata*
	Tamiza Saleh
Number of Lawyers:	18
Areas of Practice:	Full Service

Lubis Ganie & Surowidjojo

Menara Imperium, Jl. H.R. Rasuna Said Kav. 1
Jakarta 12980
Indonesia

Telephone:	62-21-831-5005
Fax:	62-21-831-5015
E-Mail:	lgs@lgslaw.co.id
Internet:	www.lgsonline.com
Partner:	*Timbul Thomas Lubis*
Number of Lawyers:	37
Areas of Practice:	Full Service

Makarim & Taira S.

Summitmas I, 17th Floor
Jalan Jenderal Sudirman Kav. 61-62
Jakarta 12069
Indonesia

Telephone:	62-21-252-1272
Fax:	62-21-252-2750
E-Mail:	Richard.cornwallis@makarin.com
Internet:	www.makarim.com
Partner:	*Ratna Iskander*
Number of Lawyers:	48
Areas of Practice:	Full Service

Mochtar, Karuwin and Komar

Wisma Metropolitan II, 14th Floor
Jalan Jenderal Sudirman Kav. 31
Jakarta 12820
Indonesia

Telephone:	62-21-571-1130
Fax:	62-21-571-1162
E-Mail:	mail@mkklaw.net
Internet:	www.mkklaw.net
Partners:	*Mochtar Kusuma-Atmadja*
	Sidik Suraputra

Number of Lawyers: 9
Areas of Practice: Full Service

Soewito, Suhardiman, Eddymurthy & Kardono

Mayapada Tower, 14th Floor
Jl. Jenderal Sudirman Kav. 28
Jakarta 12920
Indonesia

Telephone:	62-21-521-2038
Fax:	62-21-521-2039
E-Mail:	ssek@ssek.com
Internet:	www.ssek.com
Partner:	*Dyah Soewito*

Number of Lawyers: 34
Areas of Practice: Full Service

Hadiputranto, Hadinoto & Partners

Jakarta Stock Exchange Building
Tower II, 21st Floor
Sudirman Central Business District
Jl. Jenderal Sudirman Kav. 52-53
Jakarata 12190
Indonesia

Telephone:	62-21-515-5090
Fax:	62-21-515-4840
E-Mail:	tuti.hadiputranto@bakernet.com
Internet:	www.hhp.co.id
Partners:	*Tuti Hadiputranto*
	Tuti Dewi Hadinoto
Number of Lawyers:	74
Areas of Practice:	Full Service

Kartini Muljadi & Rekan

Jalan Gunawarman No. 18
Kebayoran Baru
Jakarta 12110
Indonesia

Telephone:	62-21-525-6968
Fax:	62-21-525-5561
E-Mail:	kartini.muljadi@kmuljadilaw.com
Internet:	www.kmuljadilaw.com
Partner:	*Kartini Muljadi*
Number of Lawyers:	22
Areas of Practice:	Full Service

Iran

Alexander Aghayan & Associates, Inc.

83 Sarhang Sakhai Avenue
Tehran 11354
Iran

Telephone:	98-21-6670-5056
Fax:	98-21-6670-4858
E-Mail:	aghayan@dpimail.net
Internet:	www.aghayan.com
Partner:	*Shahin Aghayan*
Other Office:	Paris
Areas of Practice:	Intellectual Property

Torossian, Avanessian & Associates

No. 17, Magnolia St., Golriz St., Ghaem Magham Farahani
Tehran 15886
Iran

Telephone:	98-21-8884-2843
Fax:	98-21-8884-1725
E-Mail:	vitorossian@taalawfirm.com
Partner:	*Vrej Terossian*
Areas of Practice:	Oil and Gas

Tavakoli & Shahabi

1946 Dr. Shariati Avenue
P.O. Box 19395-3448
Tehran 19149
Iran

Telephone:	98-21-8888-5812
Fax:	98-21-8878-4590
E-Mail:	mailroom@tavakolishahabi.com
Internet:	www.tavakolishahabi.com
Partners:	*M. Tavakoli*
	M. Shahabi

Number of Lawyers: 8
Practice Areas: Full Service

Iraq

Iraq Law Alliance, PLLC

Abunuwass, 901/21/11 Karradah Sharqeyah Khor
Bandah, Baghdad
Iraq

Telephone:	964-77-11-918-725
Fax:	253-238-6128
E-Mail:	info@iqilaw.com
Internet:	www.iqilaw.com
Partner:	*Mohamed El Roubi*
	Thomas Donovan
Number of Lawyers:	6
Other Office:	Erbil
Areas of Practice:	Full Service

Gulf International Legal Strategies, S.A.

P.O. Box 4220
Baghdad
Iraq

Telephone:	964-7901-480-888
E-Mail:	legalservices@gulflegalstrategies.com
Internet:	www.iraqlawfirm.com
Partner:	*Salem Chalabi*
Areas of Practice:	Full Service

Ireland

Arthur Cox & Co.
Earlsfort Centre
Earlsfort Terrace Dublin 2
Ireland

Telephone:	353-1-618-0000
Fax:	353-1-618-0618
E-Mail:	dublin@arthurcox.com
Internet:	www.arthurcox.com
Partners:	*Gregory Glynn*
	John Menton
	Padraig O'Riordain
Number of Lawyers:	319
Other Offices:	Belfast
	London
	New York
Areas of Practice:	Full Service

A. & L. Goodbody

International Financial Services Center
25-28 North Wall Quay
Dublin 1
Ireland

Telephone:	353-1-649-2000
Fax:	353-1-649-2649
E-Mail:	law@algoodbody.ie
Internet:	www.algoodbody.ie
Partners:	*Paul Carroll*
	Julian Yarr
	John Coman
	James Sommerville
	Michael A. Greene
	Stephen O'Riordan
	Peter Maher
Number of Lawyers:	212
Other Offices:	London
	Belfast
Areas of Practice:	Full Service

McCann FitzGerald

Riverside One
Sir John Rogerson's Quay
Dublin 2
Ireland

Telephone:	353-1-829-0000
Fax:	353-1-829-0010
E-Mail:	inquiries@mccannfitzgerald.ie
Internet:	www.mccannfitzgerald.ie
Partners:	*Ronan Molony*
	Catherine Deane
	Gerald FitzGerald
Number of Lawyers:	134
Other Offices:	London
	Brussels
Areas of Practice:	Full Service

Dillon Eustace

33 Sir John Rogerson's Quay
Dublin 2
Ireland

Telephone:	353-1-667-0022
Fax:	353-1-667-0042
E-Mail:	info@dilloneustace.ie
Internet:	www.dillonuestace.ie
Partners:	*David Dillon*
	Mark Thorne
	Kieran Cowhey
Number of Lawyers:	65
Other Offices:	Tokyo
	Cork
Areas of Practice:	Finance and Banking
	Corporate and Commercial Law
	Litigation

Eugene F. Collins, Solicitors

Temple Chambers
3 Burlington Road
Dublin 4
Ireland

Telephone:	353-1-202-6400
Fax:	353-1-667-5200
E-Mail:	lmacdermott@efc.ie
Internet:	www.efc.ie
Partners:	*Laura MacDermott*
	David Cantrell

Number of Lawyers: 78
Areas of Practice: Full Serivce

Mason Hayes & Curran

South Bank House, Barrow Street
Dublin 4
Ireland

Telephone:	353-1-614-5000
Fax:	353-1-614-5001
E-Mail:	mail@mhc.ie
Internet:	www.mhc.ie
Partners:	*Justin McKenna*
	Declan Moylan
	Emer Gilvarry
	Declan Black
	Tony Burke
	Kevin Hoy

Number of Lawyers: 89
Other Offices: London
                      New York
Areas of Practice: Full Service

Matheson Ormsby Prentice

70 Sir John Rogerson's Quay
Dublin 2
Ireland

Telephone:	353-1-232-2000
Fax:	353-1-232-3333
E-Mail:	map@mop.ie
Internet:	www.mop.ie
Partners:	*Liam Quirke*
	Robert O'Shea
	Pat English (New York)
	Elizabeth O'Connor
Number of Lawyers:	424
Other Offices:	London
	New York
	Palo Alto
Areas of Practice:	Full Service

Isle of Man

Simcocks

P.O. Box 181
Ridgeway House
Ridgeway Street
Douglas IM99 1PY
Isle of Man

Telephone:	44-1624-690300
Fax:	44-1624-690333
E-Mail:	mail@simcocks.com
Internet:	www.simcocks.com
Partner:	*Philip B. Games*
Number of Lawyers:	20
Other Office:	London
Areas of Practice:	Full Service

Laurence Keenan Advocates & Solicitors

Victoria Chambers
47 Victoria Street
Douglas IM1 2LD
Isle of Man

Telephone:	44-1624-611933
Fax:	44-1624-611893
E-Mail:	info@lklaw.com.im
Internet:	www.laurencekeenan.com
Partner:	*Laurence Keenan*
Number of Lawyers:	7
Areas of Practice:	Full Service

Israel

Zysman, Aharoni, Gayer & Ady Kaplan & Co.

Beit Zion, 41-45 Rothschild Blvd.
Tel Aviv 65784
Israel

Telephone:	972-3-795-5555
Fax:	972-3-795-5550
E-Mail:	aharoni@zag-k.co.il
Internet:	www.zag-k.co.il
Partners:	*Shmuel Zysman*
	Erez Aharoni
Number of Lawyers:	50
Other Offices:	Rosh Pina
	Eilat
Areas of Practice:	Full Service

Yigal Arnon & Co.

1 Azrieli Center
Tel Aviv 67021
Israel

Telephone:	972-3-608-7777
Fax:	972-3-608-7724
E-Mail:	info@arnon.co.il
Internet:	www.arnon.co.il
Partners:	*Paul H. Baris*
	Barry Levenfeld
Number of Lawyers:	110
Other Office:	Jerusalem
Areas of Practice:	Full Service

Haim Zadok & Co.

Rubenstein Building, 18th Floor
20 Lincoln Street
Tel Aviv 67134
Israel

Telephone:	972-3-625-4000
Fax:	972-3-625-4040
E-Mail:	general@zadokco.co.il
Internet:	www.zadokco.co.il
Partners:	*Nitza Posner*
	Ilan Shavit-Stricks
Number of Lawyers:	23
Areas of Practice:	Full Service

S. Horowitz & Co.

31 Ahad Haam Street
Tel Aviv 65202
Israel

Telephone:	972-3-567-0700
Fax:	972-3-566-0974
E-Mail:	info@s-horowitz.com
Internet:	www.s-horowitz.co.il
Partner:	*Hugh Kowarsky*
Number of Lawyers:	104
Areas of Practice:	Full Service

Efrati, Galili & Co.

6 Wissotsky Street
Tel Aviv 62338
Israel

Telephone:	972-3-545-2020
Fax:	972-3-604-0111
E-Mail:	info@eglaw.co.il
Internet:	www.egl.co.il
Partners:	*David Efrati*
	Alon Galili

Number of Lawyers: 7
Areas of Practice: Full Service

Fischer, Behar, Chen, Well, Orion & Co.

3 Daniel Frisch Street
Tel Aviv 64731
Israel

Telephone:	972-3-694-4111
Fax:	972-3-609-1116
E-Mail:	fbc@fbclawyers.com
Internet:	www.fbclawyers.com
Partners:	*Ronald Lehmann*
	Reuven Behar

Number of Lawyers: 128
Areas of Practice: Full Service

Zell & Co.

8 Geula St.
Tel Aviv 63304
Israel

Telephone:	972-3-510-1022
Fax:	972-3-510-1021
E-Mail:	telaviv@fandz.com
Internet:	www.fandz.com
Partner:	*L. Marc Zell*
Other Offices:	Jerusalem
	Washington, D.C.
	Moscow
	New York
Areas of Practice:	Full Service

Balter, Guth, Aloni & Co.

96 Yigal Alon St.
Tel Aviv 67891
Israel

Telephone:	972-3-5111-111
Fax:	972-3-642-6000
E-Mail:	bgalaw@bgalaw.co.il
Internet:	www.bgalaw.co.il
Partner:	*Moshe Balter*
Number of Lawyers:	88
Other Offices:	Jerusalem
	Haifa
	Tiberias
	Beer Sheva
	New York
Areas of Practice:	Full Service

Herzog, Fox & Neeman

Asia House
4 Weizman Street
Tel Aviv 64239
Israel

Telephone:	972-3-692-2020
Fax:	972-3-696-6464
E-Mail:	hfn@hfn.co.il
Internet:	www.hfn.co.il
Partners:	*Meir Linzen*
	Tuvia Erlich
	Janet Pahima

Number of Lawyers: 118
Areas of Practice: Full Service

Hermann, Makov & Co.

Begin 7 St. - Beit Gibor Sport
Ramat Gan 52521
Israel

Telephone:	972-3-611-4200
Fax:	972-3-611-4220
E-Mail:	main@hmlaw.co.il
Internet:	www.hmlaw.co.il
Partners:	*Isaac Winder*
	Eliahu Ben-Israel

Number of Lawyers: 26
Areas of Practice: Full Service

Alon Kaplan Law Office

1 King David Boulevard, 3rd Floor
Tel Aviv 64953
Israel

Telephone:	972-3-695-4463
Fax:	972-3-695-5575
E-Mail:	info@kaplex.com
Internet:	www.kaplex.com
Partner:	*Alon Kaplan*
Number of Lawyers:	6
Areas of Practice:	Full Service

Shibolet & Co.

Museum Tower, 4 Berkowitz St.
Tel Aviv 64238
Israel

Telephone:	972-3-777-8333
Fax:	972-3-777-8444
E-Mail:	manager@shibolet.com
Internet:	www.shibolet.com
Partner:	*Yaacov Yisraeli*
Number of Lawyers:	58
Areas of Practice:	Full Service

Y. Ben-Dror & Co.

Rubenstein Tower
25th Floor
20 Lincoln Street
Tel Aviv 67134
Israel

Telephone:	972-3-764-9200
Fax:	972-3-575-7836
E-Mail:	bendror@ybendror.co.il
Internet:	www.ybendror.com
Partner:	*Yossi Ben-Dror*
Number of Lawyers: 5	
Areas of Practice:	Full Service

Sherby & Co.

12 Menachen Begin Street
Ramat Gan 52521
Israel

Phone:	972-3-753-8668
Fax:	972-3-753-8669
E-Mail:	eric@sherby.co.il
Internet:	www.sherby.co.il
Partner:	*Eric Sherby*
Number of Lawyers: 2	
Areas of Practice:	International Litigation and Arbitration Licensing

Naschitz, Brandes & Co.

5 Tuval Street
Tel Aviv
Israel

Telephone:	972-3-623-5000
Fax:	972-3-625-5005
E-Mail:	info@nblaw.com
Internet:	www.nblaw.com
Partner:	*Hanina Brandes*
Number of Lawyers:	88
Other Office:	Haifa
Areas of Practice:	Full Service

Goldfarb, Levy, Eran, Meiri, Tzafrir & Co.

2 Weizmann Street
Tel Aviv 64239
Israel

Telephone:	972-3-608-9999
Fax:	972-3-608-9909
E-Mail:	info@goldfarb.com
Internet:	www.goldfarb.com
Partner:	*Oded Eran*
Number of Lawyers:	104
Areas of Practice:	Full Service

Italy

Gianni, Origoni, Grippo & Partners

20, Via Delle Quattro Fontane
00184 Rome
Italy

Telephone:	39-06-478-751
Fax:	39-06-487-1101
E-Mail:	rome@gop.it
Internet:	www.gop.it
Partners:	*Francesco Gianni*
	Cesare Vento
	Alessandro Giuliani (Milan)
	Nino di Bella (Milan)
	Tomaso Cenci
Other Offices:	Milan
	Padua
	Bologna
	Naples
	Turin
	New York
	London
	Brussels
Number of Lawyers:	311
Areas of Practice:	Full Service

Pavia & Ansaldo

Via Del Lauro, 7
20121 Milan
Italy

Telephone:	39-02-85581
Fax:	39-02-89011995
E-Mail:	info.milano@pavia-ansaldo.it
Internet:	www.pavia-ansaldolt.com
Partner:	*Stefano Bianchi*
Other Offices:	Rome
	Brussels
	Tokyo
	Moscow
	St. Petersburg
Number of Lawyers:	76
Areas of Practice:	Full Service

Tonucci & Partners

Via Principessa Clotilde, 7
00196 Rome
Italy

Telephone:	39-06-362-271
Fax:	39-06-323-5161
E-Mail:	mail@tonucci.it
Internet:	www.tonucci.it
Partner:	*Mario Tonucci*
Number of Lawyers:	74
Other Offices:	Milan
	Tirana
	Padua
	Florence
	Bucharest
Areas of Practice:	Full Service

Studio Legale Sutti

Via Montenapoleone, 8
20121 Milan
Italy

Telephone:	39-02-76-2041
Fax:	39-02-76204-805
E-Mail:	maildesk@sutti.com
Internet:	www.sutti.com
Partners:	*Stefano Sutti*
	Simona Cazzinga
Number of Lawyers:	167
Other Offices:	London
	Tokyo
	Bucharest
	Zagreb
	Monza
	Sofia
	Belgrade
	Genoa
	Rome
Areas of Practice:	Full Service

Macchi di Cellere e Gangemi

Via Guiseppe Cuboni, 12
00197 Rome
Italy

Telephone:	39-06-362-141
Fax:	39-06-322-2159
E-Mail:	roma@macchi-gangemi.com
Internet:	www.macchi-gangemi.com
Partners:	*Luigi Macchi de Cellere*
	Giuseppe Schiavello
Number of Lawyers:	87
Other Offices:	Milan
	Bologna
	Verona
	Paris
Areas of Practice:	Full Service

Ughi e Nunziante

Via Venti Settembre, 1
00187 Rome
Italy

Telephone:	39-06-474-831
Fax:	39-06-487-0397
E-Mail:	un.rome@unlaw.it
Internet:	www.unlaw.it
Partner:	*Marcello Gioscia*
Number of Lawyers:	60
Other Office:	Milan
Areas of Practice:	Full Service

Carabba & Partners

Via Condotti, 91
00187 Rome
Italy

Telephone:	39-06-696-701
E-Mail:	info@caplex.it
Internet:	www.caplex.it
Partners:	*Ferninando Carabba*
	Luca Mendicini
Number of Lawyers:	58
Other Office:	Milan
Areas of Practice:	Full Service

Cocuzza & Associati

Via San Giovanni Sul Mure, 18
20121 Milan
Italy

Telephone:	39-02-866-096
Fax:	39-02-862-650
E-Mail:	studio@cucuzzaeassociati.it
Internet:	www.antonellicocuzza.it
Partner:	*Claudio Cocuzza*
Number of Lawyers:	15
Areas of Practice:	Full Service

Portolano Colella Cavello

Via Santa Maria in Via 12
00187 Rome
Italy

Telephone:	39-06-696661
Fax:	39-06-69666544
E-Mail:	dcolella@portalano.it
Internet:	www.portolano.it
Partner:	*Domenico Colella*
Number of Lawyers:	23
Other Office:	Milan
Areas of Practice:	Full Service

Chiomenti Studio Legale

Via XXIV Maggio 43
00187 Rome
Italy

Telephone:	39-06-466-221
Fax:	39-06-466-22600
E-Mail:	roma@chiomenti.net
Internet:	www.chiomenti.net
Partners:	*Carlo Chiomenti*
	Giorgio Cappelli
Number of Lawyers:	192
Other Offices:	Milan
	Turin
	London
	New York
	Brussels
	Beijing
	Shanghai
	Hong Kong
Areas of Practice:	Full Service

Lombardi Molinari e Associati

Via Andregari, 4/A
2012, Milan
Italy

Telephone:	39-02-896-221
Fax:	39-02-896-22333
E-Mail:	info@lmlaw.it
Internet:	www.lmlaw.it
Partner:	Ugo Molinar
Number of Lawyers:	52
Areas of Practice:	Full Service

Lega Colucci

Via della Moscova 18
20121 Milan
Italy

Telephone:	39-027-788-751
Fax:	39-027-601-8478
E-Mail:	Milano@lcalex.it
Internet:	www.lcalex.it
Partners:	Giovanni Lega
	Paolo A. Colucci
Number of Lawyers:	30
Other Offices:	Brussels
	Beijing
	Shanghai
Areas of Practice:	Full Service

Tosetto, Weigmann e Associati

Corse Duca Delgi Abruzzi, 15
10129 Turin
Italy

Telephone:	39-11-554-5411
Fax:	39-11-518-4587
E-Mail:	guido.craveto@studiotosetto.it
Internet:	www.studiotosetto.it
Partners:	*Guido Cravetto*
	Marco Weigmann
	Marco Ricolfi
	Andrea Lanciani
Number of Lawyers:	43
Other Offices:	Milan
	Rome
Areas of Practice:	Full Service

Carnelutti Studio Legale Associato

Via Amadeo, 3
20121 Milan
Italy

Telephone:	39-02-655-851
Fax:	39-02-655-85585
E-Mail:	info@carnelutti.com
Internet:	www.carnelutti.com
Partners:	*Luca Arnaboldi*
	Margherita Barie
Number of Lawyers:	67
Other Office:	Rome
Areas of Practice:	Full Service

Law Offices of Giuseppe L. Rosa

4, Piazza G. Fracastoro
37010 Verona
Italy

Telephone:	39-045-803-0630
Fax:	39-045-803-1040
E-Mail:	glrosa@tiscalinct.it
Partner:	*Giuseppe Rosa*
Areas of Practice:	Full Service

Legance Studio Legale Associati

Via Dante 7
20123 Milan
Italy

Telephone:	39-02-896-3071
Fax:	39-02-896-7810
E-Mail:	gnardulli@legance.it
Internet:	www.legance.it
Partner:	*Giovanni Nardulli*
Number of Lawyers:	125
Other Office:	Rome
Areas of Practice:	Full Service

Jamaica

Myers Fletcher and Gordon

Park Place
21 East Street
Kingston
Jamaica

Telephone:	876-922-5860
Fax:	876-922-4811
E-Mail:	info@mfg.com.jm
Internet:	www.myersfletcher.com
Partner:	*Derek N. Jones*
Number of Lawyers:	34
Other Office:	London
Areas of Practice:	Full Service

Dunn Cox

P.O. Box 365
48 Duke Street
Kingston
Jamaica

Telephone:	876-922-1500
Fax:	876-922-9002
E-Mail:	info@dunncox.com
Internet:	www.dunncox.com
Partners:	*John Leiba*
	Janet Morrison
	Lincoln Eatmon
	Enid Chin
Number of Lawyers:	27
Areas of Practice:	Full Service

Rattray, Patterson, Rattray

15 Caledonia Avenue
Kingston 5
Jamaica

Telephone:	876-929-6680
Fax:	876-929-2840
E-Mail:	info@rattraypatterson.com
Internet:	www.rattraypatterson.com
Partner:	*Alfred Rattray*
Areas of Practice:	Full Service

Japan

Nagashima, Ohno & Tsunematsu

Kioicho Building
3-12, Kioicho
Chiyoda-Ku
Tokyo 102-0094
Japan

Telephone:	81-3-3288-7000
Fax:	81-3-5213-7800
E-Mail:	info@noandt.com
Internet:	www.noandt.com
Partners:	*Kazuo Ohtake*
	Yasuhide Watanabe (New York)
	Yoshikazu Sugino
	Soichiro Fujiwaia
Number of Lawyers:	329
Other Office:	New York
Areas of Practice:	Full Service

Oh-Ebashi LPC & Partners

Umedashinmichi Building 8F,
1-3 Dojima 1-Chome, Kita-ku
Osaka 530-0003
Japan

Telephone:	81-6-6341-0461
Fax:	81-6-6347-0688
E-Mail:	info@ohebashi.com
Internet:	www.ohebashi.com
Partners:	*Shiro Kuniya*
	Tadashi Ishikawa
Other Offices:	Tokyo
	Shanghai
Number of Lawyers:	64

Abe, Ikubo & Katayama

Fukuoka Building, 9th Floor
2-8-7 Yaesu, Chuo-ku
Tokyo 104-0028
Japan

Telephone:	81-3-3273-2600
Fax:	81-3-3273-2033
Internet:	www.aiklaw.co.jp
Partners:	*Shogo Abe*
	Yasuhiko Ikubo
	Eiji Katayama
Number of Lawyers:	42
Areas of Practice:	Full Service

Blakemore & Mitsuki

Nittochi Building, 4F
4-1, Kasumigaseki 1-chome Chiyoda-ku,
Toyko 100-0013
Japan

Telephone:	81-3-3503-5571
Fax:	81-3-3503-4707
E-Mail:	info@blakemore.gr.jp
Internet:	www.blakemore.gr.ip
Partners:	*Tetsu Tanaka*
	Yasuo Shida

Number of Lawyers: 30
Areas of Practice: Full Service

Braun Moriya Hoashi & Kubota

502 Tokyo Sakurada Building
1-3 Nishi Shinbashi,
1-chome Minato-Ku
Tokyo 105-0003
Japan

Telephone:	81-3-3504-0251
Fax:	81-3-3595-0985
E-Mail:	bmhk@mui.biglobe.ne.jp
Partner:	*Chiseko Fukuda*
Areas of Practice:	Maritime Law

Koga & Partners

Kamiyacho MT Building, 2nd Floor
3-20, Toranomon 4-chome, Minato-ku
Tokyo 105-0001
Japan

Telephone:	81-3-3578-8681
Fax:	81-3-3578-8682
E-Mail:	yoshikawa@kogapartners.com
Partners:	*Yoichiro Yamakawa*
	Seiichi Yoshikawa
Areas of Practice:	Full Service

City-Yuwa Partners

Marunouchi Mitsui Building
2-2-2 Marunouchi,Chiyoda-ku
Tokyo 100-0005
Japan

Telephone:	81-3-6212-5500
Fax:	81-3-6212-5700
Internet:	www.city-yuwa.com
Partner:	*Keisuke Ide*
Number of Lawyers:	114
Areas of Practice:	Full Service

Matsuo & Kosugi

Fukoku Seimei Building, 18th Floor
2-2-2 Uchisaiwai-cho
Chiyoda-ku, Tokyo 100-0011
Japan

Telephone:	81-3-3500-0331
Fax:	81-3-3500-0361
E-Mail:	mk@mknet.jp
Internet:	www.mknet.jp
Partners:	*Tasuku Matsuo*
	Takeo Kosugi
Number of Lawyers:	22
Areas of Practice:	Full Service

Mori Hamada & Matsumoto

Marunouchi Kitaguchi Building 1-6-5 Marunouchi,
Chiyoda-ku, Tokyo 100-8222
Japan

Telephone:	81-3-5220-1800
Fax:	81-3-5220-1700
E-Mail:	info@mhmjapan.com
Internet:	www.mhmjapan.com
Partner:	*Uchida Harumichi*
Other Offices:	Beijing
	Shanghai
Areas of Practice:	Full Service

Yuasa and Hara

Section 206, New Ohtemachi Building 2-1, Ohtemachi
2-Chome
Chiyoda-ku, Tokyo 100-0004
Japan

Telephone:	81-3-3270-6641
Fax:	81-3-3246-0233
E-Mail:	sogiso@yuasa-hara.co.jp
Internet:	www.yuasa-hara.co.jp
Partners:	*Shigeru Ohira*
	Toshiaki Makino
	Kozo Yabe

Number of Lawyers: 95
Areas of Practice: Full Service

Anderson Mori & Tomotsune

Izumi Garden Tower 6-1, Roppongi 1-Chome
Minato-Ku, Tokyo 106-6036
Japan

Telephone:	81-3-6888-1000
Fax:	81-3-6888-3028
E-Mail:	info@amt-law.com
Internet:	www.amt-law.com
Partners:	*Koichiro Nakamoto*
	Kotaro Hayashi
	Akira Kawamura
	Kazutoshi Kakuyama

Number of Lawyers: 124
Other Office: Beijing
Areas of Practice: Full Service

Nishimura & Asahi

Ark Mori Building, 28th Floor
1-12-32, Akasaka,
Tokyo 107-6029
Japan

Telephone:	81-3-5562-8500
Fax:	81-3-5561-9711
E-Mail:	mail@jurists.co.jp
Internet:	www.jurists.co.ip
Partners:	*Akira Kosugi*
	Masaki Hosaka
	Satoshi Ogishi

Number of Lawyers: 469
Areas of Practice: Full Service

Kashiwagi Sogo Law Offices

Atago Toyo Building
3-4 Atago 1-chome
Minato-ku, Tokyo 105-0002
Japan

Telephone:	81-3-5472-5050
Fax:	81-3-5472-5077
E-Mail:	email@kashiwagi-law.co.ip
Internet:	www.kashiwagi-law.co.jp
Partners:	*Shuichi Kashiwagi*
	Taku Fukui

Number of Lawyers: 14
Areas of Practice: Full Service

Kikkawa Law Offices

Aqua Douijima Bldg.
1-4-16 Doujimahama
Kita-Ku
Osaka 530 0004
Japan

E-Mail:	ohara@kikkawalaw.com
Internet:	www.kikkawalaw.com
Partners:	*Masatoshi Ohara*
	Tomoyuki Nishide
Number of Lawyers:	18
Areas of Practice:	Full Service

Jordan

Law and Arbitration Centre

P.O. Box 2696 Khelda
Amman 11821
Jordan

Telephone:	962-6-534-5777
Fax:	962-6-534-0666
E-Mail:	info@lac.com.jo
Internet:	www.lac.com.jo
Partner:	*Hamza Ahmad Haddad*

Nabulsi and Associates

Riyadh Center, 3rd Circle
P.O. Box 35116
Amman 11180
Jordan

Telephone:	962-6-465-4411
Fax:	962-6-465-7555
E-Mail:	nabulsilawfirrn@nets.com.jo
Internet:	www.nabulsilaw.com
Partner:	*Omar Nabulsi*
Number of Lawyers:	10
Areas of Practice:	Full Service

Ali Sharif Zu'bi Law Office

Jebel Amman, First Circle
Astra Building, 4th Floor
P.O. Box 35267
Amman 11180
Jordan

Telephone:	962-6-464-2908
Fax:	962-6-463-4277
E-Mail:	info@zubilaw.com
Internet:	www.zubilaw.com
Partner:	*Ali Sharif Zu'bi*
Number of Lawyers:	25
Areas of Practice:	Full Service

Safan Moubaydeen Law Firm

Emmar Towers
Building B
Zahran Street
Amman 11190
Jordan

Telephone:	962-6-577-7400
Fax:	962-6-577-7401
E-Mail:	safwan.moubaydeen@ dentonwildesapote.com
Internet:	www.dentonwildesapte.com
Partner:	*Safwan Moubaydeen*
Number of Lawyers:	5
Areas of Practice:	Full Service

Kazakhstan

Denton Wilde Sapte Kazakhstan Limited

Ken Dala Business Centre
38 Dostyk Avenue
Almaty 050010
Kazakhstan

Telephone:	7-727-258-1950
Fax:	7-727-258-1905
E-Mail:	marla.valdez@dentonwildesapte.com
Internet:	www.dentonwildesapte.com
Partner:	*Marla Valdez*
Number of Lawyers:	15
Areas of Practice:	Corporate
	M&A
	Business Law

Aequitas

47/49 Abai Avenue
Almaty, 050000
Kazakhstan

Telephone:	7-727-3968-968
Fax:	7-727-367-3037
E-Mail:	aequitas@aequitas.kz
Internet:	www.aequitas.kz
Partner:	*Yulia Chumachenko*
Number of Lawyers:	21
Other Offices:	Astana
	Atyrau
Areas of Practice:	Full Service

Grata Law Firm

104, M. Ospanov Street
Almaty 050020
Kazakhstan

Telephone:	7-727-2-445-777
Fax:	7-727-2-445-776
E-Mail:	info@gratanet.com
Internet:	www.gratanet.com
Partners:	*Akhmetzhan Abdullayev*
	Arlan Yershanov (New York)
Number of Lawyers:	85
Other Offices:	Almaty
	Tashkent
	Baku
	Bishkek
	New York
	London
	Ashgabat
	Istanbul
	Dushanabe
Areas of Practice:	Full Service

Kenya

Hamilton Harrison & Mathews

I.C.E.A. Building
Kenyatta Avenue
P.O. Box 30333
00100 Nairobi, GPO
Kenya

Telephone:	254-20-325-8000
Fax:	254-20-222-2318
E-Mail:	hhhm@hhm.co.ke
Internet:	www.hhm.co.ke
Partners:	*Kenneth Fraser*
	Richard Omwela
	Kiragu Kimani

Number of Lawyers: 22
Areas of Practice: Full Service

Kaplan & Stratton

9th Floor, Williamson House
4th 4 Ngong Avenue, Upper Hill
P.O. Box 40111
Nairobi, 00100
Kenya

Telephone:	254-20-284-1000
Fax:	254-20-273-4667
E-Mail:	info@kaplanstratton.com
Internet:	www.kaplanstratton.com
Partners:	*Fred Ojiambo*
	Peter Hime

Number of Lawyers: 23
Areas of Practice: Full Service

Korea

Bae, Kim & Lee

3rd-12th Floors, Hankook Tire Building
647-15, Yoksam-Dong, Gangnam-gu
Seoul, 135-723
Korea

Telephone:	82-2-3404-0000
Fax:	82-2-3404-0001
E-Mail:	bkl@bkl.co.kr
Internet:	www.baekimlee.com
Partners:	*Jung Hoon Lee*
	Yong Suk Oh
	Jong Ku Kang
	Ian Insoo Pyo
Number of Lawyers:	182
Other Offices:	Shanghai
	Beijing
Areas of Practice:	Full Service

Central International Law Firm

Korea Reinsurance Building 5F
80 Soosong-dong, Chongno-ku
Seoul 110-733
Korea

Telephone:	82-2-735-5621
Fax:	82-2-733-5206
E-Mail:	central@cilf.com
Internet:	www.cilf.co.kr

Partner: *Bum Rae Lee*
Number of Lawyers: 96
Areas of Practice: Full Service

Kim & Chang

Seyang Building, 5th Floor 223
Naeja-dong, Jongno-gu
Seoul 110-720
Korea

Telephone:	82-2-3703-1114
Fax:	82-2-737-9091
E-Mail:	lawkim@kimchang.com
Internet:	www.kimchang.com
Partners:	*Y.M. Kim*
	Kye Sung Chung
	Joon Park
	Kyung-Tack Jung

Number of Lawyers: 650
Areas of Practice: Full Service

Shin & Kim

Ace Tower, 4th Floor
1-170, Soonhwa-Dong, Chung-ku
Seoul 100-712
Korea

Telephone:	82-2-316-4114
Fax:	82-2-756-6226
E-Mail:	shinkim@shinkim.com
Internet:	www.shinkim.com
Partners:	*Young-Moo Shin*
	Doo Sik Kim
Number of Lawyers:	314
Areas of Practice:	Full Service

Yoon, Yang, Kim, Shin & Yu

22nd Fl., ASEM Tower
159-1 Samsung-Dong,
Gangnam-Gu
Seoul 135-798
Korea

Telephone:	82-2-6003-7000
Fax:	82-2-6003-7800
E-Mail:	dkbyun@hwawoo.com
Internet:	www.yoenyang.com
Partners:	*Dong-Geul Byun*
	Jae-Seung Byun
	Bo Hyun Kang
	Hoil Yoon
	Sam-Sung Yang
Number of Lawyers:	225
Other Office:	Tashkent
Areas of Practice:	Full Service

Lee & Ko

18th Floor, Marine Center Main Building
118, Namdaemno, Jung-gu
Seoul
Korea

Telephone:	82-2-772-4000
Fax:	82-2-772-4001
E-Mail:	mail@leeko.com
Internet:	www.leeko.com
Partners:	*Tae Hee Lee*
	Kyu Wha Lee
	Byoung Jai Kim
Number of Lawyers:	310
Other Office:	Beijing
Areas of Practice:	Full Service

Hwang Mok Park

Shinhan Bank Building, 120, 2-ka, Taepyungro, Chung-ku
Seoul 100-764
Korea

Telephone:	82-2-772-2700
Fax:	82-2-772-2800
E-Mail:	desk@hmplaw.com
Internet:	www.hmpj.com
Partners:	*Ju Myung Hwang*
	Jung Syn Suh
	Zin Hwan Kim
Number of Lawyers:	83
Areas of Practice:	Full Service

Kuwait

Al-Saleh & Partners
P.O. Box 3246, Safat
Al Anjari Complex, 2nd Floor
Ali Al-Salem Street
13033 Safat
Kuwait

Telephone:	965-246-7670
Fax:	965-243-1039
E-Mail:	asap@alsalehandpartners.com
Internet:	www.alsalehandpartners.com
Partner:	*Nazih Hameed*
	Fawzi Musaed
Number of Lawyers:	14
Areas of Practice:	Full Service

Al-Ayoub & Associates
Souk Al-Kabir Building, Block 'B'
9th Floor Fahed Al-Salem Street
P.O. Box 1714
Safat 13018
Kuwait

Telephone:	965-246-4321
Fax:	965-246-6591
E-Mail:	alayoub@al-ayoub.org
Internet:	www.al-ayoub.org
Partner:	*Abdullah Al-Ayoub*
Number of Lawyers:	22
Areas of Practice:	Full Service

Kyrgyzstan

Kalikoua & Associates

71, Erkindik Blvd.
Bishkek
Kyrgyzstan

Telephone:	996-312-66-60-60
Fax:	996-312-66-63-63
E-Mail:	lawyer@k-a.kg
Internet:	www.k-a.kg
Partner:	*Aisulu Chubarova*
Number of Lawyers:	18
Areas of Practice:	Full Service

Latvia

Klavins & Slaidins

15 Elizabetes Street
Riga, LV-1010
Latvia

Telephone:	371-7-814-848
Fax:	371-7-814-849
E-Mail:	riga@lawin.lv
Internet:	www.klavinsslaidins.lv
Partners:	*Filip Klavins*
	Liga Hartmane
	Raymond L. Slaidins

Number of Lawyers: 22
Areas of Practice: Full Service

Loze, Grunte & Cers

Blaumana 22
LV-1011, Riga
Latvia

Telephone:	371-7-830-000
Fax:	371-7-830-001
Internet:	www.lg-c.lv
Partners:	*Anis Loze*
	Gundars Cers
	Ivars Grunte

Number of Lawyers: 26
Areas of Practice: Full Service

Glimstedt and Partners

Gertrudes Street 10/12
Riga LV-1010
Latvia

Telephone:	371-6-780-3380
Fax:	371-6-780-3381
E-Mail:	eriks.blumbergs@glimstedt.lv
Internet:	www.glimstedt.lv
Partner:	*Eriks Blumbergs*
Areas of Practice:	Full Service

Lebanon

Khairallah & Chaiban

Maktabi Building, Suite 16
Clemenceau Street
Boite Postale 118336
Beirut
Lebanon

Telephone:	961-1-369-242
Fax:	961-1-200-98
E-Mail:	khairallah.chaiban@wanadvo.fr
Partner:	*Claude Chaiban*
Areas of Practice:	Full Service

Tyan & Zgheib

250 Sami el Solh Avenue, Manhattan Building
Boite Postale 175563
Beirut 2058 7706
Lebanon

Telephone:	961-1-381-006
Fax:	961-1-381-016
E-Mail:	info@tyanzgheib.com
Internet:	www.tyanzgheib.com
Partners:	*Nady Tyan*
	Mireille Richa
Number of Lawyers:	10
Areas of Practice:	Full Service

Liberia

Sannoh & Associates

Warrent Street and Camp Johnson Road
P.O. Box 2314
Monrovia
Liberia

Telephone:	231-331-064
Fax:	231-227-255
E-Mail:	sannoh.associates@yahoo.com
Partner:	*Benedict Sannoh*

Liechtenstein

Marxer & Partner

Heiligkreuz 6
Valduz FL - 9490
Liechtenstein

Telephone:	423-235-8181
Fax:	423-235-8282
E-Mail:	info@marxerpartner.com
Internet:	www.marxerpartner.com
Partners:	*Johannes Burger*
	Peter Goop

Number of Lawyers: 32
Areas of Practice: Full Service

Ritter & Wohlwend

Pflugstrasse 10
9490 Vaduz
Leichtenstein

Telephone:	423-236-5533
Fax:	423-236-5611
E-Mail:	office@lawfirm.li
Internet:	www.lawfirm.li
Partners:	*Peter Ritter*
	Chritoph Bruckschweiger
	Raphael Naescher
	Helmut Wohlwend
	Stefan Ritter

Number of Lawyers: 7
Areas of Practice: Full Service

Wanger Advokaturburo

Aeulestrasse 45
FL-9490 Vaduz
Liechtenstein

Telephone:	423-237-5252
Fax:	423-237-5253
E-Mail:	wanger@wanger.net
Internet:	www.wanger.net
Partner:	*Markus Wanger*
Number of Lawyers:	4
Areas of Practice:	Full Service

Lithuania

Lideika, Petrauskas, Valiunas and Partners
Jogailos 9/1
01116 Vilnius
Lithuania

Telephone:	370-5-268-1888
Fax:	370-5-212-5591
E-Mail:	vilnius@lawin.lt
Internet:	www.lawin.lt
Partners:	*Rolandus Valiunas*
	Giedrius Stasevieius
	Jaunius Gumbis

Number of Lawyers: 48
Areas of Practice: Full Service

Bernotas & Dominas Glimstedt
Jogailos g. 4
01116 Vilnius
Lithuania

Telephone:	370-5-269-0700
Fax:	370-5-269-0701
E-Mail:	e.bernotas@glimstedt.lt
Internet:	www.glimstedt.lt
Partner:	*Egidijus Bernotas*

Number of Lawyers: 30
Areas of Practice: Full Service

Luxembourg

Arendt & Medernach

14, rue Erasme
L-2082 Luxembourg

Telephone:	352-40-78-78-1
Fax:	352-40-78-04
E-Mail:	arineifeipel@arendt-medernach.com
Internet:	www.arendt-medernach.com
Partners:	*Guy Harles*
	Cynthia Kalathas (New York)
	Carine Feipel (New York)
Number of Lawyers:	270
Other Offices:	Brussels
	New York
	Dubai
	Hong Kong
Areas of Practice:	Full Service

Dupong & Metzler

4-6 rue de la Boucherie
L-1247 Luxembourg

Telephone:	352-46-18-38
Fax:	352-22-08-32
E-Mail:	mail@dupong-metzler.lu
Internet:	www.dupongmeltzer.lu
Partner:	*Lucy Dupong*
Number of Lawyers:	8
Areas of Practice:	Full Service

Bonn Schmitt Steichen

44 rue de la Vallee
L-2015 Luxembourg

Telephone:	352-45-58-58
Fax:	352-45-58-59
E-Mail:	mail@bsslaw.net
Internet:	www.bsslaw.net
Partners:	*Alex Schmitt*
	Guy Arendt
	Alain Steichen
Number of Lawyers:	34
Other Office:	Brussels
Areas of Practice:	Corporate Law
	Finance
	Commercial Law
	Litigation

Kremer Associes & Clifford Chance

2-4, Place de Paris
L-1011 Luxembourg

Telephone:	352-48-50-50-1
Fax:	352-48-13-85
E-Mail:	info@cliffordchance.com
Internet:	www.cliffordchance.com
Partners:	*Albert Moro*
	Christian Kremer
Number of Lawyers:	51
Areas of Practice:	Banking & Finance
	Intellectual Property
	Employment
	Litigation

Oostvogels Pfister Feyten

291, Route d'Arlon
B.P. 603/L-2016 Luxembourg

Telephone:	352-46-8383
Fax:	352-46-8484
E-Mail:	fpfister@oostvogels.com
Internet:	www.oostvogels.com
Partners:	*Francois Pfister*
	Harold Parize

Number of Lawyers: 45
Other Office: London
Areas of Practice: Full Service

Malaysia

Zaid Ibrahim & Co.
Level 19, Menara Milenium
Pusat Bandar Damansara
50490 Kuala Lumpur
Malaysia

Telephone:	603-2087-9999
Fax:	603-2094-4888
E-Mail:	send.kok.chew@zaidibrahim.com.my
Internet:	www.zaidibrahim.com.my
Partner:	*Lynette Yeow*
Other Office:	Singapore
Number of Lawyers:	186
Ares of Practice:	Full Service

Chooi & Company
Level 23, Menara Dion
No. 27 Jalan Sultan Ismail
50250 Kuala Lumpur
Malaysia

Telephone:	60-3-2055-3888
Fax:	60-3-2055-3880
E-Mail:	mail@chooi.com.my
Internet:	www.chooi.com.my
Partner:	*Chooi Mun Sou*
Number of Lawyers:	32
Areas of Practice:	Full Service

Skrine & Co.

Unit No. 50-8-1, 8th Floor,
Wisma UOA Damansara
50 Jalan Dungun, Damansara Heights
50490 Kuala Lumpur
Malaysia

Telephone:	60-3-2081-3999
Fax:	60-3-2094-3211
E-Mail:	webmaster@skrine.com
Internet:	www.skrine.com
Partners:	*Lee Tatt Boon*
	Y.C. Chin

Number of Lawyers: 72
Areas of Practice: Full Service

Shearn Delamore & Co.

7th Floor, Wisma Hamzah-Kwong Hing
No.1, Leboh Ampang
50100 Kuala Lumpur
Malaysia

Telephone:	60-3-2027-2727
Fax:	60-3-2078-2376
E-Mail:	info@shearndelamore.com
Internet:	www.shearndelamore.com
Partners:	*Wong Sai Fong*
	Rabindra Nathan

Number of Lawyers: 78
Other Office: Penang
Areas of Practice: Full Service

Azman, Davidson & Co.

Suite 13.03, 13th Floor
Menara Tan & Tan
207 Jalan Tun Razak
50400 Kuala Lumpur
Malaysia

Telephone:	60-3-2164-0200
Fax:	60-3-2164-0280
E-Mail:	adck12@azmandavidson.com.my
Internet:	www.azmandavidson.com.my
Partner:	*W.S.W. Davidson*
Number of Lawyers:	42
Areas of Practice:	Full Service

Azmi & Associates

14th Floor, Menara Keck Seng
203, Jalan Bukit Bintang
55100 Kuala Lumpur
Malaysia

Telephone:	60-3-2118-5000
Fax:	60-3-2118-511
E-Mail:	general@azmilaw.com.my
Internet:	www.azmilaw.com.my
Partner:	*Azmi Mohd Ali*
Number of Lawyers:	45
Areas of Practice:	Full Service

Malta

Cefai & Associates

5/1 Merchants Street
Valletta VLT 1171
Malta

Telephone:	356-21-222-097
Fax:	356-21-249-950
E-Mail:	info@cefaiadvocates.com
Partner:	*Renato Cefai*
Number of Lawyers:	5
Areas of Practice:	Full Service

Ganado & Associates

171 Old Bakery Street
Valletta VLT 09
Malta

Telephone:	356-21-235-406
Fax:	356-21-225-908
E-Mail:	lawfirm@jmganado.com
Internet:	www.jmganado.com
Partners:	*Louis Pullicino*
	Philip Bianchi
	Adrian Michael Gabarretta
Number of Lawyers:	26
Areas of Practice:	Full Service

Fenech & Fenech Advocates

198 Old Bakery Street
Valletta VLT 1455
Malta

Telephone:	356-21-241-232
Fax:	356-25-990-640
E-Mail:	fif@fenlex.com
Internet:	www.fenechlaw.com
Partners:	*Mark Fenech*
	Edward DeBono
	Kenneth Grima
	Ann Fenech
	Rosanne Bonnici
Number of Lawyers:	20
Areas of Practice:	Full Service

Mariana Islands

White, Pierce, Mailman & Nutting

Law Offices of Stephen J. Nutting
6th Floor, Marianas Business Plaza
Naru LP
Mariana Islands

Telephone:	670-234-6891
Fax:	670-234-6893
E-Mail:	steve@stephenjnutting.com
Internet:	www.stephenjnutting.com
Partner:	*Stephen J. Nutting*
Areas of Practice:	Full Service

Mauritius

De Comarmond & Koenig

5th Floor, Chancery House
Lislet Geoffrey Street
Port-Louis
Mauritius

Telephone:	230-212-2215
Fax:	230-208-2986
E-Mail:	koenig@intnet.mu
Internet:	www.decomermond-koenig.com
Partner:	*Thierry Koenig*
Number of Lawyers:	6
Areas of Practice:	Full Service

Juristconsult Chambers

Level 6, Newton Tower
Port-Louis
Mauritius

Telephone:	230-208-5526
Fax:	230-208-5586
E-Mail:	jurist@intnet.mu
Internet:	www.juristconsult.com
Partner:	*Marc Hein*
Number of Lawyers:	7
Areas of Practice:	Banking and Finance
	Corporate and Commercial Law
	Intellectual Property
	Hospitality and Residency
	Aircraft and Shipping

Mexico

Bryan, Gonzalez-Vargas y Gonzalez-Baz

Seneca 425, Polanco
11560 Mexico, D.F.
Mexico

Telephone:	5255-5279-3600
Fax:	5255-5279-3610
E-Mail:	mexico@bryanlex.com
Internet:	www.bryanlex.com
Partners:	*Aureliano Gonzalez-Baz*
	Hector Cortes
Number of Lawyers:	96
Other Offices:	Tijuana
	Chihuahua
	Matamoros
	Ciudad Juarez
	Reynosa
	Monterrey
	San Diego
	New Cork
	El Paso
	Mexicali
	La Paz
Areas of Practice:	Full Service

Basham, Ringe y Correa, S.C.

Paseo de los Tamarindos No. 400-A
Bosques de las Lomas
05120 Mexico, D.F.
Mexico

Telephone:	5255-5261-0400
Fax:	5255-5261-0496
E-Mail:	basham@basham.com.mx
Internet:	www.basham.com.mx
Partners:	*Miguel Peralta*
	Daniel Del Rio
Number of Lawyers:	148
Other Offices:	Monterrey
	Queretaro
Areas of Practice:	Full Service

Goodrich, Riquelme y Asociados

Paseo de la Reforma 265
06500 Mexico, D.F.
Mexico

Telephone:	5255-5533-0040
Fax:	5255-5525-1227
E-Mail:	mailcentral@goodrichriquelme.com
Internet:	www.goodrichriquelme.com
Partners:	*Julio Flores*
	Agustin Urdapilleta
	Francisco J. Velazquez
Number of Lawyers:	132
Other Office:	Paris
Areas of Practice:	Full Service

Ritch Mueller

Tone de Bosque
Boulevard Manuel Avila Camacho No. 24 Piso 20
Lomas de Chapultepec C.P.
11000 Mexico, D.F.
Mexico

Telephone:	5255-9178-7000
Fax:	5255-9178-7095
E-Mail:	info@ritch.com.mx
Internet:	www.ritch.com.mx
Partners:	*Thomas Mueller-Gastell*
	Luis A. Nicolau
	Pablo Perezalonso
	Rodrigo Conesa Labastida
	Jean Paul Farah Chajin
	Ricardo Gomez Palacio del R.
	Carlos F. Obregon Rojo

Number of Lawyers: 36
Areas of Practice: Full Service

Lexcop Abogados

Paseo Jan Jeronimo 1665
Ciudad Juarez, Chihuahua
Mexico CP 32500

Telephone:	52-656-227-0300
Fax:	52-656-618-3001
E-Mail:	agc@lexcorpabogados.com
Internet:	www.lexcorpabogados.com
Partner:	*Armando Guitierrez Cruz*
Number of Lawyers:	24
Other Offices:	Mexico City
	Queretaro
	Chihuahua
Areas of Practice:	Full Service

Von Wobeser y Sierra

Guillermo Gonzalez Camarena 1100, Piso 7
Santa Fe, Centro de Ciudad
Del. Alvaro Obregon
01210 Mexico, D.F.
Mexico

Telephone:	5255-5258-1000
Fax:	5255-5258-1098
E-Mail:	info@vwys.com.mx
Internet:	www.vonwobeserysierra.com
Partners:	*Claus Von Wobeser*
	Javier Lizardi
	Fernando Moreno
	Luis Burgueno
Number of Lawyers:	47
Areas of Practice:	Full Service

Creel, Garcia – Cuellar, Aiza y Enriquez

Paseo los Tamarindos 60
Bosques de las Lomas
05120 Mexico, D.F.
Mexico

Telephone:	5255-1105-0600
Fax:	5255-1105-0690
E-Mail:	mail@creelmx.com
Internet:	www.creelmx.com
Partners:	*Carlos Creel*
	Jorge Torres
	Samuel Garcia-Cuellar
	Carlos Aiza
	Francisco Montalvo
Number of Lawyers:	87
Other Office:	Monterrey
Areas of Practice:	Full Service

Ibanez Maroto Schriever & Hoffman

Montes Urales 635-042
Col. Lomas de Chapultepec
Mexico D.F. 11000
Mexico

Telephone:	5255-5202-1186
Fax:	5255-5202-1527
E-Mail:	ibanezmaroto@ibanezmaroto.com
Internet:	www.ibanezmaroto.com
Partners:	*Juan Carlos Maroto Oliveros*
	Mauricio Ibanez Campos

Number of Lawyers: 15
Areas of Practice: Full Service

Jauregui, Navarette, Nader y Rojas

Torre Arcos
Paseo de los Tamarindos 400-B
Bosques de las Lomas
05120 Mexico, D.F.
Mexico

Telephone:	5255-5267-4500
Fax:	5255-5258-0348
E-Mail:	jnn@jnn.com.mx
Internet:	www.jnn.com.mx
Partners:	*Miguel Jauregui*
	Gabriel Navarette

Number of Lawyers: 57
Areas of Practice: Full Service

Sanchez Mejorada Velasco y Ribe

Paseo de la Reforma 450
11000 Mexico, D.F.
Mexico

Telephone:	5255-5202-0777
Fax:	5255-5202-8222
E-Mail:	smvr@smvr.com.mx
Internet:	www.smvr.com.mx
Partner:	*Roderigo Sanchez Mejorada*
Number of Lawyers:	6
Areas of Practice:	Full Service

Santamarina y Steta

Edficio Omega
Campos Eliseos 345
Col. Chapultepec Polanco
11560 Mexico, D.F.
Mexico

Telephone:	5255-5279-5400
Fax:	5255-5280-6226
E-Mail:	infomex@s-s.com.mx
Internet:	www.s-s.com.mx
Partners:	*Fernando del Castillo*
	Aaron Levet Velasco (Tijuana)
	Jorge Barrero
	Pedro Velasco
Number of Lawyers:	87
Other Offices:	Monterrey
	Tijuana
Areas of Practice:	Full Service

Noriega y Escobedo

Sierra Mojada 626
11010 Mexico, D.F.
Mexico

Telephone:	5255-5284-3333
Fax:	5255-5284-3327
E-Mail:	info@noriegayescobedo.com.mx
Internet:	www.noriegayescobedo.com.mx
Partners:	*Miguel Escobedo*
	Pablo Cervantes

Number of Lawyers: 19
Areas of Practice: Full Service

Barrera, Siqueiros y Torres-Landa

Paseo de los Tamarindos 150-PB
Bosque de las Lomas, C.P.
05120 Mexico D.F.
Mexico

Telephone:	5255-5091-0000
Fax:	5255-5091-0123
E-Mail:	info@bstl.com.mx
Internet:	www.bstl.com.mx
Partner:	*Juan F. Torres-Landa*

Number of Lawyers: 77
Other Office: Monterrey
Areas of Practice: Full Service

Kuri Brena, Sanchez Ugarte y Aznar
Punta Santa Fe Torre "B"
Prolongacion Paseo de la Reforma No. 1015
Desarrollo Santa Fe
01376 Mexico, D.F.
Mexico

Telephone:	5255-5292-5930
Fax:	5255-5292-5928
E-Mail:	ksca@ksca.com.mx
Internet:	www.ksca.com.mx
Partners:	*AlreSantiago Corcuera*
	Jesus Sanchez-Ugarte
Number of Lawyers:	24
Areas of Practice:	Full Service

Martinez, Algaba, DeHaro, Curiel & Galvan-Duque
Paseo de los Tamarindos 400-A, Piso 20
Col. Bosques de las Lomas
05120 Mexico, D.F.
Mexico

Telephone:	5255-5258-0202
Fax:	5255-5258-0188
E-Mail:	mex@mah.com
Internet:	www.mah.com
Partners:	*Roberto Martinez Guerrero*
	Jorge de Haro
	Carlos Galvan-Duque
	Luis Lavalle
Number of Lawyers:	28
Other Office:	Monterrey
Areas of Practice:	Bankruptcy Law
	Corporate Law
	Civil Litigation

Mijares, Angoitia, Cortes y Fuentes

Montes Urales No. 505, 3er. Piso
Col. Lomas de Chapultepec
11000 Mexico, D.F.
Mexico

Telephone:	5255-5201-7400
Fax:	5255-5520-1065
Internet:	www.macf.com.mx
Partners:	*Francisco Fuentes Ostos*
	Pablo Mijares Ortiega
	Ricardo Maldonado Yanez
	Jose Raz-Guzman

Number of Lawyers: 61
Areas of Practice: Full Service

Moldova

Turcan & Turcan

Str. Puskin 47/1-5a
Chisnau, MD - 2005
Moldova

Telephone:	373-22-212-031
Fax:	373-22-223-806
E-Mail:	alexander.turcan@turcanlaw.md
Internet:	www.turcanlaw.md
Partner:	*Alexander Turcan*
Number of Lawyers:	7
Areas of Practice:	Full Service

Monaco

Gordon S. Blair Law Offices

3 Rue Louis Aureglia, Boite Postale 449
MC 98011 Monte Carlo
Monaco

Telephone:	377-9325-8525
Fax:	377-9325-7958
E-Mail:	info@gordonblair.com
Internet:	www.gordonblair.com
Partner:	*Oliver Gaultier*
	Simon Huxford

Number of Lawyers: 12

Jean-Charles S. Gardetto

Villa Marcel
19 Boulevard des Moulins
MC 98000 Monte Carlo
Monaco

Telephone:	377-92-16-16-17
Fax:	377-93-50-42-41
E-Mail:	gardetto.lawoffice@wanadoo.fr
Partner:	*Jean-Charles Gardetto*
Areas of Practice:	Full Service

Morocco

Seddik Zaari Law Offices

121 Avenue Hassan II
Casablanca
Morocco

Telephone:	212-22-27-77-56
Fax:	212-2-264-712
E-Mail:	zaari@menara.ma
Partner:	*Seddik Zaari*

Hajji & Associes

28, Bd Moulay Youssef
20000 Casablanca
Morocco

Telephone:	212-22-48-74-74
Fax:	212-22-48-74-75
Internet:	www.ahlo.ma
Partner:	*Amin Hajji*
Number of Lawyers:	4
Areas of Practice:	Full Service

Mozambique

Vasconcelos Porto & Associados

Av. Dos Martires de Inhaminga, 170, -4 Andar
Maputo
Mozambique

Telephone:	258-2131-2070
Fax:	258-2131-2060
E-Mail:	avp@vasconcelosporto.com.mz
Partner:	*Antonio deVasconcelos Porto*
Number of Lawyers:	16
Other Offices:	Johannesburg
	Lisbon
	Nampula
Areas of Practice:	Full Service

Myanmar

U Myint Lwin

No. 162, 35th Street
Kyauktada Township
Yangan 11182
Myanmar

Telephone:	95-1-372712
Fax:	95-1-371990
Internet:	myint.advocate@mptmail.net.mm
E-Mail:	mlwinku@mptmail.net.mm
Partner:	*U Myint Lwin*
Areas of Practice:	Intellectual Property

Namibia

Fisher Quarmby & Pfeifer

P.O. Box 37
Windhoek
Namibia

Telephone:	61-233-171
Fax:	61-228-286
E-Mail:	fpc@fqp.com.na
Internet:	www.fqp.com.na
Partners:	*F.P. Coetzee*
	Christian Johan Gouws
Number of Lawyers:	6
Areas of Practice:	Full Serivice

Nepal

Dhruba Bar Singh Thapa & Associates

Anam Nagar
PO Box 828
Kathmandu
Nepal

Telephone:	977-1-425-7991
Fax:	977-1-425-2610
E-Mail:	lexnepal@ntc.net.np
Partner:	*Sajjan Bar Singh Thapa*
Number of Lawyers:	5
Areas of Practice:	Full Service

Netherlands Antilles

STvB Advocaten

Johan van Walbeekplein 11
Willemstad, Curacao
Netherlands Antilles

Telephone:	599-9-465-5055
Fax:	599-9-465-5720
E-Mail:	stvb@stvb.an
Internet:	www.stvb.nl
Partner:	*Gerhard Smeets*
Number of Lawyers:	17
Other Office:	Amsterdam
Areas of Practice:	Full Service

Van Eps Kunneman Van Doorne

Julianaplein 22
P.O. Box 504
Willemstad, Curacao
Netherlands Antilles

Telephone:	599-9-461-3400
Fax:	599-9-461-2023
E-Mail:	info@ekvandoorne.com
Internet:	www.ekvandoorne.com
Partners:	*Frank Kunneman*
	J.M.R. Statius van Eps
Number of Lawyers:	25
Areas of Practice:	Full Service

Netherlands Antilles *continued*

Curacaolaw

Kaya W.F.G. Mensing 27
P.O. Box 4920
Willemstad, Curacao
Netherlands Antilles

Telephone:	599-9-465-7777
Fax:	599-9-465-7666
E-Mail:	info@curacaolaw@na-law.com
Internet:	www.curacaolaw.com
Partners:	*Erich W.H. Zielinski*
	Freida Pais-Fruchter
	Altagracia Juliana
	Lex Gonzales

Number of Lawyers: 3
Other Office: Bonaire
Areas of Practice: Full Service

Bonairelaw

J.A. Abraham Blvd. 82
Bonaire
Netherlands Antilles

Telephone:	599-9-563-8290
E-Mail:	lgonzales@bonairelaw.com
Internet:	www.curacaolaw.com
Partner:	*Alex C. A. Gonzales*

Areas of Practice: Full Service

Gomez & Bikkerlaw Offices

Caya Dr. J.E.M. Arends #14
Punta Brabo
Oranjestad
Aruba
Netherlands Antilles

Telephone:	297-588-7355
Fax:	297-588-7533
E-Mail:	info@gobiklaw.com
Internet:	www.gobiklaw.com
Partner:	*Lincoln Gomez*
Number of Lawyers:	5
Areas of Practice:	Full Service

The Netherlands

Stibbe

Stibbetoren
Strawinskylaan 2001
1077 ZZ Amsterdam
The Netherlands

Telephone:	31-20-546-0606
Fax:	31-20-546-0123
E-Mail:	info@stibbe.nl
Internet:	www.stibbe.nl
Partners:	*Jaap Willeumier*
	Maarten de Bruin
	Derk Lemstra
	Jean-Paul van den Berg (New York)
	Lennaert Posch (New York)
	Hans Witteveen (London)
	Heleen Kersten
	Duco de Boer (New York)
	Michael Molenaars
	Frans Corpeleijn
Number of Lawyers:	342
Other Offices:	Dubai
	New York
	London
Areas of Practice:	Full Service

Houthoff Buruma

Gustav Mahlerplein 50
1082 MA Amsterdam
The Netherlands

Telephone:	31-20-605-6000
Fax:	31-20-605-6700
E-Mail:	info@houthoff.com
Internet:	www.houthoff.com
Partners:	*Jan van der Horst*
	Casper Banz
Number of Lawyers:	186
Other Offices:	The Hague
	Rotterdam
	London
	Brussels
	Luxembourg
Areas of Practice:	Full Service

De Brauw Blackstone Westbroek

Claude Debussylaan 80
1082 MD Amsterdam
The Netherlands

Telephone:	31-20-577-1771
Fax:	31-20-577-1775
E-Mail:	amsterdam@debrauw.com
Internet:	www.debrauw.com
Partners:	*Dirk Meerburg*
	Rutger de Witt Wijnen
	Pierre Nijnens
	Kees Peijster
	Paul Cronheim
	Jaap Winter
	Berend Crans
	Tobias Cohen Jehoram
	Niek Biegman
	Bernard Spoor (London)
	Frans Rosendaal
	Ton Schutte (New York)
	Paul Sleurink
Number of Lawyers:	376
Other Offices:	New York
	London
Areas of Practice:	Full Service

Allen & Overy

Apollolaan 15
1070 AK Amsterdam
The Netherlands

Telephone:	31-20-674-1000
Fax:	31-20-674-1111
Internet:	www.allenovery.com
Partners:	*Rob Abendroth*
	Tom Ottervanger
	Bart Meesters
Number of Lawyers:	Numerous
Other Offices:	Numerous
Areas of Practice:	Full Service

Loyens & Loeff

Fred Roeskestraat 100
1076 ED Amsterdam
The Netherlands

Telephone:	31-20-578-5785
Fax:	31-20-578-5800
E-Mail:	info@loyensloeff.com
Internet:	www.loyensloeff.com
Partners:	*Maarten van der Weijden*
	Thomas Claassens
	Mark van Casteren
	Guido Portier
	Philip van Verschuer
	Jack Berk (New York)
	Lodewijk Berger (New York)
Other Offices:	Paris
	Tokyo
	Singapore
	Luxembourg
	Antwerp
	Aruba
	Brussels
	Curacao
	Dubai
	Rotterdam
	Frankfurt
	Geneva
	Zurich
	New York
	London
Number of Lawyers:	811
Area of Practice:	Full Service

Boekel de Neree NV

Gustav Mahlerplein 2
10820 MA
Amsterdam
The Netherlands

Telephone:	3120-795-3305
Fax:	3120-517-9268
E-Mail:	info@boekeldeneeree.com
Internet:	www.bokeldeneeree.com
Partners:	*Peter H. Ariens Kappers*
	Christiaan Toorman

Number of Lawyers: 173
Areas of Practice: Full Service

Nauta Dutilh

Strawinskylaan 1999
1077 XV Amsterdam
The Netherlands

Telephone:	31-20-717-1000
Fax:	31-20-717-1111
E-Mail:	info@nautadutilla.com
Internet:	www.nautadutilh.com
Partners:	*Marc Blom*
	Dirk Van Gerven
	Willem J.L. Calkoen (Rotterdam)
	Elizabeth van Schilfgaarde (NewYork)

Number of Lawyers: 412

Other Offices:	Rotterdam
	Brussels
	New York
	London
	Luxembourg
Area of Practice:	Full Service

Simmons & Simmons

WTC H Tower
Zuidplein 100
1077 XV Amsterdam
The Netherlands

Telephone:	31-20-890-9900
Fax:	31-20-890-9999
Internet:	www.simmons-simmons.com
E-Mail:	Amsterdam@simmons-simmons.com
Partners:	*R.P. Kroner*
	Gerhard Gispen
Number of Lawyers:	Numerous
Other Offices:	Numerous
Areas of Practice:	Full Service

Van Mens & Wisselink

Piet Heinkade 55
Amsterdam 1019 6M
The Netherlands

Telephone:	31-20-301-6633
Fax:	31-20-301-6622
E-Mail:	info@vmwtaxand.nl
Internet:	www.vmwtaxand.nl
Partner:	*Frans Duynstee*
Number of Lawyers:	54
Areas of Practice:	Tax
	Corporate
	Intellectual Property

New Zealand

Russell McVeagh

Vero Centre
48 Shortland Street
Auckland
New Zealand

Telephone:	649-367-8000
Fax:	649-367-8163
Internet:	www.russellmcveagh.com
E-Mail:	info@russellmcveagh.com
Partners:	*David Hoare*
	Cameron Fleming
Number of Lawyers:	92
Other Office:	Wellington
Areas of Practice:	Full Service

Simpson Grierson

Lumley Centre
88 Shortland Street
Private Bag 92518
Auckland 1141
New Zealand

Telephone:	649-358-2222
Fax:	649-307-0331
Internet:	www.simpsongrierson.com
E-Mail:	enquires@simpsongrierson.com
Partners:	*Gregory Towers*
	Peter Stubbs
	Denis McNamara
	Stephen Flynn (Wellington)
Number of Lawyers:	114
Other Office:	Wellington
Areas of Practice:	Full Service

Chapman Tripp

23-29 Albert Street
Auckland 1140
New Zealand

Telephone:	649-357-9000
Fax:	649-957-9099
Internet:	www.chapmantripp.com
E-Mail:	info@chapmantripp.com
Partners:	*Rupert Wilson (Wellington)*
	Lindsey Jones
	Jack Hodder
	Mark Reese
	Stephen Lowe
	Peter Bennett (Wellington)
	Barry Brown (Wellington)
Number of Lawyers:	192
Other Offices:	Wellington
	Christchurch
Areas of Practice:	Full Service

Quigg Partners

Level 7, The Bayleys Building
28 Brandon Street
PO Box 3035
Wellington 6140
New Zealand

Telephone:	644-472-7471
Fax:	644-472-7871
E-Mail:	davidquigg@quiggpartners.com
Internet:	www.quiggpartners.com
Partners:	*David Quigg*
Number of Lawyers:	11
Areas of Practice:	Full Service

Nicaragua

Alvarado y Asociados

Planes de Altimira III Etapa
Semaforos ENITELVILLA fontana 2
CaudrasalEstc, 2 ½ Guadras al Note
Managua
Nicaragua

Telephone:	505-2278-7708
Fax:	505-2278-7491
Internet:	www.alvaradoyasociados.com.ni
E-Mail:	info@alvaradoyasociados.com.ni
Partner:	*Jose Antonio Alvarado*
Number of Lawyers:	13
Areas of Practice:	Full Service

Delaney & Associates

KM 10 ½ Carretera Sur y Calle Santa Anita
Managua
Nicaragua

Telephone:	505-265-8081
Fax:	505-265-8819
E-Mail:	mail@delaney.com.ni
Partner:	*Tomas Delaney*
Number of Lawyers:	10

Hueck, Manzanares, Ortega & Sanchez

Altimira D'Este
Rotonda Madrid #235
Managua
Nicaragua

Telephone:	505-277-0485
Fax:	505-278-3820
E-Mail:	fortega@cablenet.com.ni
Partner:	*Francisco Ortega Gonzalez*
Areas of Practice:	Full Service

Francisco Ortega & Asociados

Altamira D'Este
Rotonda Madrid #235
Apartado 2813
Managua
Nicaragua

Telephone:	505-8882-5714
E-Mail:	fortega@iurisfirm.com
Internet:	www.iurisfirm.com
Partners:	*Francisco Ortega Gonzalez*
	J. Ortega Orozco
Number of Lawyers: 7	
Areas of Practice:	Full Service

Nigeria

Abuka & Partners

Western House, 10th Floor
8-10 Broad Street
P.O. Box 7022
Lagos
Nigeria

Telephone:	234-1-263-3024
Fax:	234-1-263-1687
E-Mail:	patrickabuka@abukapartners.com
Internet:	www.abukapartners.com
Partner:	*Patrick Abuka*
Number of Lawyers:	14
Other Offices:	Port Harcourt
	Abuja
Areas of Practice:	Full Service

Udo Udoma & Belo-Osagie

St. Nicholas House
Catholic Mission Street
Lagos
Nigeria

Telephone:	234-1-263-6957
Fax:	234-1-263-4541
E-Mail:	uubo@uubo.org
Internet:	www.uubo.org
Partners:	*Udoma Udo Udoma*
	Aniekan Ukpanah
Number of Lawyers:	43
Other Office:	Port Harcourt
Areas of Practice:	Full Service

Allan & Ogunkeye

Western House, 7th Floor
8/10 Broad Street
P.O. Box 51769
Lagos
Nigeria

Telephone:	234-1-271-6910
Fax:	234-280-2018
E-Mail:	admin@allanogunkeye.com
Internet:	www.allanogunkeye.com
Partners:	*Obatosin Ogunkeye*
	Marlies Allan
Number of Lawyers:	8
Areas of Practice:	Full Service

Chief Rotimi Williams Chambers

1, Shagamu Avenue
Ilupeju
Lagos
Nigeria

Telephone:	234-1-8121192
Fax:	234-1-2615354
E-Mail:	info@frawilliams.com.ng
Internet:	www.frawilliams.com
Partners:	*Chief Rotimi Williams*
	Abimbola Williams
Number of Lawyers:	17
Areas of Practice:	Full Service

AE LEX

Marble House, 7th Floor
1 Kingsway Road
Lagos
Nigeria

Telephone:	234-1-267-2032
Fax:	234-1-269-2072
E-Mail:	lagos@aelex.com
Internet:	www.aelex.com
Partners:	*Laurence Anga*
	Soji Awogbade
Number of Lawyers:	26
Other Offices:	Port Harcourt
	Abuja
Areas of Practice:	Full Service

Kusamotu & Kusomotu

Greenfish Chambers
D45 Dolphin Plaza
Dolphin Estate- Ikoyi
Lagos State
Nigeria

Telephone:	234-1-876-3935
E-Mail:	enquires@kusamotu.com
Internet:	www.kusamotu.com
Partner:	*Ayo Kusamotu*
Number of Lawyers:	10
Areas of Practice:	Full Service

Aluko & Oyebode

35 Moloney Street
Marina
Lagos
Nigeria

Telephone:	234-1-462-8360
Fax:	234-1-462-8377
E-Mail:	lagos@aluko-oyebate.com
Internet:	www.aluko-oyebode.com
Partner:	*Gbenga Oyebode*
Number of Lawyers:	52
Other Offices:	Abuja
	Port Harcourt
Areas of Practice:	Full Service

Northern Ireland

Carson McDowell

Murray House
4/5 Murray Street
Belfast BT1 6DN
Northern Ireland

Telephone:	44-28-9024-4951
Fax:	44-28-9024-5768
E-Mail:	law@carson-mcdowell.com
Internet:	www.carson-mcdowell.com
Partners:	*Michael Johnston*
	Tom Adairt

Number of Lawyers: 31
Areas of Practice: Full Service

Cleaver Fulton Rankin

50 Bedford Street
Belfast BT2 7FW
Northern Ireland

Telephone:	44-28-9024-3141
E-Mail:	info@cfrlaw.co.uk
Internet:	www.cfrlaw.co.uk
Partners:	*Jennifer Ebbage*
	Alistair Rankin

Number of Lawyers: 30
Areas of Practice: Full Service

Norway

Wiersholm, Mellbye & Bech

Ruselokkveien 26, 10th Floor
0251 Oslo
Norway

Telephone:	47-210-210-00
Fax:	47-210-210-01
E-Mail:	firma@wiersholm.no
Internet:	www.wiersholm.no
Partners:	*Per Raustol*
	Erling Lind
	Erik Thyness
	Erik Ramm

Number of Lawyers: 120
Areas of Practice: Full Service

Bugge, Arentz-Hansen & Rasmussen

Stranden 1
P.O. Box 1524 Vika
Oslo 1 0117
Norway

Telephone:	47-22-83-02-70
Fax:	47-22-83-07-95
E-Mail:	post@bahr.no
Internet:	www.bahr.no
Partners:	*Ole Lund*
	Beret Sundet

Number of Lawyers: 110
Areas of Practice: Full Service

Haavind

Bygdoy
Alle 2
0101 Oslo
Norway

Telephone:	47-22-43-30-00
Fax:	47-22-43-30-01
E-Mail:	post@haavind.no
Internet:	www.haavind.no
Partners:	*Harald Arnkvaern*
	Amund Bugge
	Geir Steinberg

Number of Lawyers: 96
Areas of Practice: Full Service

Advokatfirmaet Hjort DA

Akersgaten 51
P.O. Box 471 Sentrum
0105 Oslo
Norway

Telephone:	47-22-47-1800
Fax:	47-22-47-1818
E-Mail:	advokatfirmaet@hjort.no
Internet:	www.hjort.no
Partners:	*Erik Keiserud*
	Monica Syrdal

Number of Lawyers: 55
Areas of Practice: Full Service

Foyen Advokatfirma DA

C.J. Hambros Pl. 2A
0130 Oslo
Norway

Telephone:	47-21-93-10-00
Fax:	47-21-93-10-01
E-Mail:	post@foyen.no
Internet:	www.foyen.no
Partners:	*Arve Foyen*
	Heiki Giverholt
	Karl Marthinussen

Number of Lawyers: 28
Areas of Practice: Full Service

Advocatfirmaet Thommessen

P.O. Box 1484 Vika
N-0116 Oslo
Norway

Telephone:	47-23-11-11-11
Fax:	47-23-11-10-10
E-Mail:	firmapost@thommessen.no
Internet:	www.thommessen.no
Partners:	*Kim Dobrowen*
	Hans Arnesen

Number of Lawyers: 147
Other Office: Bergen
Areas of Practice: Full Service

Advokatfirmaet Steenstrup Strodrange DA

P.O. Box 1829 Vika
0123 Oslo
Norway

Telephone:	47-22-81-45-00
Fax:	47-22-81-45-01
E-Mail:	lawyers@steenstrup.no
Internet:	www.steenstrup.no
Partners:	*Morten Steenstrup*
	Preben Aas
Other Offices:	Tonsberg
	Stavanger
	Bergen
	Trondheim
	Tromso
	Alesund
Areas of Practice:	Full Service

<u>Oman</u>

Al Busaidy, Mansoor Jamal & Co.

Muscat International Centre, Mezzanine Floor
Central Business District
Bait Al Falaj Street
P.O. Box 686, Ruwi, Postal Code 112
Muscat
Oman

Telephone:	968-2481-4466
Fax:	968-2481-2256
E-Mail:	mj-co@omantel.net.om
Internet:	www.amjoman.com
Partners:	*Mansoor Jamal Malik*
	Said Al Busaidy
Number of Lawyers:	35
Areas of Practice:	Full Service

Pakistan

Hassan & Hassan

PAAF Building
7-D Kashmir-Egerton Road
Lahore 54000
Pakistan

Telephone:	92-42-6360-800
Fax:	92-42-6360-811
E-Mail:	phassan@brain.net.pk
Internet:	www.hnh.com.pk
Partners:	*Dr. Parvez Hassan*
	Jawad Hassan
Number of Lawyers:	10
Other Office:	Rawalpindi
Areas of Practice:	Full Service

Orr, Dignam & Co.

Building No. 1B
State Life Square I.I.
Chundrigar Road
Karachi 74000
Pakistan

Telephone:	92213-2415384
Fax:	92213-2418924
E-Mail:	orrdignam@pakpages.com
Internet:	www.orrdignam.com
Partners:	*Maudood Khan*
	Aliya Yusaf
Number of Lawyers:	22
Other Office:	Islamabad
Areas of Practice:	Full Service

Sattar & Sattar

United Bank Building
I.I. Chundrigar Road
PO. Box 6699
Karachi
Pakistan

Telephone:	9221-241-5001
Fax:	9221-241-4728
E-Mail:	lawstar@cyber.net.pk
Internet:	www.sattar-attorneys.com
Partners:	*Abdul R. Sattar*
	Kader Sattar
Number of Lawyers:	12
Other Offices:	Islamabad
	Lahore
Areas of Practice:	Full Service

Surridge & Beecheno

Finlay House
I.I. Chundrigar Road
Karachi 74000
Pakistan

Telephone:	9221-324-272-92
Fax:	9221-324-168-30
E-Mail:	info@surridgeandbeecheno.com
Internet:	www.surridgeandbeecheno.com
Partners:	*Aftab Kahn (Lahore)*
	Mohammad Naeem
Number of Lawyers:	25
Other Offices:	Lahore
	Dubai
Areas of Practice:	Full Service

Kabraji & Talibuddin

64-A/1, Gulshal-E-Faisal, Bath Island
Karachi 75530
Pakistan

Telephone:	9221-3583-8874
Fax:	9221-3583-8871
E-Mail:	kandt@kandtlaw.com
Partners:	*Kairas Kabraji*
	Salman Talibuddin

Number of Lawyers: 12
Areas of Practice: Full Service

Vellani & Vellani

148 18th East Street, Phase I
Defence Officers' Housing Authority
Karachi 75500
Pakistan

Telephone:	9221-3580-1000
Fax:	9221-3580-2120
E-Mail:	khi@vellani.com
Internet:	www.vellani.com
Partner:	*Fatehali Vellani*
	Badaruddin Vellani

Number of Lawyers: 23
Areas of Practice: Full Service

Amhurst Brown

64 Nazimuddin Road Sector F8-4
Islamabad
Pakistan

Telephone:	9251-285-5890
Fax:	9251-285-5893
E-Mail:	mail@amhurstbrown.com
Internet:	www.amhurstbrown.com
Partner:	*Munawar A. Akhtar*
Areas of Practice:	Full Service

Palestinian Territories

Al Zaeem & Associates

Omar el Mokhtar Street
P.O. Box 1135
Gaza City
Palestinian Territories

Telephone:	0097282820445
E-Mail:	alzaeem@alzaeem.ps
Internet:	www.alzaeem.ps
Partner:	*Sharhabeel Y. Al Zaeem*
Number of Lawyers:	9
Areas of Practice:	Full Service

Panama

Icaza, Gonzalez-Ruiz, & Aleman

Calle Aquilino de la Guardia No. 8
IGRA Building
P.O. Box 0823-02435
Panama City 7
Panama

Telephone:	507-205-6000
Fax:	507-269-4891
E-Mail:	igranet@icazalaw.com
Internet:	www.icazalaw.com
Partner:	*Alvaro R. Aleman*
Number of Lawyers:	11
Areas of Practice:	Full Service

Cajigas & Co.

Bonanza Building, Planta Baja
Ave. Manuel Ma. Icaza
Panama City
Panama

Telephone:	507-264-6111
Fax:	507-264-5749
E-Mail:	cajigas@cajigaslaw.com
Internet:	www.cajigaslaw.com
Partner:	*Enrique Cajiga*
Areas of Practice:	Full Service

Fabrega, Molino, & Mulino

Samuel Lewis Avenue, 53 Street
Omega Building, Mezzanine
Panama City 5
Panama

Telephone:	507-301-6600
Fax:	507-301-6606
E-Mail:	fmm@fmm.com.pa
Internet:	www.fmm.com.pa
Partner:	*Juan Pablo Fabrega*
Number of Lawyers:	19
Areas of Practice:	Full Service

Patton, Moreno & Asvat

Paseo Roberto Motta
Capital Plaza, Floor 8
Costa del Este
Panama

Telephone:	507-306-9600
Fax:	507-263-7887
E-Mail:	info@pmalawyers.com
Internet:	www.pmalawyers.com
Partners:	*Brett Patton*
	Ebrahim Asva
Number of Lawyers:	14
Other Offices:	Tortola
	Montevideo
	Anguilla
	Nassau
	Belize City
	Hong Kong
	London
Areas of Practice:	Full Service

Arias, Fabrega, & Fabrega

Plaza 2000 Building, 16th Floor, 50th Street
Panama City 5
Panama

Telephone:	507-205-7000
Fax:	507-205-7001
E-Mail:	panama@arifa.com
Internet:	www.arifa.com
Partners:	*Fernando Cardoze*
	Gabriel A. Galindo

Arosemena, Noriega & Contreras

Interseco Building
Calle Elvira Mendez Street, 10
Panama City 5
Panama

Telephone:	507-366-8400
Fax:	507-264-4569
E-Mail:	anc@anorco.com.pa
Internet:	www.anorco.com
Partner:	*Julio Contreras*
Number of Lawyers:	18
Areas of Practice:	Full Service

Durling & Durling

Edificio Vallarino — Penthouse Calle Elvira Mendez, 52
PO Box 0816-06805
Panama City
Panama

Telephone:	507-263-8244
Fax:	507-263-8234
E-Mail:	adm@durlinglaw.com
Internet:	www.durlinglaw.com
Partner:	*Ricardo Durling*
Number of Lawyers:	8
Areas of Practice:	Full Service

Morgan & Morgan

MMG Tower, 16th Floor
53 E Street, Urbanizacion Marbella 0832-00232
Panama City
Panama

Telephone:	507-265-7777
Fax:	507-265-7700
E-Mail:	info@morimor.com
Internet:	www.morimor.com
Partner:	*Eduardo Morgan*
Number of Lawyers:	63
Areas of Practice:	Full Service

Pardini & Associates

Plaza 2000 Tower
10th Floor 50th Avenue
PO Box 0815-01117
Panama City 4
Panama

Telephone:	507-223-7222
Fax:	507-264-4730
E-Mail:	pardini@padela.com
Internet:	www.pardinilaw.com
Partner:	*Juan Pardini*
Number of Lawyers:	14
Areas of Practice:	Full Service

Papua New Guinea

Allens Arthur Robinson

Level 5, Pacific Place
Cnr. Musgrave Street & Champions Parade
Port Moresby
Papua New Guinea

Telephone:	675-320-2000
Fax:	675-320-0588
E-Mail:	vincent.bull@aar.com.au
Internet:	www.aar.com.au
Partner:	*Vincent Bull*
Number of Lawyers:	3
Areas of Practice:	Full Service

Paraguay

Vouga & Olmedo

Av. Peru Nr. 505 and Av. Espana
Asuncion
Paraguay

Telephone:	595-21-207-185
Fax:	595-21-200-284
E-Mail:	lawfirm@vouga-olmedo.py
Internet:	www.vouga-olmedo.com
Partners:	*Gustavo Olmedo*
	Rodolfo Vouga

Lumber of Lawyers: 39
Areas of Practice: Full Service

Peroni, Sosa, Tellechea, Burt & Narvaja

Eulogio Estigarribia St. 4846
Asuncion
Paraguay

Telephone:	595-21-663-536
Fax:	595-21-600-448
E-Mail:	pstbn@pstbn.com.py
Internet:	www.pstbn.com.py
Partners:	*Esteban Burt*
	Guillermo F. Peroni

Number of Lawyers: 14
Areas of Practice: Full Service

Fiorio, Cardozo & Alvarado

Avda Peru 708
1560 Asuncion
Paraguay

Telephone:	595-21-205-052
Fax:	595-21-610-240
Internet:	www.alfio.com.py
Partner:	*R. Marcelo Alvarado*
Number of Lawyers:	18
Areas of Practice:	Full Service

Estudio Juridico Gross Brown

Benjamin Constant 624, P.O. Box 730
Asuncion
Paraguay

Telephone:	595-21-444-426
Fax:	595-21-498-169
E-Mail:	estudiojuridico@grossbrown.com.py
Internet:	www.grossbrown.com.py
Partners:	*Jorge R. Gross Brown*
	Atilio Gomez Grassi
Number of Lawyers:	20
Areas of Practice:	Full Service

Berkemeyer

Benjamin Constant 835
Asuncion
Paraguay

Telephone:	595-21-446-706
Fax:	595-21-449-694
E-Mail:	law@berke.com.py
Internet:	www.berke.com.py
Parners:	*M. Yolanda Pereira*
	Luis Breur
	Hugo T. Berkemeyer

Number of Lawyers: 37
Areas of Practice: Full Service

Peru

Estudio Aurelio Garcia Sayan

Av. Reducto 1310
Miraflores
Lima
Peru

Telephone:	511-615-0202
Fax:	511-615-0222
E-Mail:	postmaster@garciasayan.com.pe
Internet:	www.garciasayan.com.pe
Partner:	*Jose Miguel Morales Dasso*
Number of Lawyers:	35
Areas of Practice:	Full Service

Estudio Osterling

Av. Sarb Torbo 143
San Isidro
Lima
Peru

Telephone:	511-611-8385
Fax:	511-611-8284
E-Mail:	osterling@osterlingfirm.com
Internet:	www.osterlingfirm.com
Partners:	*Felipe Osterling Parodi*
	Arturo Tello Diaz
Number of Lawyers:	26
Areas of Practice:	Full Service

Estudio Rubio, Leguia, Normand & Asociados

Avenida Dos de Mayo 1321
San Isidro
Lima 27
Peru

Telephone:	511-442-4900
Fax:	511-442-3511
E-Mail:	abogados@erubio.com.pe
Internet:	www.erubio.com.pe
Partners:	*Alfonso Rubio A.*
	Victor Ferro D.
Number of Lawyers:	49
Other Office:	Cajamarca
Areas of Practice:	Full Service

Pierola & Asociados

P.O. Box 18-0715
Lima 18
Peru

Telephone:	511-447-2454
Fax:	511-447-2450
E-Mail:	pierola@terra.com.pe
Internet:	www.pierola-asociados.com
Partners:	*Jose de Pierola*
	Christel de Pierola
Number of Lawyers:	10
Areas of Practice:	Intellectual Property

Estudio Flint

198 Mariscal Sucre
Miraflores
Lima
Peru

Telephone:	511-440-6011
Fax:	511-442-5398
E-Mail:	estudioflint@flintgroup.com.pe
Internet:	www.flintgroup.com.pe
Partner:	*Pinkas J. Flint*
Number of Lawyers:	10
Areas of Practice:	Full Service

Barrios Fuentes Arias

Arias Araguez 250
Lima 18
Peru

Telephone:	511-610-6100
Fax:	511-445-1015
E-Mail:	lawfirm@bafur.com.pe
Internet:	www.bafur.com.pe
Partners:	*Raul Barrios*
	Julio Gallo
Number of Lawyers:	28
Areas of Practice:	Full Service

Estudio Echecopar

Avide la Floresta 497
Lima
Peru

Telephone:	511-618-8500
Fax:	511-372-7374
E-Mail:	estudio@echecopar.com.pe
Internet:	www.echecopar.com.pe
Partner:	*Jose Ramirez Gaston Roe*
Number of Lawyers:	67
Areas of Practice:	Full Service

Fort, Bertorini, Godoy Pollari & Carcelen Abogados

Av. Camino Real 456
Torre Real
Lima
Peru

Telephone:	511-442-4646
Fax:	511-442-1287
E-Mail:	postmaster@fobego.com.pe
Internet:	www.fobego.com.pe
Partner:	*Fernando Fort*
Number of Lawyers:	6
Areas of Practice:	Full Service

Estudio Olaechea

Bernardo Monteagudo 201, San Isidro
Lima 27
Peru

Telephone:	511-219-0400
Fax:	511-219-0420
E-Mail:	postmaster@esola.com.pe
Internet:	www.esola.com.pe
Partner:	*Jose Antonio Olaechea*
Number of Lawyers:	36
Areas of Practice:	Full Service

Berninzon, Loret deMola, Benavides & Fernandez

Camino Real 390, Torre Central of 801
San Isidro
Lima
Peru

Telephone:	511-222-5252
Fax:	511-421-4816
E-Mail:	postmaster@berlegal.com
Internet:	www.blmblegal.com
Partners:	*Eduardo Benavides*
	Francisco Berninzon
Areas of Practice:	Full Service

Benites, Forno & Ugaz

Marconi 165
San Isidro, Lima
Peru
Telephone:	511-615-9090
Fax:	511-615-9091
E-Mail:	bdfu@bdfu.com
Internet:	www.bdfu.com
Partner:	*Hugo Forno*
Number of Lawyers:	37
Other Office:	Trujillo
Area of Practice:	Full Service

Muniz, Ramirez, Perez-Taiman & Olaya

Las Begonias 475
San Isidro, Lima 27
Peru
Telephone:	511-611-7000
Fax:	511-611-7030
E-Mail:	contactus@munizlaw.com
Internet:	www.munizlaw.com
Partner:	*Jorge Perez-Taiman*
Number of Lawyers:	106
Other Offices:	Trujillo
	Arequipa
	Ica
	Chincha
	Piura
	Quito
	Guayaquil
Areas of Practice:	Full Service

Rodrigo, Elias & Medrano

Avenida San Felipe 758
Lima 11
Peru

Telephone:	51-16-191-900
Fax:	51-16-191-919
E-Mail:	jpchabaneix@estudioradrigo.com
Internet:	www.estudiorodrigo.com
Partners:	*Jorge Velarde*
	Alex Morris
	Jean Paul Chabeneix
Number of Lawyers:	120
Other Office:	Madrid
Areas of Practice:	Full Service

Philippines

Sycip, Salazar, Hernandez & Gatmaitan

SSHG Law Centre
105 Paseo de Roxas
Makati City 1226, Metro Manila
Philippines

Telephone:	632-817-9811
Fax:	632-817-3896
E-Mail:	sshg@syciplaw.com
Internet:	www.syciplaw.com
Partners:	*Domingo G. Castillo*
	Andres G. Gatmaitan
	Rafael A. Morales
Other Offices:	Cebu
	Davao
	Subic
Areas of Practice:	Full Service

Philippines *continued*

Angara Abello Concepcion Regala & Cruz

ACCRA Building
122 Gamboa Street, Legaspi Village 0770 Makati, Metro Manila
Philippines

Telephone:	632-830-8000
Fax:	632-816-0119
E-Mail:	accra@accralaw.com
Internet:	www.accralaw.com
Partners:	*Avelino Cruz*
Number of Lawyers:	115
Other Offices:	Cebu City
	Davao
Areas of Practice:	Full Service

Quasha Ancheta Pena & Nolasco

Don Pablo Building
114 Amorsolo St.
Makati, Metro Manila 1229
Philippines

Telephone:	632-892-3011
Fax:	632-817-6423
E-Mail:	quasha@quasha-interlaw.com
Internet:	www.quasha-interlaw.com
Partners:	*Alonzo Ancheta*
	Nilo Pena
Number of Lawyers:	31
Areas of Practice:	Full Service

Castillo Laman Tan Pantaleon & San Jose

Valero Tower
122 Valero Street, Salcedo Village,
Makati City, Metro Manila 1227
Philippines

Telephone:	632-817-6791
Fax:	632-819-2725
E-Mail:	counsel@cltpsj.com.ph
Internet:	www.cltpsj.com.ph
Partners:	*Polo Pantaleon*
	Victoria Sarmiento

Number of Lawyers: 53
Areas of Practice: Full Service

Romulo Mabanta Buenaventura Sayoc & De Los Angeles

Citibank Tower
8741 Paseo de Roxas
Makati City, Metro Manila 3117
Philippines

Telephone:	632-848-0114
Fax:	632-815-3172
E-Mail:	rmbsa@rmbsa.com
Internet:	www.rmbsa.com
Partners:	*Ricardo Romulo*
	Eduardo De Los Angeles

Number of Lawyers: 52
Other Office: Hong Kong
Areas of Practice: Full Service

Poland

Wardynski & Partners

Al Ujazdowskie 10
00-478 Warsaw
Poland

Telephone:	48-22-437-8200
Fax:	48-22-437-8201
E-Mail:	warsaw@wardynski.com.pl
Internet:	www.wardynski.com.pl
Partners:	*Tomasz Wardynski*
	Tomasz Zasacki
Number of Lawyers:	137
Other Offices:	Wroclaw
	Poznan
	Brussels
Areas of Practice:	Full Service

Forystek & Partnerzy

Bud. Pasaz Saski
Ul. Grzybowska 12/14
00-132 Warsaw
Poland

Telephone:	48-22-890-9630
Fax:	48-22-890-9631
E-Mail:	jozef.forystek@forystek.pl
Internet:	www.forystek.pl
Partner:	*Jozef Forystek*
Number of Lawyers:	36
Areas of Practice:	Full Service

Laszczuk & Partners
Plac Pilsudskiego 2
00-073 Warsaw
Poland
Telephone:	48-22-351-0067
Fax:	48-22-351-0068
E-Mail:	warsaw@laszczuk.pl
Internet:	www.laszczuk.pl
Partners:	*Maciej Laszczuk*
	Andrej Polimirski

Number of Lawyers: 22
Areas of Practice: Full Service

Lukowicz, Swierzewski & Partners
13 Mazowiecka Str.
00-052 Warsaw
Poland
Telephone:	48-22-827-3322
Fax:	48-22-826-8319
E-Mail:	office@lukowicz.pl
Internet:	www.lukowicz.pl
Partner:	*Olgierd Swierzewski*

Number of Lawyers: 39
Other Offices:	Bucarest
	Sofia
	Kiev

Areas of Practice: Full Service

Drzewiecki, Tomaszek & Partners

Spolka Komandytowa ul. Krupnicza 13/306a
50 075 Wroclaw
Poland

E-Mail:	a.tomaszek@dt.com.pl
Internet:	www.dt.com.pl
Partner:	*Andrzej Tomaszek*
Number of Lawyers:	59
Other Office:	Warsaw
Areas of Practice:	Full Service

Portugal

Morais Leitao, Galvao Teles Soares Da Silva & Associados

Rua Castilho, 165
1070-050 Lisbon
Portugal

Telephone:	351-213-817-400
Fax:	351-213-817-499
E-Mail:	mlgtslisboa@mlgts.pt
Internet:	www.mlgts.pt
Partners:	*Jose Manuel GalvaoTeles*
	Antonio Pinto Leite
Number of Lawyers:	82
Other Offices:	Oporto
	Funchal
Areas of Practice:	Full Service

Carlos de Sousa Brito & Associados

Rua Castilho, 71
1250-068 Lisbon
Portugal

Telephone:	351-21-384-6200
Fax:	351-21-386-1735
E-Mail:	csba@csbadvogados.pt
Internet:	www.csbadvogados.pt
Partner:	*Carlos de Sousa e Brito*
Number of Lawyers:	34
Areas of Practice:	Full Service

Miranda, Correia, Amendoeira & Associados

The Stock Exchange Building
Ru Soeiro Pereira Gomes
1600-196 Lisbon
Portugal

Telephone:	351-21-781-4800
Fax:	351-21-781-4802
E-Mail:	lisbon@mirandalawfirm.com
Internet:	www.mirandalawfirm.com
Partners:	*Rita Correia*
	Ricardo Silva
	Rui Amendoeira
Number of Lawyers:	118
Other Office:	Madeira
Areas of Practice:	Full Service

Franco Caiado Guerreiro & Associades

Rua Castilho, 39
1250-058 Lisbon
Portugal

Telephone:	351-213-717-000
Fax:	351-213-717-001
E-Mail:	jguerreiro@fcguerreiro.com
Internet:	www.fcguerreiro.com
Partners:	*J.C. Guerreiro*
	Ricardo Costa Mecedo
Number of Lawyers:	53
Other Offices:	Maputo
	Cape Verde
Areas of Practice:	Full Service

Cuatrecasas, Goncalves Pereira

Praca Marques de Pombal, 2
1250-160 Lisbon
Portugal

Telephone:	351-21-355-3800
Fax:	351-21-353-2362
E-Mail:	Lisboa@gpcb.pt
Internet:	www.gpcb.pt
Partners:	*Andres Goncalves Pereira*
	Carlos de Almeida Sampaio
Number of Lawyers:	Numerous
Other Offices:	Numerous
Areas of Practice:	Full Service

Abreu Advogados

Av. Das Forcas Armadas, 125
1600-029 Lisbon
Portugal

Telephone:	351-21-723-1800
Fax:	351-21-723-1899
E-Mail:	Lisboa@abreuadvogados.com
Internet:	www.abreuadvogados.com
Partners:	*Duarte Athayede*
	Pedro Pais De Almedia
Number of Lawyers:	114
Other Offices:	Oporto
	Madeira
	Angola
Areas of Practice:	Full Service

Portugal _{continued}

Chaves, Roquette, Matos, Azevedo & Associados

Rua das Amoreiras, 70
1269-105 Lisbon
Portugal

Telephone:	351-213-826-000
Fax:	351-213-866-571
E-Mail:	lawfirm@crma.pt
Internet:	www.crma.pt
Partner:	*Henrique Chaves*
Number of Lawyers:	9
Areas of Practice:	Full Service

Puerto Rico

Goldman Antonetti & Cordova

Suite 1400, American International Plaza
250 Munoz Rivera Avenue
San Juan 00918
Puerto Rico

Telephone:	787-759-8000
Fax:	787-767-9333
E-Mail:	vantonetti@gaclaw.com
Internet:	www.gaclaw.com
Partners:	*Maria Lake*
	Carlos A. Rodriguez-Vidal
	Vicente J. Antonetti

Number of Lawyers: 37
Areas of Practice: Full Service

Law Offices of Benjamin Acosta

331 Recinto Sur Street
San Juan 00901
Puerto Rico

Telephone:	787-722-2363
Fax:	787-724-5970
E-Mail:	benacosta@lobajr.com
Internet:	www.lobajr.com
Partner:	*Ben Acosta*

Number of Lawyers: 5
Areas of Practice: Insurance
Litigation

McConnell Valdes

270 Munoz Rivera Avenue
San Juan 00918
Puerto Rico

Telephone:	787-759-9292
Fax:	787-759-9225
E-Mail:	webmaster@mcvpr.com
Internet:	www.mcvpr.com
Partners:	*Jorge Gonzalez*
	Richard Graffam
Number of Lawyers:	104
Other Office:	Washington, D.C.
Areas of Practice:	Full Service

O'Neill & Borges

American International Plaza
250 Munoz Rivera Avenue
San Juan 00918
Puerto Rico

Telephone:	787-764-8181
Fax:	787-753-8944
E-Mail:	info@oneillborges.com
Internet:	www.oneillborges.com
Partners:	*Raymond C. O'Neill*
	Walter Chow
Number of Lawyers:	89
Areas of Practice:	Full Service

Lasa, Monroig & Veve

Westernbank World Plaza
268 Munoz Rivera Avenue
San Juan 00918
Puerto Rico

Telephone:	787-774-0400
Fax:	787-773-1171
E-Mail:	info@lmvlaw.com
Internet:	www.lmvlaw.com
Partners:	*Armando Lasa Ferrer*
	Antonio Monroig
Number of Lawyers:	10
Other Offices:	Washington, D.C.
	Reston, Virginia
Areas of Practice:	Full Service

Reichard & Escalera

MCS Plaza, 10th Floor
255 Ponce de Leon Avenue
San Juan 00917
Puerto Rico

Telephone:	787-777-8888
Fax:	787-765-4225
E-Mail:	counsellors@reichardescalera.com
Internet:	www.recounsel.com
Partner:	*Hector Reichard*
Number of Lawyers:	10
Areas of Practice:	Full Service

Manuel San Juan

Banco Popular Building, 8th Floor
P.O. Box 9023587
San Juan 00902-3587
Puerto Rico

Telephone:	787-723-6669
Fax:	787-725-2932
E-Mail:	sanjuanm@sanjuanlawfirm.com
Internet:	www.sanjuanlawfirm.com
Partner:	*Manuel San Juan*
Number of Lawyers:	1
Areas of Practice:	Litigation

Qatar

Hassan A. Alkhater Law Office

P.O. Box 1737
20464 Doha
Qatar

Telephone:	974-443-7770
Fax:	974-443-7772
E-Mail:	haklegal@qatar.net.qu
Partner:	*Hassan A. Alkhater*
Number of Lawyers:	4
Areas of Practice:	Full Service

Khalid bin Mohd Al-Attiya

1 Building, 5th Floor P.O. Box 9228
Brooq
Bin Mahmood Street
Doha
Qatar

Telephone:	974-436-4447
Fax:	974-436-4449
E-Mail:	info@alattiya-legal.com
Internet:	www.alattiya-legal.com
Partner:	*Khalid bin Mohd Al-Attiya*
Number of Lawyers:	10
Areas of Practice:	Full Service

Romania

Nestor Nestor Diculescu Kingston Peterson
Bucharest Business Park
lA Bucuresti-Ploiesti National Road, 1st District
013681, Bucharest
Romania

Telephone:	40-21-201-1200
Fax:	40-21-201-1210
E-Mail:	office@nndkp.ro
Internet:	www.nndkp.com
Partner:	*Ion Nestor*
Number of Lawyers:	105
Areas of Practice:	Full Service

Musat & Associatii
43, Aviatorilor Boulevard
1st District
011853 Bucharest
Romania

Telephone:	40-21-202-5900
Fax:	40-21-223-3957
E-Mail:	general@musatro
Internet:	www.musat.ro
Partner:	*Gheorghe Musat*
Number of Lawyers:	85
Other Office:	Cluj
Areas of Practice:	Full Service

Russia

Monastyrsky, Zyuba, Semenov & Partners

3/1 Novinsky Boulevard
Moscow 121099
Russia

Telephone:	7495-231-4222
Fax:	7495-231-4223
E-Mail:	moscow@mzs.ru
Internet:	www.mzs.ru
Partner:	*Alexander Zyuba*
Number of Lawyers:	26
Areas of Practice:	Full Service

Mikhailov & Partners

2 Begovaya Street
Moscow 125284
Russia

Telephone:	7095-945-4463
Fax:	7095-945-2706
E-Mail:	mp@mnp.ru
Internet:	www.mnp.ru
Partner:	*Oleg Mikhailov*
Other Office:	Bonn
Areas of Practice:	Full Service

Jurinflot International Law Firm

34, Marxistskaya Str.
Moscow
Russia

Telephone:	7495-792-5701
Fax:	7495-792-5700
E-Mail:	jurin@jurinflot.ru
Internet:	www.jurinflot.ru
Partner:	*Stanislav Kondrashin*
Number of Lawyers:	17
Areas of Practice:	Full Service

Egorov Puginsky Afanasiev & Partners

40/4 Bol. Ordynka
Mosco 119017
Russia

Telephone:	7-495-935-8010
Fax:	7-495-935-8011
E-Mail:	Mow_office@epam.ru
Internet:	www.epam.ru
Partner:	*Ilya Victorovich Nikiforov*
Other Offices:	St. Petersburg
	London
Areas of Practice:	Full Service

Pepeliaev Group

54 Shpalernaya St.
Golden Shpalernaya Business Center
St. Petersburg 191015
Russia

E-Mail:	s.sosnovsky@pgplaw.ru
Internet:	www.pgplaw.ru
Partners:	*Sergey Sosnovsky*
	Sergey Papeliaev (Moscow)
	Sergey Spasennov
Number of Lawyers:	180
Other Office:	Moscow
Areas of Practice:	Full Service

Saudi Arabia

Law Firm of Salah Al-Hejailan
Al-Dahna Center
54 A1-Ahsaa Street, Malaz District
P.O. Box 1454
Riyadh 11431
Saudi Arabia

Telephone:	966-1-479-2200
Fax:	966-1-479-1717
E-Mail:	Lfshriyadh@hejailanlaw.com
Internet:	www.hejailanlaw.com
Partners:	*Salah Al-Hejailan*
	Robert Thomas
Number of Lawyers:	24
Other Office:	Jeddah
Areas of Practice:	Full Service

Law Offices of Dr. Mujahid M. Al-Sawwaf
P.O. Box 5840
Jedda 21432
Saudi Arabia

Telephone:	966-2-669-0751
Fax:	966-1-665-5052
E-Mail:	msawwaf@sbm.netsa
Partner:	*Mujahid M Al-Sawwaf*
Number of Lawyers:	7
Other Office:	Riyadh
Areas of Practice:	Full Service

Scotland

Dundas & Wilson

Saltire Court
20 Castle Terrace
Edinburgh EH1 2EN
Scotland

Telephone:	44-131-228-8000
Fax:	444-131-228-888
Internet:	www.dundas-wilson.com
Partners:	*David Hardie*
	Donald Shaw
	John Rothwell Verrill (London)
Number of Lawyers:	403
Other Offices:	Glasgow
	London
Areas of Practice:	Full Service

Maclay Murray & Spens

151 St. Vincent Street
Glasgow G2 5NJ
Scotland

Telephone:	44-141-248-5011
Fax:	44-141-248-5819
E-Mail:	magnus.swanson@mms.co.uk
Internet:	www.mms.co.uk
Partner:	*Magnus Swanson*
Number of Lawyers:	296
Other Offices:	Edinburgh
	London
	Aberdeen
	Brussels
Areas of Practice:	Full Service

McGrigor's

Pacific House
141 Bothwell Street
Glasgow G2 7EQ
Scotland

Telephone:	44-141-567-8400
Fax:	44-141-567-8401
E-Mail:	enquiries@mcgrigors.com
Internet:	www.mcgrigors.com
Partner:	*Ewan Alexander*
Number of Lawyers:	318
Other Offices:	Aberdeen
	Belfast
	Edinburgh
	Falklands
	London
	Manchester
Areas of Practice:	Full Service

Brodies LLP

15 Atholl Crescent
Edinburgh EH3 8HA
Scotland

Telephone:	44-131-228-3777
Fax:	44-131-228-3878
E-Mail:	mailbox@brodies.com
Internet:	www.brodies.co.uk
Partners:	*Grant Campbell*
	William Drummond
	Joan Cradden
Number of Lawyers:	240
Other Office:	Glasgow
Areas of Practice:	Full Service

Senegal

Fall & Sow

P.O. Box 30063
Dakar
Senegal

Telephone:	221-824-9490
Fax:	221-824-9490
E-Mail:	fall_aboubacar@yahoo.fr
Partner:	*Aboubacar Fall*

Cabinet Maitre Cheikh Fall

48, rue Vincens
P.O. Box 32319
Dakar
Senegal

E-Mail:	cgfall@orange.sn
Internet:	www.avocat-cheikhfall.com
Partner:	*Cheikh Fall*
Number of Lawyers:	4
Areas of Practice:	Full Service

Serbia

Popovic, Popovic, Samardzija & Popovic

Takovska 19
11120 Belgrade
Serbia

Telephone:	381-11-323-9442
Fax:	381-11-324-2646
E-Mail:	office@ppsp.rs
Internet:	www.ppsp.rs
Partners:	Srdja Popovic
	Petar A. Samardzija

Number of Lawyers: 5
Areas of Practice: Full Service

Ninkovic

Balkansta 49
11000 Belgrade
Serbia

Telephone:	381-11-3614-632
Fax:	381-11-3613-832
E-Mail:	legal@ninkovic.co.rs
Internet:	www.ninkovic.rs
Partners:	Djurdje Ninkovic
	Dejan Ducic

Number of Lawyers: 13
Areas of Practice: Full Service

Sierra Leone

Basma & Macaulay

26 Main Motor Road
Brookfields
Freetown
Sierra Leone

Telephone:	232-22-222-798
Fax:	232-22-224-248
E-Mail:	info@basmaandmacaulay.com
Internet:	www.basmaandmacaulay.com
Partner:	*Shakib Basma*
Areas of Practice:	Full Service

Macauley, Bangura & Co

UMC Building, 4th Floor
31 Lightfoot Boston Street
Freetown
Sierra Leone

Telephone:	232-22-226164
Fax:	232-22-222115
E-Mail:	info@mbclegal.org
Internet:	www.mbclegal.org
Partner:	*Centus O. Macauley*
Number of Lawyers:	6
Areas of Practice:	Full Service

Singapore

Drew & Napier

20 Raffles Place
Ocean Towers 17-00
Singapore 048620

Telephone:	656-535-0733
Fax:	656-535-4906
E-Mail:	mail@drewnapier.com
Internet:	www.drewnapier.com
Partner:	*Davinder Singh*
Number of Lawyers:	242
Areas of Practice:	Full Service

Rodyk & Davidson

80 Raffles Place
33-00 UOB Plaza 1
Singapore 048624

Telephone:	656-225-2626
Fax:	656-225-1838
E-Mail:	mail@rodyk.com
Internet:	www.rodyk.com
Partners:	*Christopher Chong*
	Helen Yeo
	Doreen Sim
Other Office:	Shanghai
Areas of Practice:	Full Service

Wong Partnership

1 George Street
#20-01
Singapore 049145

Telephone:	65-6416-8000
Fax:	65-6532-5722
E-Mail:	contactus@wongpartnership.com
Internet:	www.wongpartnership.com
Partners:	*Meng Meng Wong*
	Alvin Yeo
Number of Lawyers:	246
Other Offices:	Shanghai
	Abu Dhabi
	Doha
Areas of Practice:	Full Service

Shook Lin & Bok

1 Robinson Road
#18-00 AIA Tower
Singapore 048542

Telephone:	656-535-1944
Fax:	656-535-8577
E-Mail:	slb@shooklin.com.sg
Internet:	www.shooklin.com
Partner:	*Sarjit Singh Gill*
Number of Lawyers:	112
Areas of Practice:	Full Service

Donaldson & Burkinshaw

24 Raffles Place
15-00 Clifford Centre
Singapore 048621

Telephone:	656-533-9422
Fax:	656-533-7806
E-Mail:	enquiries@donburk.com.sg
Internet:	www.donburk.com.sg
Partner:	*Tan Bok Hoay*
Number of Lawyers:	104
Areas of Practice:	Full Service

Kelvin Chia Partnership

6 Temasek Boulevard
Suntec Tower Four, 29th Floor
Singapore 038986

Telephone:	656-220-1911
Fax:	656-224-4118
E-Mail:	info@kcpartnership.com
Internet:	www.kcpartnership.com
Partners:	*Kelvin Chia*
	Cheah Swee Gim
Number of Lawyers:	65
Other Offices:	Bangkok
	Hanoi
	Ho Chi Minh City
	Pyongyany
	Shanghai
	Tokyo
	Isahgon
Areas of Practice:	Full Service

Stamford Law Corporation

9 Raffles Place
#32-00 Republic Plaza
Singapore 048619

Telephone:	65-6389-3000
Fax:	65-6389-3099
E-Mail:	legal@stamford.com.sg
Internet:	www.stamfordlaw.com.sg

Partner: _Suet Fern Lee_
Number of Lawyers: 82
Areas of Practice: Full Service

Slovak Republic

Cechova & Partners

Sturova 4
811 02 Bratislava
Slovak Republic

Telephone:	421-2-54-41-44-41
Fax:	421-2-54-43-45-98
E-Mail:	office@cechova.sk
Internet:	www.cechova.sk
Partners:	*Katarina Cechova*
	Tomas Maretta
Number of Lawyers:	12
Other Office:	Brussels
Areas of Practice:	Full Service

Detvai Ludik Maly Udvaros

Cukrova 14
813 39 Bratislava
Slovak Republic

Telephone:	421-2-52-92-36-28
Fax:	421-2-52-92-60-02
E-Mail:	detvai@dlmu.sk
Internet:	www.dlmu.sk
Partners:	*Jozef Maly*
	Stefan Detvai
Number of Lawyers:	26
Areas of Practice:	Full Service

Ruzicka Csekes

Vysoka 2/B
811 06 Bratislava
Slovak Republic

Telephone:	421-2-3233-3444
Fax:	421-2-3233-3443
E-Mail:	office-ba@rc-cmsisk
Internet:	www.re-cms.sk
Partner:	*Erika Csekes*
Number of Lawyers:	17
Other Office:	Dunajska Streda
Areas of Practice:	Full Service

Peterka & Partners

Kapitulska 18/A
811 01 Bratislava
Slovak Republic

Telephone:	421-2-544-18-700
Fax:	421-2-544-18-701
E-Mail:	office@peterkapartners.sk
Internet:	www.peterkapartners.com
Partner:	*Premysl Marek*
Number of Lawyers:	9
Other Offices:	Prague
	Moscow
	Kiev
	Sofia
Areas of Practice:	Full Service

Slovenia

Janezic & Jarkovic

Tavcarjeva 8
1000 Ljubljana
Slovenia

Telephone:	386-1-230-9000
Fax:	386-1-230-9010
E-Mail:	info@jjlex.si
Internet:	www.jjlex.si
Partners:	*Aleksandra Janezic*
	Andrej Jarkovic

Number of Lawyers: 5
Areas of Practice: Full Service

South Africa

Bowman Gilfillan Inc.

SA Reserve Bank Building
60 St. Georges Mall
Cape Town
South Africa

Telephone:	27-21-480-7800
Fax:	27-21-424-1688
E-Mail:	cpt_info@bowman.co.za
Internet:	www.bowman.co.za
Partners:	*David Anderson (Johannesburg)*
	Bobby Bertrand
Number of Lawyers:	118
Other Offices:	Johannesburg
Areas of Practice:	Full Service

Cliffe Dekker Hofmeyr

1 Protea Place
Sandton 2196
South Africa

Telephone:	27-11-290-7000
Fax:	27-11-290-7300
Internet:	www.cliffedekkerhofmeyr.com
Partner:	*Chris Ewing*
Number of Lawyers:	187
Other Office:	Cape Town
Areas of Practice:	Full Service

Cox Yeats

Victoria Maine
71 Victoria Embankment
Durban, 4001
South Africa

Telephone:	27-31-304-2851
Fax:	27-31-301-3540
E-Mail:	coxyeats@coxyeats.co.za
Internet:	www.coxyeats.co.za
Partner:	*Graham C. Cox*
Number of Lawyers:	52
Areas of Practice:	Full Service

Werksmans

155 5th Street
Sandton
South Africa

Telephone:	27-11-535-8000
Fax:	27-11-535-8600
E-Mail:	vbunyan@werksmans.co.za
Internet:	www.werksmans.co.za
Partner:	*Des Williams*
Other Offices:	Cape Town
	Paarl
	Stellenbosch
	Tyger Valley
Areas of Practice:	Full Service

Webber Wentzel

10 Fricker Road
Johannesburg 2001
South Africa

Telephone:	27-11-530-5000
Fax:	27-11-530-5111
E-Mail:	webmaster@webberwentzel.com
Internet:	www.webberwentzel.com
Partners:	Peter Leon
	Selwyn Hockey (Cape Town)
	Murray Thompson
Number of Lawyers:	295
Other Office:	Cape Town
Areas of Practice:	Full Service

Deneys Reitz

82 Maude Street
Sandton 2196
South Africa

Telephone:	27-11-685-8500
Fax:	27-11-883-4000
E-Mail:	krc@deneysreitz.co.za
Internet:	www.deneysreitz.co.za
Partners:	Theuns Steyn (Cape Town)
	Philip Geromont (Cape Town)
	Kevin Cron
Number of Lawyers:	142
Other Offices:	Cape Town
	Durban
Areas of Practice:	Full Service

Fairbridges

16th Floor, Main Tower
Standard Bank Centre
Heerengracht
Cape Town 8001
South Africa

Telephone:	27-21-405-7300
Fax:	27-21-419-5135
E-Mail:	attorneys@fairbridges.co.za
Internet:	www.fairbridges.co.za
Partners:	*Louis G. Rood*
	Richard Cheeseman
Number of Lawyers:	29
Other Office:	Johannesburg
Areas of Practice:	Full Service

Spain

Uria & Menendez

Principe de Vergara 187
Madrid 28002
Spain

Telephone:	34-915-860-400
Fax:	34-915-860-403
E-Mail:	madrid@uria.com
Internet:	www.uria.com
Partners:	*Charles Coward (Barcelona)*
	Fernando Calbacho
	Antonio Herrera (New York)
	Carlos de Cardenas Smith
	Eduardo Geli (Barcelona)
	Rafael Sebastián
Number of Lawyers:	497
Other Offices:	Numerous
Areas of Practice:	Full Service

B. Cremades y Asociados

Calle Goya 18
28001 Madrid
Spain

Telephone:	34-914-23-7200
Fax:	34-915-769-794
E-Mail:	bcremades-mad@bcremades.com
Internet:	www.cremades.com
Partner:	*Bernardo Cremades*
Number of Lawyers:	14
Areas of Practice:	Full Service

Cuatrecasas, Goncalves Pereira

Velazquez, 63
28001 Madrid
Spain

Telephone:	34-91-524-7000
Fax:	34-91-524-7124
E-Mail:	madrid@cuatracasas.com
Internet:	www.cuatrecasas.com
Partners:	*Javier Villasante*
	Emilio Cuatrecasas
	Albert Garrofe (New York)
	Javier Rodríguez (New York)
	Javier Asensio
	Sonia Velasco
	Gerhard Hernandez (Barcelona)
	Victor Xercavins
Number of Lawyers:	1000
Other Offices:	Numerous
Areas of Practice:	Full Service

Gomez-Acebo & Pombo

Paseo del la Castellana, 216
28046 Madrid
Spain

Telephone:	34-91-582-9100
Fax:	34-91-582-9114
E-Mail:	info@gomezacebo-pombo.com
Internet:	www.gomezacebo-pombo.com
Partners:	_Ignacio Gomez-Acebo_
	Fernando Pombo
	Richard Silberstein (Barcelona)
	Manuel Martin
	Daniel Marin Moreno (Barcelona)
Number of Lawyers:	366
Other Offices:	Barcelona
	Bilbao
	Malaga
	Valencia
	Brussels
	London
Areas of Practice:	Full Service

Garrigues

Calle Hermosilla, 3
28001 Madrid
Spain

Telephone:	34-91-514-5200
Fax:	34-91-399-2408
E-Mail:	communicaciones@garrigues.com
Internet:	www.garrigues.com
Partners:	*Eduardo Abad*
	Susan Cabrera
	Antonio Garriguez
	Ricardo Gomez-Barreda
	Fernando Vives
Number of Lawyers:	2137
Other Offices:	Numerous
Areas of Practice:	Full Service

Montero Aramburu Abogados

Avenida Republica Argentina, 24
41011 Seville
Spain

Telephone:	34-954-990-267
Fax:	34-954-990-301
E-Mail:	Leonardo.neri@montero-arambus.com
Internet:	www.montero-aramburu.com
Partner:	*Leonardo Neri*
Number of Lawyers:	71
Other Offices:	Santa Cruz de Tenerife
	Las Palmas
	Cordoba
Areas of Practice:	Full Service

Roca Junyent

Aribau, 198
08036 Barcelona
Spain

Telephone:	34-93-240-2841
E-Mail:	bcn@rocajunyent.com
Internet:	www.rocajunyent.com
Partners:	*Miguel Roca Junyet*
	Joan Roca Sagaria
	Jordi Casas Thio
Number of Lawyers:	192
Areas of Practice:	Full Service

Sri Lanka

Julius & Creasy

Hong Kong Bank Building
No 41 Janadhipathi Mawatha (Queen Street)
P.O. Box 154
Colombo 1
Sri Lanka

Telephone:	94-11-2422-601
Fax:	94-11-2446-663
E-Mail:	jandc@juliusandcreasy.com
Internet:	www.juliusandcreasy.com
Partners:	*R. Senathi Rajah*
	Amila Fernando
Number of Lawyers:	49
Areas of Practice:	Full Service

John Wilson Partners

365 Dam Street
Colombo 12
Sri Lanka

Telephone:	94-11-2324579
Fax:	94-11-2446954
E-Mail:	general@srilankalaw.com
Internet:	www.srilankalaw.com
Partner:	*John Wilson*
Number of Lawyers:	5
Areas of Practice:	Full Service

Sudath Perera Associates

51, Kassapa Road
Colombo 05
Sri Lanka

Telephone:	94-11-255-9944
E-Mail:	sudath@sudathpereraassociates.com
Internet:	www.sudathpereraassociates.com
Partners:	*Sudath Perera*
	Ali Tyebkhan
Areas of Practice:	Full Service

St. Kitts & Nevis

Vernon S. Veira & Associates

#3 Church Street
Basseterre
St. Kitts & Nevis

E-Mail:	Vgasklaw@caribsurf.com
Partner:	*Vernon S. Veira*
Other Office:	Charlestown
Areas of Practice:	Full Service

Sudan

Mahmoud Elsheikh Omer & Associates

P.O. Box 1569
Khartoum 1111
Sudan

Telephone:	249-183-772-270
Fax:	249-183-777-362
E-Mail:	info@mahmoudelsheikh.com
Internet:	www.mahmoudelsheikh.com
Partner:	*Tarig Mahmoud Elsheikh*
Number of Lawyers:	13
Areas of Practice:	Full Service

Sweden

Vinge

Smalandsgatan 20
Box 1703
5-111 87 Stockholm
Sweden

Telephone:	468-614-3000
Fax:	468-614-3190
E-Mail:	michael.wigg.vinge.se
Internet:	www.vinge.se
Partners:	*Michael Wigge*
	Anders Forkman (Malmo)
	Par Remnelid
	Jan Bystrom
Number of Lawyers:	284
Other Offices:	Gothenburg
	Malmo
	Helsingborg
	Brussels
	Hong Kong
	Shanghai
Areas of Practice:	Full Service

Magnusson Wahlin Qvist Stanbrook

Norrmalmstong 1
Box 7009
SE-103 86 Stockholm
Sweden

Telephone:	46-8-407-0900
Fax:	46-8-407-0910
E-Mail:	stockholm@se.maqs.com
Internet:	www.mags.com
Partner:	_Lars Boman_
Other Offices:	Copenhagen
	Riga
	Warsaw
	Vilnius
	Tallinn
	Gothenburg
	Malmoe
Areas of Practice:	Full Service

Alwa Law Firm

Strandvagen 7B
SE-114 56 Stockholm
Sweden

Telephone:	46-8-662-0051
Fax:	46-8-6601440
E-Mail:	jessica.sandberg@alwaadvocal.se
Internet:	www.alaadvocat.se
Partner:	_Jessica Sandberg_
Other Office:	Helsingborg
Areas of Practice:	International Business
	EU Law
	Family Law

Advokatfirman Sodermark

Strandvagen 1
PO Box 14055,
SE-104 40 Stockholm
Sweden

Telephone:	46-8-670-5750
Fax:	46-8-663-6720
E-Mail:	mail@sodermark.se
Internet:	www.eversheds.com
Partners:	*Bertil Brinck*
	Magnus Andren
Other Offices:	Numerous
Areas of Practice:	Full Service

Mannheimer Swartling

Norrlandsgatan 21
P.O. Box 1711
S-111 87 Stockholm
Sweden

Telephone:	468-595-060-00
Fax:	468-595-060-01
E-Mail:	info@msa.se
Internet:	www.mannheimerswartling.se
Partners:	*Peter Alhanko*
	Andre Andersson
	Hans Andreasson
	Tore Wiwen-Nilsson (Malmo)
	Tommy Pettersson
	Sven-Ake Bergkvist
	Johan Coyet
	Johan Carle
Number of Lawyers:	340
Other Offices:	Malmo
	Moscow
	New York
	St. Petersburg
	Gothenburg
	Frankfurt
	Hong Kong
	Shanghai
	Berlin
	Brussels
	Helsingborg
Areas of Practice:	Full Service

Gernandt & Danielsson

Hamngatan 2
P.O. Box 5747
SE-114 87 Stockholm
Sweden

Telephone:	468-670-6600
Fax:	468-662-6101
E-Mail:	info@gda.se
Internet:	www.gda.se
Partner:	*Johan Josjo*
Number of Lawyers:	67
Areas of Practice:	Full Service

Setterwalls

Arsenalsgatan 6
S-111 47 Stockholm
Sweden

Telephone:	468-598-890-00
Fax:	468-598-890-90
E-Mail:	stockholm@setterwalls.se
Partners:	*Hakan Fohlin*
	Anders Heintze
Number of Lawyers:	115
Other Offices:	Malmo
	Gothenburg
Areas of Practice:	Full Service

Hellstrom Law

Sodra Kungstornet
Kungsgatan 33, P.O. Box 7305
S-103 90 Stockholm
Sweden

Telephone:	468-220-900
Fax:	468-204-090
E-Mail:	info@hellstromlaw.com
Internet:	www.hellstromlaw.com
Partners:	*Mats Hellstrom*
	Staffan Michelson
Number of Lawyers:	28
Areas of Practice:	Corporate Finance
	Mergers and Acquisitions
	Banking and Finance

Switzerland

Pestalozzi

Lowenstrasse 1
CH-8001 Zurich
Switzerland

Telephone:	411-217-9111
Fax:	411-217-9217
E-Mail:	zrh@pestalozzilaw.com
Internet:	www.pestalozzilaw.com
Partners:	*Robert Furter*
	Guy-Philippe Rubeli (Geneva)
Number of Lawyers:	94
Other Offices:	Geneva
	Brussels
Areas of Practice:	Full Service

Bar & Karrer

Brandschenkestrasse 90
CH-8027 Zurich
Switzerland

Telephone:	41-58-261-5000
Fax:	41-58-261-5001
E-Mail:	zurich@baerkarrer.ch
Partners:	*Thomas A. Bar*
	Robert Karrer
Number of Lawyers:	123
Other Offices:	Zug
	Geneva
	Lugano
Areas of Practice:	Full Service

Switzerland *continued*

Froriep Renggli

Bellerivestrasse 201
CH-8034 Zurich
Switzerland

Telephone:	41-44-386-6000
Fax:	41-44-383-6050
E-Mail:	zurich@froriep.ch
Internet:	www.froriep.com
Partners:	*Hans Stuber*
	Eric Haymann
Number of Lawyers:	80
Other Offices:	Geneva
	Zug
	London
	Lausanne
	Madrid
Areas of Practice:	Full Service

Secretan Troyanov

2, Rue Charles-Bonnet
P.O. Box 189
1211 Geneva 12
Switzerland

Telephone:	41-22-789-7000
Fax:	41-22-789-7070
E-Mail:	gva.mail@secretantroyanov.com
Internet:	www.secretantroyanov.com
Partners:	*Horace Gautier*
	Eric W. Fiechter
	Cyril Troyanov
Number of Lawyers:	15
Areas of Practice:	Full Service

Budin & Partners

20, rue Senebier CP 166
1211 Geneva 12
Switzerland

Telephone:	41-22-818-0808
Fax:	41-22-818-0818
E-Mail:	budinlaw@budin.ch
Internet:	www.budin.ch
Partner:	*Patrick Bittel*
Number of Lawyers:	28
Other Office:	Lausanne
Areas of Practice:	Full Service

Dietrich, Baumgartner & Partners

Sihlporte 3/Talstrasse
P.O. Box 3580
8021 Zurich
Switzerland

Telephone:	41-44-217-4747
Fax:	41-44-217-4700
E-Mail:	dbp@dbp.ch
Internet:	www.dbp.ch
Partners:	*Andres Baumgartner*
	Fabio Delco
Number of Lawyers:	9
Areas of Practice:	Full Service

Lalive

35, rue de la Mairie
1207 Geneva
Switzerland

Telephone:	41-22-319-8700
Fax:	41-22-319-8760
E-Mail:	info@lalive.ch
Internet:	www.lalive.ch
Partners:	*Pierre Lalive*
	Michael Schneider
Number of Lawyers:	44
Other Office:	Zurich
Areas of Practice:	Full Service

Neupert & Partners

Dufourstrasse 58
8702 Zurich
Switzerland

Telephone:	41-44-396-8080
Fax:	41-44-396-8088
E-Mail:	mail@nplaw.ch
Partners:	*Dieter Neupert*
	Alexander Faber
Number of Lawyers:	8
Areas of Practice:	Full Service

Altenburger & Partners

Seestrasse 39
8700 Zurich
Switzerland

Telephone:	41-44-914-8888
Fax:	41-44-914-8880
E-Mail:	zurich@altenburger.ch
Internet:	www.altenburger.ch
Partners:	*Peter R. Altenburger*
	Leonhard Toenz
Number of Lawyers:	25
Other Office:	Geneva
Areas of Practice:	Full Service

Lenz & Staehelin

58 Bleicherweg
8027 Zurich
Switzerland

Telephone:	41-44-204-1212
Fax:	41-44-204-1200
E-Mail:	zurich@lenzstaehelin.com
Internet:	www.lenzstaehelin.com
Partners:	*Harold Frey*
	Martin Lutz
Number of Lawyers:	165
Other Offices:	Geneva
	Lausanne
Areas of Practice:	Full Service

Switzerland *continued*

Roesle, Frick & Partner

Bleicherweg 18
P.O. Box 2745
8022 Zurich
Switzerland

Telephone:	41-43-344-2222
Fax:	41-43-344-2211
E-Mail:	rfpzh@rfplegal.ch
Internet:	www.rfplegal.ch
Partners:	*Max Roesle*
	Bruno Frick
Number of Lawyers:	8
Other Office:	Pfaffikon
Areas of Practice:	Full Service

Perreard, de Boccard, Kohler, Ador & Partners

44, Avenue Krieg
1208 Geneva
Switzerland

Telephone:	41-22-839-1111
Fax:	41-22-839-1100
E-Mail:	legal@pbka.ch
Internet:	www.pbka.ch
Partners:	*Georges E. Perreard*
	Andre Tombet
	Philippe de Boccard
Number of Lawyers:	21
Areas of Practice:	Full Service

Gloor & Sieger

Utoquai 37
P.O. Box 581
CH-8024 Zurich
Switzerland

Telephone:	41-44-254-6161
Fax:	41-44-254-6171
E-Mail:	lawyers@gloor-sieger.ch
Internet:	www.gloor-sieger.ch
Partners:	*Alain Gloor*
	Daniel Marugg
	Kurt Sieger
	Daniel Wehrli
Number of Lawyers:	11
Areas of Practice:	Full Service

Schellenberg Wittmer

Lowenstrasse 19
P.O. Box 6333
8023 Zurich
Switzerland

Telephone:	41-44-215-5252
Fax:	41-44-215-5200
E-Mail:	zurich@swlegal.ch
Internet:	www.swlegal.ch
Partners:	*Georg von Segesser*
	Martin Bernet
	Manuel Liatowitsch
Number of Lawyers:	102
Other Office:	Geneva
Areas of Practice:	Full Service

Walder Wyss & Partners

Seefeldstrasse 123
Ch-8034 Zurich
Switzerland

Telephone:	41-44-498-9898
Fax:	41-44-498-9899
E-Mail:	dhofmann@wwp.ch
Internet:	www.wwp.ch
Partners:	*Dieter Hofmann*
	Veli Sommer
Number of Lawyers:	111
Areas of Practice:	Full Service

Zwicky Windlin & Partner

Seepank/Gardenstrasse 4
CH-6304 Zug
Switzerland

Telephone:	41-44-728-7161
Fax:	41-41-728-7166
E-Mail:	info@zwlawyers.com
Internet:	www.zwlawyers.com
Partner:	*Markus Ziday*
Number of Lawyers:	10
Areas of Practice:	Full Service

Hartmann Muller Partner

Zurichbergstrasse 66
CH-8044 Zurich
Switzerland

Telephone:	41-43-268-8300
Fax:	41-43-268-8301
E-Mail:	contact@hmp.ch
Internet:	www.hmp.ch
Partners:	*Jurg E. Hartmann*
	Niklaus B. Muller
	Christoph Martig
Number of Lawyers:	10
Areas of Practice:	Full Service

Bratschi Wiederkehr & Bnob

Bahnofstrasse 46/106
CH-8021- Zurich
Switzerland

Telephone:	
Fax:	41-58-258-1099
E-Mail:	zuerich@bratschi-law.ch
Internet:	www.bratschi-law.ch
Partner:	*Florian Stefan Jorg*
Number of Lawyers:	62
Other Offices:	Bern
	St. Gallen
	Basel
	Zug
Areas of Practice:	Full Service

Switzerland continued

Homburger

Weinbergstrasse 56/58
8006 Zurich
Switzerland

Telephone:	41-43-222-1000
Fax:	41-43-222-1500
E-Mail:	lawyers@homburger.ch
Internet:	www.homburger.ch
Partners:	*Dieter v. Schulthess*
	Peter Widmer
	Markus H. Wirth

Number of Lawyers: 102

Python & Peter

Rue Firmin-Massot 9
1206 Geneva
Switzerland

Telephone:	41-22-702-1515
Fax:	41-22-702-1414
E-Mail:	mail@pplex.ch
Internet:	www.pplex.ch
Partner:	*Pierre-Yves Gunter*
Number of Lawyers:	67
Other Offices:	Lausanne
	Bern
	Sion
	Zug
	Brussels
	Tokyo
Areas of Practice:	Full Service

Syria

Law Offices of Dr. Moustafa Al-Sayed

23, Bahsa Street
Damascus
Syria

Telephone:	11-221-9177
Fax:	11-224-1251
E-Mail:	sayed-law@net.sy
Partner:	*Dr. Moutafa Al-Sayed*
Areas of Practice:	Full Service

Ghazi S. Ghazzi

Salhieh-Asia Clothes Building
Damascus
Syria

Telephone:	963-11-222-9798
Fax:	963-11-222-7648
E-Mail:	ahmadg@gsg-net.org
Partner:	*Ghazi S. Ghazzi*

Taiwan

Lee and Li

7th Floor, Formosa Plastics Building
201, Tun Hua North Road
P.O. Box 118-619
Taipei 10508
Taiwan

Telephone:	886-2-2715-3300
Fax:	886-2-2713-3966
E-Mail:	attorneys@leeandli.com
Internet:	www.leeandli.com
Partners:	*C. V. Chen*
	Chao-Tung Chang
Number of Lawyers:	530
Other Offices:	Hsinchu
	Taichung
	Kaohsiung
Areas of Practice:	Full Service

Formosa Transnational Attorneys at Law

13ᵗʰ Floor, Lotus Building
136, Jen-Ai Road, Section 3
Taipei 106
Taiwan

Telephone:	886-2-2755-7366
Fax:	866-2-2755-6486
E-Mail:	ftlaw@taiwanlaw.com
Internet:	www.taiwanlaw.com
Partners:	*John C. Chen*
	Paiff Huang
Number of Lawyers:	71
Other Office:	Kaohsiung
Areas of Practice:	Full Service

Tsar & Tsai Law Firm

8ᵗʰ Floor, 245 DunHua S. Road, Section 1
Taipei 106
Taiwan

Telephone:	886-2-2781-4111
Fax:	886-2-2721-3834
E-Mail:	tm@tsartsai.com.tw
Internet:	www.tsartsai.com.tw
Partners:	*Lillian Chu*
	C.Y. Huang
Number of Lawyers:	68
Other Office:	Hsinchu City
Areas of Practice:	Full Service

Huang & Partners

9th Floor, No. 563 Chung Hsiao East Road,
Section 4 Taipei
Taiwan

Telephone:	886-2-2746-0868
Fax:	886-2-2764-2448
E-Mail:	unilaw@ms2.hinet.net
Internet:	www.hungandpartners.com.tw
Partners:	*T.C. Huang*
	Jamie C.M. Huang

Number of Lawyers: 11
Areas of Practice: Full Service

Pamir Law Group

116 Nanking East Road
Section 2
Taipei
Taiwan

Telephone:	886-2-2536-9788
E-Mail:	nchen@pamirlaw.com
Internet:	www.pamirlaw.com
Partners:	*Nicholas Chen*
	Michael David Lee

Number of Lawyers: 10
Areas of Practice: Full Service

Tanzania

Mkono & Company

9th Floor, PPF Tower
Garden Avenue/Ohio Street
P.O. Box 4369
Dar Es Salaam
Tanzania

Telephone:	255-22-211-8790
Fax:	255-22-211-6635
E-Mail:	info@mkono.com
Internet:	www.mkono.com
Partners:	*Nimrod Elireheemah Mkono*
	Wilbert B.L. Kapinga
Number of Lawyers:	20
Other Office:	Bujumbura
Areas of Practice:	Full Service

Thailand

Dej-Udom & Associates

Charn Issara Tower 9th Floor
942/142-3 Rama IV Road
Bangkok 10500
Thailand

Telephone:	66-2-233-0055
Fax:	66-2-236-6681
E-Mail:	dei-udom@dejudom.com
Internet:	www.dejudomlaw.com
Partners:	*Dej-Udom Krairit*
	Worawut Krairit

Number of Lawyers: 5
Areas of Practice: Full Service

Chandler and Thong-Ek Law Offices Limited

7th-9th Floors, Bubhajit Building
20 North Sathom Road
Bangkok 10500
Thailand

Telephone:	66-2-266-6485
Fax:	66-2-266-6483
E-Mail:	chandler@ctlo.com
Internet:	www.ctlo.com
Partners:	*Albert T Chandler*
	Niwes Phancharoenworakul

Number of Lawyers: 37
Areas of Practice: Full Service

Tilleke & Gibbins International Ltd.

Supalai Grand Tower
1011 Rama 3 Road
Chongnosi, Yannawa
Bangkok 10120
Thailand

Telephone:	66-2653-5555
Fax:	66-2653-5678
E-Mail:	bangkok@tillekeandgibbins.com
Internet:	www.tillekeandgibbins.com
Partners:	*David Lyman*
	Alan Adcock
Other Offices:	Phuket
	Hanoi
	Ho Chi Minh City
Number of Lawyers:	94
Areas of Practice:	Full Service

Vickery & Worachai Ltd.

16th Floor, GPF Witthayu Tower A
93/1 Wireless Road
Lumpini, Pathumwan
Bangkok 10330
Thailand

Telephone:	66-2-256-6311
Fax:	66-2-256-6317
E-Mail:	vwlaw@loxinfo co.th
Internet:	www.v-w.co.th
Partners:	*Harold K Vickery, Jr.*
	Dusit Ali-Ishak
	Worachai Bhicharnchitr
Number of Lawyers:	16
Areas of Practice:	Full Service

Seri Manop & Doyle

21 Soi Amnuaywat
Sutthisan Road
Samsen Nok
Huaikwang
Bangkok 10310
Thailand

Telephone:	66-2-693-2036
Fax:	66-2-693-4189
E-Mail:	info@serimanop.com
Internet:	www.serimanop.com
Partners:	*Manop Nagadatta*
	Michael Doyle
Number of Lawyers:	14
Areas of Practice:	Full Service

Trinidad & Tobago

Fitzwilliam, Stone, Furness-Smith & Morgan
48-50 Sackville Street
P.O. Box 75
Port of Spain
Trinidad & Tobago

Telephone:	868-623-1618
Fax:	868-623-0605
E-Mail:	fitzstone@fitzwilliamstone.com
Internet:	www.fitzwilliamstone.com
Partners:	*Winston Alfred Thompson*
	Vishma Jaisingh
	Tara Mary Allum
Number of Lawyers:	22
Areas of Practice:	Full Service

Pollonais, Blanc, de la Bastide & Jacelon
Pembroke Court
17-19 Pembroke Street
P.O. Box 350
Port of Spain
Trinidad & Tobago

Telephone:	868-623-7496
Fax:	868-625-8415
E-Mail:	sdaly@trinidad.net
Partners:	*Edward A. Collier*
	Stephanie Daly
	Courtenay Braemar Williams
Number of Lawyers:	15
Other Office:	San Fernando
Areas of Practice:	Full Service

Tunisia

Al-Namouchi & Associates
5 Rue De Russie
Tunis 1000
Tunisia

Telephone:	216-132-3402
Fax:	216-132-1910
E-Mail:	alnamouchi.lawfirm@planet.tn
Partner:	*Moktar Namouchi*
Areas of Practice:	Full Service

Turkey

Birsel Law Offices

Inonu Caddesi, No. 53 Ongan Apartmani K: 4 Gumussuyu
34439 Istanbul
Turkey

Telephone:	90-212-245-5015
Fax:	90-212-245-5025
E-Mail:	istanbul@birset.com
Partners:	*Mahmut Tevfik Birsel*
	Arzu Aksac Yesilirmak
Other Offices:	Izmir
	Ankara
Number of Lawyers:	27
Areas of Practice:	Full Service

Herguner Bilgen Ozeke

Suleyman Seba Cad.
Siraevler 55, Akaretler
34357 Besiktas, Istanbul
Turkey

Telephone:	90-212-310-1800
Fax:	90-212-310-1899
E-Mail:	info@herguner.av.tr
Internet:	www.herguner.av.tr
Partners:	*Umit Herguner*
	Ayse Bilgen
	Ender Ozeke
	Tolga Danisman
Number of Lawyers:	45
Areas of Practice:	Full Service

Pekin & Pekin

Lamartine Caddesi 10
Taksim 34437
Istanbul
Turkey

Telephone:	90-212-313-3500
Fax:	90-212-313-3535
E-Mail:	postmaster@pekin-pekin.com
Partners:	*Ahmed Pekin*
	Fethi Pekin
	Vural Gunal
Number of Lawyers:	40
Areas of Practice:	Full Service

Turkmenistan

Grata Law Firm

7, Ainy Street
Ashgabat
Turkmenistan

Telephone:	998-90-188-6789
Fax:	998-71-120-4779
E-Mail:	zmalikov@gratanet.com
Internet:	www.gratanet.com
Partner:	*Zafar Malikov*
Other Offices:	Almaty
	Tashkent
	Baku
	Bishkek
Areas of Practice:	Full Service

AK Counsel

Trading Centre "Paytagt"
10 yil Abadanchilik St. 60
Ashgabat 74400
Turkmenistan

Telephone:	993-12-477-668
Fax:	993-12-477-669
E-Mail:	marla.valdez@dentonwildesapte.com
Internet:	www.dentonwildesapte.com
Partner:	*Marla Valdez*
Areas of Practice:	Business and Commercial Law

Turks and Caicos Islands

Misick & Stanbrook

Richmond House
P.O. Box 127
Leeward Highway
Providenciales
Turks and Caicos Islands

Telephone:	649-946-4732
Fax:	649-946-4734
E-Mail:	info@misickstanbrook.tc
Internet:	www.misickstanbrook.tc
Partners:	*Ariel R. Misick*
	Conrad Griffiths
Number of Lawyers:	12
Areas of Practice:	Full Service

Saunders & Co.

Town Centre Building
P.O. Box 257
Providenciales
Turks and Caicos Islands

Telephone:	649-941-4500
Fax:	649-941-4533
E-Mail:	saunders@ticway.tc
Internet:	www.tcilaw.com
Partner:	*Norman B. Saunders*
Number of Lawyers:	7
Areas of Practice:	Full Service

Uganda

Katende, Ssempebwa and Company

2nd Floor, Radiant House Building Plot 20, Kampala Road
P.O. Box 2344
Kampala
Uganda

Telephone:	256-414-233-770
Fax:	256-414-257-544
E-Mail:	kats@kats.co.ug
Internet:	www.kats.co.ug
Partner:	*John W. Katende*
Number of Lawyers:	21
Areas of Practice:	Full Service

Lex Uganda

8th Floor, Communications House
Plot 1, Colville Street
Kampala
Uganda

Telephone:	256-041-4232733
Fax:	256-041-4254721
E-Mail:	advocates@lexuganda.com
Internet:	www.lexuganda.com
Partners:	*Charles Odere*
	Mathias Nalyanya
	Edmund Kafanka Wakida
Number of Lawyers:	9
Areas of Practice:	Full Service

Synergy Solicitors & Advocates

Soliz House
23 Lumumba Avenue
Nakasero
Kampala
Uganda

Telephone:	256-774-594818
E-Mail:	bernard.katureebe@synergyadvocates.co.ug
Internet:	www.synergyadvocates.co.ug
Partners:	*Bernard Katureebe*
	Alexander Kibandama

Number of Lawyers: 8
Areas of Practice: Full Service

Ukraine

Vasil Kisil & Partners

Leonardo Business Centre
17/52A Bogdana
Khmelnistkogo Str
Kiev 01030
Ukraine

Telephone:	380-44-581-7777
Fax:	380-44-581-7770
E-Mail:	vkp@vkp.kiev.ua
Internet:	www.kisilandpartners.com
Partners:	*Vasil I. Kisil*
	Oleg A. Makarov
	Oleg Y Alyoshin
Number of Lawyers:	60
Areas of Practice:	Full Service

Konnov & Sozanovsky

23 Shota Rustaveli Street, Suite 3
Kiev 01019
Ukraine

Telephone:	380-44-490-5400
Fax:	380-44-490-5490
E-Mail:	info@konnov.com
Internet:	www.konnov.com
Partners:	*Sergei Sozanovsky*
	Sergei Konnov
Number of Lawyers:	50
Other Offices:	Chernovtsy
	London
	Moscow
	Nicosia
Areas of Practice:	Full Service

Noerr Tov

Vul. Khreschatyk, 7/11
01001 Kiev
Ukraine

Telephone:	380-44-495-3080
Fax:	380-44-495-3090
E-Mail:	m.pr@noree.com
Internet:	www.noerr.com
Partners:	*Mansur Pour Rafsendhani*
	Alexander Weigelt
Number of Lawyers:	13
Areas of Practice:	Full Service

Magisters

38 Volodymyrska St.
Kiev, 01034
Ukraine

Telephone:	380-44-492-8282
Fax:	380-44-206-7766
Internet:	www.magisters.com
Partner:	*Andrew Mac*
Number of Lawyers:	31
Other Offices:	Astana
	London
	Minsk
	Moscow
Areas of Practice:	Full Service

United Arab Emirates

All H. Ghosheh & Partners

Suite 1002, 10th Floor
The Blue Tower, Khalifa Street, P.O. Box 767
Abu Dhabi
United Arab Emirates

Telephone:	97-12-627-2323
Fax:	97-12-627-2979
E-Mail:	agosheh@emirates.net.ac
Partner:	*Ali H. Ghosheh*
Number of Lawyers:	4
Areas of Practice:	Full Service

Al Tamimi & Company

Dubai International Financial Centre
6th Floor, Building 4 East
Sheikh Zayed Road
P.O. Box 9275
Dubai
United Arab Emirates

Telephone:	971-43-641-641
Fax:	971-43-641-777
E-Mail:	info@tamimi.com
Partners:	*Essam Al Tamimi*
	Hasam Hourani
Number of Lawyers:	250
Other Offices:	Abu Dhabi
	Sharjah
	Riyadh
	Amman
	Doha
	Kuwait
	Baghdad
Areas of Practice:	Full Service

United Kingdom

Herbert Smith

Exchange House
Primrose Street
London EC2A 2HS
England

Telephone:	44-20-7374-8000
Fax:	44-20-7374-0888
E-Mail:	contact@herbertsmith.com
Internet:	www.herbertsmith.com
Partners:	*Christopher Harrison*
	Richard Fleck
	Clive Barnard
Number of Lawyers:	811
Other Offices:	Brussels
	Paris
	Moscow
	Dubai
	Abu Dhabi
	Hong Kong
	Beijing
	Shanghai
	Tokyo
	Bangkok
	Singapore
	Madrid
Areas of Practice:	Full Service

Allen & Overy

One Bishops Square
London E1 6AD
England

Telephone:	44-20-3088-0000
Fax:	44-20-3088-0088
E-Mail:	information@allenovery.com
Internet:	www.allenovery.com
Partners:	*Michael Reynolds (Brussels)*
	David Morley
	James Grandolfo (Hong Kong)
	Thomas Jones (Hong Kong)
	Harmut Krause (Frankfurt)
	Adam Farlow
	Stephen Denyer (Frankfurt)
	Wim Dejonghe (Brussels)
	Jeffrey Golden
	Anne Baldock
Number of Lawyers:	2100
Other Offices:	Numerous
Areas of Practice:	Full Service

Stone Chambers

4 Field Court
Gray's Inn
London WC1R 5EF
England

Telephone:	44-2-7440-6900
Fax:	44-20-7242-0197
E-Mail:	clerks@stonechamber.com
Partner:	*Steven Gee*
Number of Lawyers:	24
Areas of Practice:	Litigation
	Arbitration

CMS Cameron McKenna

Mitre House
160 Aldersgate Street
London EC1A 4DD
England

Telephone:	44-20-7367-3000
Fax:	44-20-7367-2000
E-Mail:	law-now.administrator@cms-cmck.com
Internet:	www.cms-cmck.com
Partners:	*Duncan Aldred*
	Edward Benzecry
	Fiona Woolf
	Penelope Warne
Number of Lawyers:	2240
Other Offices:	Numerous
Areas of Practice:	Full Service

Clyde & Co.

51 Eastcheap
London EC3M 1JP
England

Telephone:	44-020-7623-1244
Fax:	44-020-7623-5427
Internet:	www.clydeco.com
Partners:	*Chris Harris*
	Conrod Walker
Number of Lawyers:	463
Other Offices:	Numerous
Areas of Practice:	Full Service

Clifford Chance LLP

10 Upper Bank Street
London E14 5JJ
England

Telephone:	44-207-006-1000
Fax:	44-207-006-5555
E-Mail:	info@cliffordchance.com
Internet:	www.cliffordchance.com
Partners:	*David R. Childs*
	Jeremy V. Sandelson
	Stuart G. Popham
	David Harkness
Number of Lawyers:	3500
Other Offices:	Numerous
Areas of Practice:	Full Service

Reynolds Porter Chamberlain

Tower Bridge House
St. Katharine's Way
London E1W 1AA
England

Telephone:	44-203-060-6000
Fax:	44-203-060-7000
E-Mail:	enquiries@rpc.co.uk
Internet:	www.rpc.co.uk
Partners:	*Robert Hogarth*
	Jonathan Wafmough
Number of Lawyers:	260
Areas of Practice:	Full Service

Simmons & Simmons

Citypoint
One Ropemaker Street
London EC2Y 9SS
England

Telephone:	44-20-7628-2020
Fax:	44-20-7628-2070
E-Mail:	enquiries@simmons-simmons.com
Internet:	www.simmons-simmons.com
Partners:	_Jan Cullen_
	Peter Manning
	David Dickinson
	Andrew Wingfield (Doha)
	Mark Dawkins
	John Slater (Hong Kong)
Number of Lawyers:	782
Other Offices:	Numerous
Areas of Practice:	Full Service

Fox Williams LLP

Ten Dominion Street
London EC2M 2EE
England

Telephone:	44-20-7628-2000
Fax:	44-20-7628-2100
E-Mail:	mail@foxwilliams.com
Internet:	www.foxwilliams.com
Partners:	_Tina Williams_
	Paul Osborne
Number of Lawyers:	42
Areas of Practice:	Full Service

Linklaters

One Silk Street
London EC2Y 8HQ
England

Telephone:	44-20-7456-2000
Fax:	44-20-7456-2222
E-Mail:	info@linklaters.com
Internet:	www.linklaters.com
Partners:	*William Buckley*
	David Cheyne
	Simon Davies
	Caird Forbes-Cockell (New York)
	Guy Brannan
Number of Lawyers:	2,700
Other Offices:	Numerous
Areas of Practice:	Full Service

Travers Smith

10 Snow Hill
London EC1A 2AL
England

Telephone:	44-20-7295-3000
Fax:	44-20-7295-3500
E-Mail:	Andrew.lilley@traverssmith.com
Internet:	www.traverssmith.com
Partners:	*Andrew Lilley*
	Chris Carroll
	Chris Hale
	Spencer Summerfield
	David Patient
	Andrew Gillen
Number of Lawyers:	255
Other Office:	Paris
Areas of Practice:	Full Service

Charles Russell

5 Fleet Place
London EC4A 7RD
England

Telephone:	44-20-7203-5000
Fax:	44-20-7203-0200
E-Mail:	enquiries@charlesrussell.co.uk
Internet:	www.charlesrussell.co.uk
Partners:	*James Holder*
	Michael Bennett
	David Berry
	James Hyne
Number of Lawyers:	161
Other Offices:	Guildford
	Geneva
	Oxford
	Cheltenham
	Cambridge
	Bahrain
Areas of Practice:	Full Service

Freshfields Bruckhaus Deringer

65 Fleet Street
London EC4Y 1HS
England

Telephone:	44-20-7936-4000
Fax:	44-20-7832-7001
E-Mail:	enquiries@freshfields.com
Internet:	www.freshfields.com
Partners:	*Stuart Axford*
	Chris Barratt
	Peter Green
Number of Lawyers:	2554
Other Offices:	Numerous
Areas of Practice:	Full Service

Lovells

Atlantic House
Holborn Viaduct
London EC1A 2FG
England

Telephone:	44-20-7296-2000
Fax:	44-20-7296-2001
E-Mail:	information@lovells.com
Internet:	www.lovells.com
Partners:	*John T. Young*
	David Latham
	Philip Gershuny
	Chris Grierson
	Karen Hughes
Number of Lawyers:	2660
Other Offices:	Numerous
Areas of Practice:	Full Service

Fladgate LLP

25 North Row
London W1K6DJ
England

Telephone:	44-20-7323-4747
Fax:	44-20-7629-4414
E-Mail:	fladgate@fladgate.com
Internet:	www.fladgate.com
Partners:	*Paul Howcroft*
	Paul Leese
Number of Lawyers:	112
Areas of Practice:	Full Service

Norton Rose

3 More London Riverside
London SE1 2AQ
England

Telephone:	44-20-7283-6000
Fax:	44-20-7283-6500
E-Mail:	info@nortonrose.com
Internet:	www.nortonrose.com
Partners:	*Nick Adams*
	Stephen Parrish
	Deirdre Walker
	Peter Martyr
	Caroline May
	Mark Jones
Number of Lawyers:	1812
Other Offices:	Numerous
Areas of Practice:	Full Service

Slaughter & May

One Bunhill Row
London EC 1Y 8YY
England

Telephone:	44-20-7600-1200
Fax:	44-20-7090-5000
E-Mail:	mail@slaughterandmay.com
Internet:	www.slaughterandmay.com
Partners:	*Graham White*
	Nigel Boardman
	Chris Saul
	Andrew Balfour
	George Seligman
	Philip Snell
Other Offices:	Hong Kong
	Brussels
	Beijing
Areas of Practice:	Full Service

DLA Piper UK LLP

3 Noble Street
London EC2V 7EE
England

Telephone:	44-8700-111-111
Fax:	44-207-796-6666
E-Mail:	info@dlapiper.com
Internet:	www.dlapiper.com
Partners:	*Catherine Usher*
	Nigel Knowles
	Elisabeth Bremner
	Andrew Darwin
Number of Lawyers:	Numerous
Other Offices:	Numerous
Areas of Practice:	Full Service

Field Fisher Waterhouse

35 Vine Street
London EC3N 2AA
England

Telephone:	44-20-7861-4000
Fax:	44-20-7488-0084
E-Mail:	info@ffw.com
Internet:	www.ffw.com
Partners:	*Charles Whiddington*
	Moira Gilmore
	Nicholas Thompsell
Number of Lawyers:	366
Other Offices:	Brussels
	Hamburg
	Manchester
	Paris
Areas of Practice:	Full Service

Dundas & Wilson

Northwest Wing
Bush House
Aldwych
London WC2B 4EZ
England

Telephone:	44-20-7240-2401
Fax:	44-20-7240-2448
E-Mail:	john.verrill@dundas-wilson.com
Partner:	*John Rothwell Verrill*
Number of Lawyers:	403
Other Offices:	Glasgow
	Edinburgh
Areas of Practice:	Full Service

Brabners Chaffe Street

Horton House
Exchange Flags
Liverpool L2 3YL
England

Telephone:	44-151-600-3000
Fax:	44-151-227-3185
E-Mail:	maurice.watkins@brabnerscs.com
Internet:	www.brabnerschaffestreet.com
Partners:	*Mark Brandwood*
	Maurice Watkins
Number of Lawyers:	222
Other Offices:	Manchester
	Preston
Areas of Practice:	Full Service

Berwin Leighton Paisner

Adelaide House
London Bridge
London EC4R 9HA
England

Telephone:	44-20-7760-1000
Fax:	44-20-7760-1111
E-Mail:	info@blplaw.com
Internet:	www.blplaw.com
Partners:	*Harold Paisner*
	Neville Eisenberg
Number of Lawyers:	1,300
Other Offices:	Brussels
	Abu Dhabi
	Moscow
	Paris
	Singapore
Areas of Practice:	Full Service

Denton Wilde Sapte

One Fleet Place
London EC4M 7WS
England

Telephone:	44-20-7242-1212
Fax:	44-20-7246-7777
E-Mail:	info@dentonwildesapte.com
Internet:	www.dentonwildesapte.com
Partners:	*Howard Morris*
	Guy Fifield
	Ingrid Silver
	Jerry Katzman
	Nick Graham
	Ibraham Elsadig (Dubai)
	Robert Finney
	Neil Cuthbert (Dubai)
	Simon Cook
	Martin Kitchen
Number of Lawyers:	965
Other Offices:	Numerous
Areas of Practice:	Full Service

Olswang

90 High Holborn
London WC1V 6XX
England

Telephone:	44-20-7067-3000
Fax:	44-20-7067-3999
E-Mail:	london@olswang.com
Internet:	www.olswang.com
Partners:	*Steven Baker*
	Marcus Barclay
Other Offices:	Thames Valley
	Brussels
	Berlin

Ashurst

Broadwalk House
5 Appold Street
London EC2A 2HA
England

Telephone:	44-20-7638-1111
Fax:	44-20-7638-1112
E-Mail:	enquiries@ashurst.com
Internet:	www.ashurts.com
Partners:	*Geoffrey Green*
	Charlie Geffen
	Daniel R. Bushner
	Simon Bromwich
Number of Lawyers:	900
Other Offices:	Numerous
Areas of Practice:	Full Service

Eversheds

1 Wood Street
London EC2V 7W5
England

Telephone:	44-20-7919-4500
Fax:	44-20-7919-4919
E-Mail:	online@eversheds.com
Internet:	www.eversheds.com
Partners:	*Comelius Medvei*
	Anthony Arter
	Bryan Hughas
	David Gray
Number of Lawyers:	1200
Other Offices:	Numerous
Areas of Practice:	Full Service

Withers LLP

16 Old Bailey
London EC4M 7 EG
England

Telephone:	44-20-7597-6000
Fax:	44-20-7597-6543
Internet:	www.withersworldwide.com
Partners:	*Richard Cassell*
	Anthony Indaimo
Number of Lawyers:	387
Other Offices:	Geneva
	Milan
	Tortola
	New York
	New Haven
	Greenwich
	Hong Kong
Areas of Practice:	Full Service

Uruguay

Guyer & Regules

Plaza Independencia 811
11100 Montevideo
Uruguay

Telephone:	598-2-902-1515
Fax:	598-2-902-5454
E-Mail:	post@guyer.com.uy
Internet:	www.guyer.com.uy
Partners:	*Nicolas Herrera*
	Alvaro Tarabal
Number of Lawyers:	72
Areas of Practice:	Full Service

Ferrere

Av. Dr. Luis A. de Herrera
1248 World Trade Center, Torre B
Montevideo
Uruguay

Telephone:	598-2-623-0000
Fax:	598-2-628-2100
E-Mail:	ferrere@ferrere.com
Internet:	www.ferrere.com
Partners:	*Daniel M. Ferrere*
	Alberto Varela Rellan
Other Offices:	Numerous
Areas of Practice:	Full Service

Hughes & Hughes

25 de Mayo, 455
11000 Montevideo
Uruguay

Telephone:	598-2-916-0988
Fax:	598-2-916-1003
E-Mail:	h&h@hughes.com.uy
Internet:	www.huges.com.uy
Partners:	*Marcela Hughes*
	Haroldo Espalter

Number of Lawyers: 23
Areas of Practice: Full Service

Olivera & Delpiazzo

Misiones 1424, 2nd Floor
11000 Montevideo
Uruguay

Telephone:	598-2-916-5859
Fax:	598-2-916-5863
E-Mail:	olidelp@olidelp.com
Internet:	www.oliveraydelpiazzo.com
Partners:	*Ricardo Olivera Garcia*
	Carlos Delpiazzo

Number of Lawyers: 19
Areas of Practice: Full Service

Posadas, Posadas & Vecino

Juncal 1305, P. 21
CP 11100
Montevideo
Uruguay

Telephone:	598-2-916-2202
Fax:	598-2-916-2429
E-Mail:	mail@ppv.com.uy
Internet:	www.ppv.com.uy
Partners:	*German Vecino Sanchez*
	Ignacio de Posadas Montero
Number of Lawyers:	31
Areas of Practice:	Full Service

U.S. Virgin Islands

Birch, Dejongh & Hindels

Pointsetta House at Bluebeard's Castle
1330 Estate Taarenberg
Charlotte Amalie, St. Thomas 00802
U.S. Virgin Islands
Telephone: 340-774-1100
Fax: 340-774-7300
E-Mail: birchdej@viaccess.net
Partner: *James Hindels*
Number of Lawyes: 3
Areas of Practice: Full Service

Bolt Nagi PC

Corporate Place
5600 Royal Dane Mall
St. Thomas 00802-6410
U.S. Virgin Islands
Telephone: 340-774-2944
Fax: 340-776-1639
E-Mail: tbolt@vilaw.com
Internet: www.vilaw.com
Partner: *Tom Bolt*
Number of Lawyers: 8
Areas of Practice: Full Service

Dudley Clark & Chan

9720 Estate Thomas
Havensight Executive Tower
St. Thomas 00802
U.S. Virgin Islands

Telephone:	340-776-7474
Fax:	340-776-8044
E-Mail:	info@dudleylaw.com
Internet:	www.dudleylaw.com
Partners:	*Adriane J. Dudley*
	Bennett Chan

Number of Lawyers: 11
Areas of Practice: Full Service

Uzbekistan

Denton Wilde Sapte CA Limited
90 Acad. Vosit Vkhidov St.
Yakkasarayskiy District
Tashkent 100031
Uzbekistan

Telephone:	998-71-120-6946
Fax:	998-71-120-6185
E-Mail:	marla.valdez@dentonwildesapte.com
Internet:	www.dentonwildesapte.com
Partner:	*Marla Valdez*
Number of Lawyers:	4
Areas of Practice:	Full Service

Venezuela

Benson, Perez Matos, Antakly & Watts

Edificio Centro Altamira
Avenida San Juan Bosco
Urb. Altamira
Apartado Postal 69056
Caracas 1062-A
Venezuela

Telephone:	58-212-265-38-01
Fax:	58-212-261-24-93
E-Mail:	bpmawccs@bpmaw.com
Internet:	www.bpmaw.com
Partners:	*Farid Antakly*
	R. Alberto Parra-Febres
Number of Lawyers:	25
Other Offices:	Maturin
	Barcelona
	Puerto Diaz

Hoet Pelaez Castillo & Deque

Centro San Ignacio
Av. Blandin, Torre Kepler
La Castellana
Caracas 1060
Venezuela

Telephone:	58-212-201-8611
Fax:	58-212-263-7744
E-Mail:	infolaw@hpcd.com
Internet:	www.hpcd.com
Partners:	*Franklin Hoet-Linares*
	Fernando Pelaez-Pier
	Francisco M Castillo-Garcia
	Roman Jose Duqe-Corredor
Number of Lawyers:	42
Areas of Practice:	Full Service

Travieso Evans Arria Rengel & Paz

Torre La Castellana, Piso 6
Principal De La Castellana, Urb. La Castellana
Caracas 1060
Venezuela

Telephone:	58-212-277-3333
Fax:	58-212-277-3334
E-Mail:	legal@traviesoevans.com
Internet:	www.traviesoevans.com
Partners:	*Francisco Paz Parra*
	Olga Nass de Massiani
Number of Lawyers:	36
Other Offices:	Maturin
	Maracaibo
	Valencia
	Puerto La Cruz
Areas of Practice:	Full Service

De Sola Pate & Brown

Torre Domus, Av. Abraham Lincoln
Caracas 1050-A
Venezuela

Telephone:	58-212-793-9898
Fax:	58-212-793-9043
E-Mail:	dplaw@desolapate.com
Internet:	www.desolapate.com
Partners:	*John R. Pate*
	Arturo De Sola Lander
Number of Lawyers:	10
Areas of Practice:	Full Service

Tinoco, Travieso, Planchart & Nunez

Avenida Francisco de Miranda
Torre Country Club, Pisos 2 y 3
Caracas 1050
Venezuela

Telephone:	58-212-952-9033
Fax:	58-212-953-1053
E-Mail:	ttpn@ttpn.com.ve
Internet:	www.ttpn.com.ve
Partners:	*Gustavo Planchart Manrique*
	Alfredo Travieso Passios
	Jose Santiago Nunez Gomez
Number of Lawyers:	31
Areas of Practice:	Full Service

Imery Urdaneta Calleja Itriago Flamarique

Multicentro Empresarial del Este
Torre Libertador Nucleo A
Av. Libertador, Chacao 1060
Caracas
Venezuela

Telephone:	58-212-265-9745
Fax:	58-212-265-9723
E-Mail:	purdaneta@imeryurdaneta.com
Internet:	www.imerygurdaneta.com
Partner:	*Pedro Urdaneta*
Number of Lawyers:	15
Areas of Practice:	Full Service

Raffalli de Lemos Halvorssen Ortega y Ortiz

Torre Forum
Calle Guaicaipuro El Rosal
Caracas 1060
Venezuela

Telephone:	58-212-952-0995
Fax:	58-212-952-4415
E-Mail:	info@rdhoo.com
Internet:	www.rdhoo.com
Partners:	*Rafael de Lemos*
	Jose Manuel Ortega
Number of Lawyers:	17
Areas of Practice:	Full Service

Vietnam

Tran H.N. & Associates

1 Nguyen Gia Thieu
P.O. Box 456
Hanoi
Vietnam

Telephone:	84-4-942-0020
Fax:	84-4-942-0040
E-Mail:	than@hn.vnn.vn
Internet:	www.than.com
Partners:	*Tran Huu Nam*
	Nguyen Quoc Hung
Number of Lawyers:	3
Areas of Practice:	Intellectual Property

Kelvin Chia Partnership

Unit 1801 Saigon Tower
29 Ton Doc Thang Street
Riverside Office Center District 1
Ho Chi Minh City
Vietnam

Telephone:	84-8-3822-4986
Fax:	84-8-3824-5441
E-Mail:	Kelvin.chia@kcpartnership.com
Partners:	*Kelvin Chia*
	Cheah Swee Gim
Number of Lawyers:	65
Other Offices:	Singapore
	Hanoi
	Yangon
	Shanghai
	Pyongyang
	Phnom Penh
	Bangkok
	Tokyo
Areas of Practice:	Full Service

Duane Morris Vietnam LLC

Suite 809, Saigon Tower
29 Le Duan Street
District 1, Ho Chi Minh City
Vietnam

Telephone:	84 8 3827 9460
Fax:	84 8 3827 9470
E-Mail:	gtcooper@duanemorris.com
Internet:	www.duanemorris.com
Partner:	*Giles T. Cooper*
Number of Lawyers:	700 (6 in Vietnam)
Other Offices:	Numerous
Areas of Practice:	Full Service

Yemen

Law Offices of Sheikh Tariq Abdullah

P.O. Box 148
Al-Sabeel Street
Crater
Aden
Yemen

Telephone:	967-2-255-305
Fax:	967-2-251-638
E-Mail:	relevant@y.net.ye
Internet:	www.yemenlaw-relevant.com
Partners:	*Sheikh Tariq Abdullah*
	Fuad Abdul Hameed

Number of Lawyers: 4
Areas of Practice: Full Service

Zambia

Ezugha, Musonda and Company

Angoni House
Obote Avenue
Kitwe
Zambia

Telephone:	260-2-224843
Fax:	260-2-220-539
E-Mail:	ezugham@zammet.zm
Partner:	*William B. Nyirenda*

Sharpe & Howard

Anglo American Annex Building
Plot 74
Independence Avenue
P.O. Box 32587
Lusaka
Zambia

Telephone:	260-1-256-424
E-Mail:	nicola.sharpe@sharpehoward.com
Partners:	*Nicola Sharpe-Phiri*
	Andrew Howard
Number of Lawyers:	6
Areas of Practice:	Full Service

Zimbabwe

Atherstone & Cook

7th Floor, Mercury House
24 Geroge Silundika Avenue
P.O. Box 2625
Harare
Zimbabwe

Telephone:	263-4-704-244
Fax:	263-4-705-180
E-Mail:	generalr@praetonco.zw
Partners:	*Simon Burl*
	Linda Cook
Number of Lawyers:	14
Areas of Practice:	Full Service

Coghlan Welsh & Guest

Executive Chambers
14-16 George Silundika Avenue
P.O. Box 53
Harare
Zimbabwe

Telephone:	263-4-758-472
Fax:	263-4-756-268
E-Mail:	email@cwg.co.zw
Internet:	www.cwg.co.zw
Partner:	*David Morgan*
Number of Lawyers:	10
Areas of Practice:	Full Service

Gill Godlonton & Gerrans

Beverley Court
100 Nelson Mandela Avenue
Harare
Zimbabwe

Telephone:	263-4-707-023
Fax:	263-4-707-380
E-Mail:	ggg@ggg.co.zw
Internet:	www.ggg.co.zw
Partner:	_James Henry Pennell Black_
Number of Lawyers: 9	
Areas of Practice:	Full Service

Excerpt from

THE ABA GUIDE TO INTERNATIONAL BUSINESS NEGOTIATIONS (3d Ed.)

Chapter 10
"Selecting and Dealing with Foreign Lawyers"
by Henry T. King, Jr. & James R. Silkenat

1. Introduction

Like all businesses in this age of increasing globalization, continuing on an accelerated basis, the move toward truly global, transnational business continues to expand daily. Like any business, large law firms are becoming transnational in their structure. At the same time, new technology is helping smaller law firms form alliances and transact business regardless of national boundaries. A remarkable sensitivity to discrete cultures and legal systems is required of international lawyers and businesspeople. This, in turn, requires both small and large law firms to bring the best of both worlds to bear on the needs of their international and foreign clientele: local law firm savvy matched with twenty-first-century resources.

The world has changed greatly in its handling of international transactions, and the number of countries participating in the global market has grown rapidly. This makes life interesting, but also makes it more complex, because the approaches for dealing with this diversity have to be.

2. Selecting a Foreign Lawyer

Foreign lawyers are a primary means for bridging the gulf between U.S. negotiators and foreign parties. The selection of a foreign lawyer may well influence the success or failure of the negotiation. In light of this potential impact on transactions, a foreign lawyer must be selected with great care, and the differences between negotiating domestic transactions and international transactions must be recognized. Frequently, these differences are based on culture, religion, and historical background. The foreign lawyer is helpful by virtue of being a product of his national culture, but at the same time he must meet certain requirements.

In selecting foreign lawyers or law firms, keep in mind the need for technical skills and knowledge. Experience gained from other transactions is also important because almost inevitably it will be useful in your transaction. Particularly when government clearances are involved, a foreign lawyer doing multiple transactions needs to have a good feel for what will be approved and not approved. Furthermore, the lawyer may have the governmental contacts that will facilitate these approvals.

The foreign lawyer's objectivity in telling you what you need to know is important. He should have an understanding of what is doable and what is not doable, both in terms of the local context and in terms of your relationship with your client's preferred partner or any other party involved in the transaction.

American business operates with a sense of urgency. But this is not necessarily the way business is done in other countries. You need to find a lawyer with the same sense of the need for getting things done within a defined time frame as you have.

In some countries, particularly in the Far East, negotiations take significant amounts of time, almost by definition. Progress seems glacial, and your lawyer (wisely selected) can advise you on the time frame with which you are dealing. He can tell you when delaying tactics are being used and when time delays are simply par for the course and may actually be ways for the parties involved to get to know one another better. Bear in mind that business is, in general, more personal outside the United States, and that once a personal relationship has been established, it may well stand the test of time and indeed be more lasting than in countries where quick rapport is firmed up almost immediately.

An excellent working knowledge of both English and the host country language is mandatory for an effective foreign counsel. This enables your local counsel to brief you on the slang, innuendos, and double meanings of the foreign language, and helps ensure that both parties fully understand the contractual relationship into which they are entering. The depth of understanding achieved will be insurance toward making the contract work for both parties.

It is also important that a foreign lawyer have as good an awareness of the U.S. context as possible. He needs to have an appreciation of our legislative ethics in dealing with foreign government officials. Our Foreign Corrupt Practices Act, for example, is different from the laws of many other countries that have such statutes, in that it is rigidly enforced. Indeed, both Germany and Japan have enacted similar legislation, but we do not know whether it will be followed by U.S.-style enforcement. The foreign lawyer needs to know what will and what will not fly under the law and be prepared to apprise you immediately of any unacceptable activities.

A sense of empathy can be an important glue in the relationship between the U.S. negotiator and a foreign counsel. There has to be a free exchange of ideas between you and your foreign counterpart. Any fears you have should be conveyed to your foreign counsel with complete candor and without holding anything back.

If possible, select a lawyer with good business sense. After all, the success of your negotiation will be determined by the bottom-line results of what you have negotiated. Some appreciation of the host-country tax context and how it relates to the U.S. tax context is, for example, a strong plus. A foreign lawyer's feel for the cost of any contract concessions you may have to consider is also important.

In negotiating a foreign contract you may have to sell the terms of the contract both to the foreign party and also to your own principal. Your foreign counsel's persuasiveness and credibility may go a long way in helping you establish the credibility of the results of the negotiation with your client.

Normally, your relationship with the foreign lawyer will not end with signing the contract. The foreign lawyer may well have to help you make the contract work. This means that his continuing relationship with the other parties to the contract will be critical. He must be loyal to you, yet maintain some working relationship with the other parties to the contract. He will probably be there as the results of the contract unfold and needs to keep you posted on how matters are progressing in the operation of the contract.

In the last analysis, your relationship with a foreign lawyer is a matter of trust and confidence. This will not come quickly but must develop over a period of time. When it has developed, it can be very fulfilling for both sides. But it takes time, and you always have to be aware of the context in which the foreign lawyer is operating when judging performance.

Thus, many highly specialized legal markets can only be served by establishing relationships with foreign firms as local counsel. This practice has resulted in an interesting hybrid: the large international firm staffed by that region's local legal elite. In some cases, this might offer the best of all worlds: sensitivity to and expertise in complex local cultural and legal issues, matched with the resources and expertise of a large "mega" firm.

Meanwhile, no assumptions should be made. The name and logo of a world-renowned firm do not in any way guarantee that this optimal fusion exists. One must carefully study the level of integration between the local office and the rest of the firm. Are the firm's offices technologically linked, so that information, including conflict checks, is shared across offices? Is the management structure of the firm such that local autonomy is grounded in the best practices of the larger firm as a whole? Further, is the staff of the local office a collection of home office transplants, or has the firm invested in cultivating high-quality local lawyers?

3. Region and Country-Specific Observations

Following are some brief characterizations of foreign lawyers and their approach to the law on a country-specific basis, grouped under the various regions of the world. These observations, while necessarily simplifications, are designed. to highlight some of the differences and similarities between foreign and U.S. lawyers that we have observed over a considerable period of time. Keep in mind that in a number of countries, particularly in Europe, American law firms have offices and their own way of doing things that may affect the style of local lawyers and the way they handle international transactions. Where available, they may well be a valuable resource.

3.1 Latin America

Argentina. There has not been much economic or political certainty in Argentina in recent years, and the lawyers there have had to adjust to it. Given the context, there is a high degree of professionalism and integrity, but it is incumbent at times to include a sense of urgency so that matters get done within a preplanned time frame. Just as you make demands for performance, see that your foreign counsel is paid in a timely manner. There are a number of excellent firms with which to work here.

Brazil. In Brazil, the caliber of lawyers varies widely, and the step down from top-flight to the next level is frequently significant. This means that a close check of possible Brazilian counsel before retaining them is essential.

Mexico. Mexican lawyers are technically and ethically sound, but delays are frequently the order of the day. It is sometimes very difficult to secure a prompt response to questions posed. The day starts later in Mexico, which means that Mexican working hours parallel ours to only a limited extent. On the other hand, some Mexican lawyers work very late. If you want to get the job done, you may have to adjust your working hours to those of your Mexican colleagues.

3.2 Europe

United Kingdom. In the United Kingdom, the caliber of lawyers is impressive, but they sometimes have a different business orientation than lawyers in the United States. At times they seem very legalistic, perhaps overly so. It is important, therefore, to make sure that U.K. counsel is aware of the business objectives behind the transaction on which you are seeking assistance, as well as the proposed time frame. Ethical standards are quite high.

Germany. German lawyers are generally very business-oriented and direct. In the international sector, they have a very good command of English. You can easily communicate what you want to accomplish in a few words, and can count on them to be very responsive. It is best to have German counsel who is tax-oriented. In the tax area, the line of demarcation between law firms and accounting firms is not clearly defined, and there are growing tendencies in companies to rely on accounting firms rather than law firms for tax advice.

Eastern Europe. Business lawyers, in the broad U.S. sense, did not exist under the previous communist regimes in the region. Lawyers familiar with international trade, finance, licensing, or joint ventures were few in number and employees of the communist governments. Currently, the legal profession in Central and Eastern Europe, like the legal system, is undergoing significant changes. The active study of western legal systems, associations with western law firms, and the emergence of new laws are all positive forces, as lawyers in these areas become familiar with a market economy system. Consequently, when selecting a local lawyer in Central or Eastern Europe, you should, with diligence, find numerous lawyers familiar with local laws and regulations, knowledgeable about required governmental approvals, and helpful with the language, culture, and local customs.

France. The French legal system seems in certain respects to be very conceptualistic and formalistic. There are ways of dealing with such matters, and French lawyers have learned how to utilize these approaches. French lawyers tend to be responsive and business-oriented. Documentation is almost always in French, but language is rarely a problem in negotiations. On the major questions of structuring transactions to limit tax exposure, French lawyers are quite knowledgeable. On tax matters involved in the operation of French companies, however, there is a tendency to refer such matters to firms of tax advisors (consisting of former French government officials) or to accounting firms.

Italy. In Italy, because of the nature of the Italian legal context, exchanges with Italian counsel may well be complex and extended. When exchanging legal views with Italian counsel, it is always important to keep your eye on the target and to make sure that the answer received responds to the question asked.

Spain. Spanish international lawyers are busy people. Additionally, significant legal work in Spain has until quite recently been concentrated in just a few firms, with the result that there has not always been an adequate supply of competent Spanish legal talent available to meet the foreign investor's needs. It is necessary to define priorities clearly so that your Spanish counsel has a good grasp of what is most important from your standpoint.

Switzerland. There are some fine Swiss corporate lawyers, but they often lack the tax sophistication that is necessary for U.S. client purposes. It can be awkward to get knee-deep in a transaction and then find that your Swiss lawyer is not tax-oriented. If your reasons for being in Switzerland are tax-related, you can save yourself a lot of pain and suffering if you thoroughly check out your prospective Swiss lawyer's tax experience. This may take time, but it is well worth the effort.

Turkey. There is not as much transactional experience historically in Turkey as in other European countries, and the role of your counsel, therefore, assumes special importance. As for location, you have two choices: Istanbul and Ankara. If it means an hour's flight to Ankara to get the right counsel, you should not be reluctant to make the trip. It may well save you much grief later on.

3.3 The Middle East

Iraq. The situation here is sufficiently complex that any summary would be outdated before this volume reaches print. The position of local counsel is likely to remain unsettled for some time.

Egypt. When selecting counsel in Egypt, a review of their capacity and competence should relate to their responsiveness and ability to serve you on a timely basis. One of the fine inheritances of Egypt from its colonial days is a very good legal system, but you need strong Egyptian legal assistance to make it work for you, and you need to be selective in locating such help because of the time pressures that will be on you.

Saudi Arabia. It is always good to have a counsel who knows what the government will and will not allow you to do. Frequently, lawyers with this qualification have worked at some time in their careers in a government capacity. Governmental experience gives a prospective counsel an excellent feel for how things work in Saudi Arabia and is invaluable in problem solving.

3.4 The Far East

Indonesia. There are a limited number of law firms in Indonesia that can adequately service international clients. To get the services you need, you may have to commit to a retainer arrangement. Get your arrangements with Indonesian counsel worked out prior to using the firm. If you have to go ahead on a retainer basis, by all means do so, but there should be a clear understanding between the parties as to just what legal areas the retainer arrangements cover.

Taiwan. Good legal services are available in Taiwan, but they do not come cheap. Internationally oriented law firms in Taiwan frequently have lawyers on board who have studied in the United States, so they are generally aware of U.S. requirements. Because of the distance from the United States, you will want an on-the-spot counsel who can promptly field many of the legal questions raised by the operating people who will be running your client's production facilities. It will be of particular importance to retain readily available counsel with whom your operating people feel compatible and with whom they can discuss proposed actions freely and candidly. Your Taiwan counsel should always be aware that it is his or her obligation to bring you into the loop on sensitive and important issues.

Former British Connections in Asia. Fortunately, Australia, New Zealand, Singapore, and Hong Kong have a common legal tradition. Lawyers from all these areas speak a common language, thereby avoiding the problems caused by translations. U.S. lawyers can generally expect prompt, courteous, and efficient service from their foreign counterparts in these jurisdictions.

Japan. In Japan, the situation has changed recently because of steps taken to open up to foreign lawyers the right to render legal services in that country. Previously, the few firms with western partners admitted to practice in Japan were at a premium and could pick and choose among the clients they served. The door has begun to open for U.S. lawyers who wish to practice in Japan, and the pressure is on the Japanese to widen that opening. This is a continuing process.

China. Chinese law firms of considerable talent and depth have emerged in the last decade. Several of them have offices in the U.S. and in multiple cities in China. English-language capacity can still be an issue, as can review of relevant conflict situations. The growth in sophistication of this market has been quite dramatic.

4. Conclusion

The capacity and status of foreign lawyers varies widely from country to country. In some instances, the pace of living is much different than that in the United States, and there can be less of a sense of urgency to finish a job. In other countries, the coverage of legal areas is not as well defined or complete as it is in this country, and there are gaps that foreign lawyers must try to fill with sound reasoning and good judgment.

Finally, the ethical climate for business in many countries can vary greatly from that in the United States. The role of the foreign lawyer in these countries assumes special importance because the lawyer may need to deal with both legal and ethical questions. What is more, he must have the confidence of the local management so that these questions are raised ahead of time, not after the fact. The role of counsel overseas in the greater business context is subject to wide variations. Our impression is that in the Middle East, it is best to have your documents prepared by U.S. counsel to the maximum extent possible. In Germany and certain other European countries, on the other hand, this is not as necessary. In fact, in Germany, lawyers prepare major transactions in their own desired form and frequently with great clarity and an economy of words.

In the tax area, which always has bottom-line impact, lawyers play a role that varies from country to country. We have always found tax competence to be a plus. But on matters such as reorganizations and mergers, as well as on operating problems, accounting firms are playing a more important role than in the past. There is often a good mesh between legal and accounting firms, but this is by no means always the case. The U.S. counsel's role is to see that matters requiring attention do not fall between the cracks.

Legal services overseas do not come cheap. You are sometimes charged the senior partner's rates (which will be quite high and may exceed US. rates) even though associates may actually be doing the legwork on a legal problem. It is, therefore, important that you think through problems prior to contacting foreign counsel. Often you will need to look into the foreign attorney's mind and see how he will view the question in his own context. By being precise with your questions, you can save time and money. For good order's sake and for the record, your questions to foreign counsel should always be by e-mail, fax, or letter. Telephone service in many areas of the world is still not good; moreover, recollections of an oral exchange may vary widely when the going gets rough.

The selection of foreign local counsel by US. companies needs to be done with a good sense of the legal context in which the foreign lawyer will operate. Some factors to be considered in your search include:

- Legal experience, including the handling of U.S. clients.
- Independence of judgment, particularly where the ethical context of business in the country is clouded.
- Business orientation or, specifically, an understanding of the bottom-line effects of particular legal approaches.
- Responsiveness: whether the proposed foreign counsel's track record and staffing equip the firm to handle your needs.
- Costs: These may, in some instances, be hard to establish beforehand, but must be considered in light of bottom-line requirements.

Excerpt from

the ABA Section of International Law and Practice's INTERNATIONAL LAWYER'S DESKBOOK (2d Ed.)

Chapter 26

"Selecting and Working With Foreign Counsel"
by William M. Hannay

* * *

II.　Selecting outside foreign counsel — where to look and factors to consider

A.　Outline the Matter/Expectations

Before U.S. counsel interviews and selects outside foreign counsel, it is important to take the time to sketch out the parameters of the international matter. What exactly does the client need? Is it researching local laws, drafting, negotiating, meeting with local government officials, handling litigation? Or is it limited to performing due diligence?

U.S. counsel should outline what is expected of foreign counsel. These expectations should then be reviewed with the client to confirm their accuracy. The client's short- and long-term objectives must be known as fully as possible, at the outset, in order to select appropriate outside foreign counsel and other advisors.

B.　Understand the Type of Lawyers that Are Available

Most law schools provide little or no training concerning the differences in the structure of the legal profession in different countries. Depending upon the jurisdictions involved, U.S. counsel may be working with more than one type of legal system. In some systems, the legal profession in organized differently from that in the U.S. The U.S. lawyer needs to understand the profession's local structure to determine whom to retain to fulfill his needs.

* * *

C. What Sort of Legal Services Does the U.S. Counsel Need?

Before U.S. counsel picks up the phone and starts calling foreign lawyers, it is essential to be clear what sort of legal services U.S. counsel needs. U.S. counsel should prepare an outline or summary of expectations and determine, to the extent possible, the client's/company's short- and long-term objectives. For example:

- Is U.S. counsel looking for advice on an isolated transaction? Or is U.S. counsel looking to begin a long-term relationship for the client/company because it expects to have significant in-country presence or on-going transactions?

- Is U.S. counsel looking for a general litigator in a foreign jurisdiction to handle a minor local business dispute? Or does U.S. counsel need an expert in a highly specialized subject matter?

- Is U.S. counsel looking for someone to make sure that the client/company is following the proper procedures to do business in a foreign country? Or is U.S. counsel looking for someone to help smooth the way in obtaining business from a foreign government?[1]

Once U.S. counsel has clearly in mind the nature of the assignment and the client's/company's needs, U.S. counsel can begin the search process for locating foreign counsel.

---

1   If it is the latter, U.S. counsel need to keep in mind the requirements of the Foreign Corrupt Practices Act and the risks associated with using local 'consultants' to obtain business from a foreign government.

D. Where to Look for Outside Foreign Counsel

How does U.S. counsel find the right lawyer? Selecting the proper outside foreign counsel to represent U.S. counsel in an international matters can be difficult. Where should U.S. counsel start? Who can U.S. counsel call? Are there any available directories to consult? If so, are they neutral sources or self-serving? Are they complete?

There are many sources to tap in creating a list of potential outside foreign counsel choices. Consult several sources, and look for recurrent names. If one lawyer's name keeps coming up, especially from word-of-mouth, that is a positive sign. The list below represents several typical sources that may be helpful:

- The Client's/Company's Regular U.S. Counsel – * * *
- Word of Mouth I: Other Lawyers – * * *
- Word of Mouth II: Other Professionals – * * *
- Multinational vs. National Firms – * * *
- "Multi-Disciplinary Practice" Firms – * * *
- Legal Directories – * * *
- Internet – * * *
- Government sources – * * *
- CLE Speakers or Authors – * * *

E. Factors to Consider When Retaining Foreign Counsel

Once U.S. counsel have compiled a list of potential outside foreign counsel, U.S. counsel are ready to embark on the process of contacting them via telephone, e-mail, or fax. Of course, if U.S. counsel have the opportunity to meet the candidate in person, by all means do so. This is especially important if the work will be long-term, expensive or strategically critical to the client.

* * *

1. The Comfort Level

Determine the foreign lawyer's qualifications. How comfortable does U.S. counsel feel that he has the types of experience the client's transaction will require? For example, if the deal involves multiple parties from multiple countries, does U.S. counsel feel confident that the potential foreign counsel has the requisite expertise?

Typically, U.S. counsel starts with an inquiry as to the attorney's education and training and then move on to his general experience. Constantly ask: what skills does the lawyer need for this engagement? For instance, will U.S. counsel benefit from retaining a lawyer with U.S. education (legal or other relevant graduate course work) or U.S. training? Is experience in representing clients from the U.S. important; or stated another way, is it important for the foreign lawyer to know the mindset of U.S. businessmen or lawyers?

Assess the lawyer's work environment. Is his office equipped with the technological resources needed for prompt responses? Is the equipment and software compatible with the working requirements of U.S. counsel and/or the client?

Does the lawyer exhibit any cultural biases? And, remember to ensure at the outset that there are no conflicts of interest (different jurisdictions have different standards).

2. Existing Representation in the Client's Industry

If the firm or contact lawyer represents clients in the client's industry, this will eliminate much time in explaining how the U.S. company does business, industry terms and paperwork, etc. If the foreign lawyer has experience representing clients in the industry, he will be able to flag issues and identify more concerns in much less billable time than a lawyer who has no background in the client's industry. Another potential benefit from retaining a lawyer with experience is that he may apprise the client of other business opportunities.

On the other hand, existing representations within the industry may be a negative if the firm or lawyer happens to represent the client's main competitor. In highly specialized areas of practice, it may be difficult to find an experienced practitioner that does not, especially in some countries where the pool of qualified potential counsel is relatively small.

If the lawyer has little or no previous industry experience, U.S. counsel and the client may lose valuable time explaining the basics. However, depending upon the client's business and philosophy, U.S. counsel might prefer a lawyer who does not represent clients in its industry and thereby reduce the risk of a conflict of interest.

The foreign lawyer should be expected to provide the client with the highest degree of expertise possible, all dependent upon the economic resources at hand, the amount to be invested and the potential risks.

3. References

It is important to obtain a list of other clients whom the foreign counsel has represented in similar engagements, including the name and telephone or e-mail address of a contact person at the client or of the lead attorney with whom he worked. Possibly there may be some local law restrictions or client confidentiality issues, but the prospective local counsel should be willing to help U.S. counsel work around them.

Once identified, U.S. counsel should contact the references. When doing so, one should be inquisitive. Ask for a general sketch of what was involved in past or present matters. What were the obstacles and significant achievements? Ask about the current status and the future outlook. U.S. counsel should then evaluate this information in order to draw independent conclusions.

4. Substantive Expertise

Evaluate the prospective counsel's expertise by issue area. For instance, can he provide U.S. counsel with the necessary tax guidance? (Keep in mind that lawyers in many countries may not be as specialized as those in the United States.)

If the client is looking for a suitable country in which to locate overseas manufacturing, are there tax incentives to help the client decide where to locate the business? Will it make a difference if the principal office is located in, for example, Holland or Belgium? The answer to these issues may not be obvious, and U.S. counsel should probe such issues during the initial consultation. Depending on the locale of the transaction, U.S. counsel might decide to seek tax advice from an accounting firm, and not an attorney.

During the initial meeting, the prospective foreign attorney can demonstrate his abilities by identifying big picture issues and providing U.S. counsel with a thumbnail sketch of the legal issues facing the project or litigation to review with the client.

U.S. counsel may also need to determine whether one firm will be able to provide advice on all of the areas of law implicated by the matter, *e.g.,* trademark, tax, labor/employment, and environmental. If not, U.S. counsel will need to retain multiple lawyers/firms.

It is equally important to assess prospective counsel's awareness of business and political as well as legal trends in his country. Assess, for example, what he knows of current business developments – *e.g.,* what is the competition doing and what industry trends are developing – that may positively or adversely affect the matter. If the lawyer lacks awareness in the business area, what assurances does U.S. counsel have that he keeps current on changes in local laws and key legal decisions?

5. Connections

It is important to explore whether the potential foreign counsel knows any individuals who are connected to the matter, *e.g.,* the president of the company the client intends to acquire, potential investors, key government officials, existing customers, potential customers, and/or the competition? For instance, if the transaction will require the government's consent (*e.g.,* permits), U.S. counsel may be well served with local foreign counsel who has already worked successfully with local government officials. However, this can be a double-edged sword. Foreign counsel may be related to a local official and make an inadvertent disclosure. Also, beware of connections without substance (*i.e.,* the person who is only well-connected), and of the U.S. [FCPA] law risks associated with payments to foreign officials. Consider including no-bribery pledges in an engagement letter if the transaction involves significant work with government officials and the country involved has a reputation for bribery.

6. Language Skills

While many sophisticated foreign attorneys and businessmen speak fluent English, it is not universally true, and it is certainly not to be expected in less developed areas of the world. To assess the language issues, begin at home: do the key participants at the client and/or U.S. counsel speak or read the language spoken in the foreign location and among the major players in the deal? How fluent are they? Be honest. U.S. counsel could be called upon to interpret a deal-breaking provision. If U.S. counsel does not possess expert language skills (and most U.S. lawyers do not), U.S. counsel need to select a foreign lawyer who does. Otherwise, U.S. counsel and the client will be at a disadvantage.

* * *

7. Flexibility, Technology, and Accommodation

A key question is how accommodating the lawyer will be. What is the candidate's degree of willingness to travel, work around the schedule, and the time tables for the deal? Does he have the flexibility and commitment to provide quality service and be mindful of budgetary considerations? Will U.S. counsel be charged for travel time?

Are he and his firm technologically up-to-date? Does he regularly use e-mail? Does his e-mail system readily accept document attachments? Does his office use word processing software that is compatible with the own? Finally, don't make assumptions about work habits or hours (*e.g.,* working weekends) and whether they will stay in communication with U.S. counsel if they are on holiday.

When interviewing potential outside foreign counsel, ask for clarification of what work the lawyer himself would do and what would be assigned to others. Also U.S. counsel need to make it quite clear what work will be performed by U.S. counsel or the client and what work the foreign lawyer will do. U.S. counsel may wish to prepare the first draft of documents or perform legal research to the extent logistically possible, collect information, and perform other necessary tasks in an effort to hold down costs. It is vital to clarify the expectations in this regard up front and make sure that the prospective foreign counsel is willing to accommodate them.

* * *

8. Worst-Case Scenarios

Before U.S. counsel and the client make a final selection of foreign counsel, it is critical to assess "worst case scenarios." What do the potential foreign counsel tell U.S. counsel can happen if the deal falls apart or if the litigation is unsuccessful? If two potential counsel differ radically in their opinions as to worst-case liabilities, seek out other counsel and call upon whatever other resources are available so that U.S. counsel and the client can draw their own conclusions.

* * *

9. Firmwide Capabilities

It is important to understand who will actually perform work on the matter and what their qualifications are. If this is not done, the client may find that it has hired the lawyer's associates when U.S. counsel intended to obtain the services of a particular individual whose skills and experience the client needed. U.S. counsel should review background information on the firm's expertise, the expertise of its members and the firm's office locations. Depending on the nature of the transaction or litigation, a firm with multiple locations or with firm members who have practiced or trained in various countries may give the client an advantage. This could depend upon the number of countries involved in the deal. One factor to consider is whether there is any additional cost, such as travel time and expenses, by using lawyers from multiple locations.

10. Fee Factors

There is no right or wrong answer when it comes to the issue of attorney's fees. However, make sure U.S. counsel understand from the beginning on what basis the client will be billed by the prospective foreign counsel. Determine at the outset what types of services and individuals (secretary, assistant, paralegal) for which/whom the firm intends to bill. Also, specify whether U.S. counsel prefer to limit the number (or identity) of lawyers working on the matter.

* * *

11. Attorney-Client Confidentiality

Do not presume that communications between foreign counsel and the client or between foreign counsel and U.S. counsel will be treated as privileged and confidential as they are in the United States. In some countries, inside attorneys are not considered "lawyers" and communications between them and company employees are not privileged. Particularly in litigation matters, it is important to find out the rules and to modify communication patterns and expectations accordingly. Depending on the nature of the services the client is seeking from foreign counsel, this factor could be highly significant.

On the other hand, in some jurisdictions, client listings are kept confidential. Even if they are not, U.S. counsel may prefer to keep their relationship with outside counsel confidential and specifically instruct him not to disclose the relationship.

* * *